NEW RULES FOR CLASSIC GAMES

R. Wayne Schmittberger

John Wiley & Sons, Inc.

New York • Chichester • Brisbane • Toronto • Singapore

The author gratefully acknowledges the following inventors, who gave permission to adapt their rules: Robert Abbott, for Eleusis and Epaminondas; Sid Sackson, for Fields of Action and Haggle; and Christiaan Freeling, for Emergo, The Glass Bead Game, Havannah, Hexade, Hexdame, Lotus, Medusa, and Grand Chess. Inventors of other games and game variations decribed in this book are credited in the appropriate chapters, when known.

Interior design by Laura Cleveland of WordCrafters Editorial Services Inc.

Diagrams by the author, using Aldus Freehand 2.02

Typesetting by the author, using QuarkXPress 3.0

Library of Congress Cataloguing-in-Publication Date

Schmittberger, R. Wayne, 1949-
    New rules for classic games / R. Wayne Schmittberger
        p.   cm.
    Includes index.
    ISBN 0-471-53621-0
    1. Games—Rules.   2. Board games—Rules.   I. Title
GV1201.42.S36   1992
793—dc20   91-22386

Printed in the United States of America

10 9 8 7 6 5 4 3 2 1

To Jean, Kim, and Bonnie

TRADEMARKS AND ACKNOWLEDGMENTS

Abalone is a registered trademark of Abalone Games.

Acquire, Civilization, and Sleuth are registered trademarks of Avalon Hill.

Aldus Freehand is a trademark of Aldus Corporation.

Boggle, Domination, Parcheesi, and Scrabble are registered trademarks of Milton Bradley.

Frisbee is a registered trademark of Wham-O.

MasterMind is a registered trademark of Pressman.

Mhing is a registered trademark of Suntex International.

Monopoly, Nerf, Trivial Pursuit, Pente, Risk, Clue, and Sorry! are registered trademarks of Parker Brothers.

Othello is a registered trademark of Tsukuda Company.

Pictionary is a registered trademark of Pictionary, Incorporated.

Ping Pong is a registered trademark of India Industries.

QuarkXPress is a registered trademark of Quark, Inc.

Wiffle is a registered trademark of Wiffle Ball, Inc.

Reference to the name of a game or other product without a trademark symbol does not imply lack of trademark status for that game or product.

Rules and diagrams for Phutball have been adapted from *Winning Ways for Your Mathematical Plays*, ©1982, by Elwyn Berlekamp, John Conway, and Richard Guy, and are reprinted by permission of Academic Press. Rules of Eleusis are adapted from *The New Eleusis*, ©1977 by Robert Abbott, and are reprinted by permission.

PREFACE

No matter how good a game is, chances are that it can be improved upon, or at least varied in an interesting way. By experimenting with the rules of a game, players can create new challenges, add excitement, and customize the game to meet their own needs and tastes.

Players should not view the rules that come in a game box as inviolate. Game inventors, by necessity, make many arbitrary decisions in choosing their final set of rules. How many cards should each player be dealt? In which directions should pieces be allowed to move? How much money should players start with? Game inventors cannot possibly test every possible combination of rules—and even if they could, they might end up having to choose between variations in which the "best" one is just a matter of taste. Inventors can always use help from you, the player, to refine their games.

Sometimes a game variation becomes so popular that it replaces the original game. Many of today's best-known games have evolved this way, such as backgammon from Tabula, contract bridge from Whist, and modern chess from Shatranj.

Sports organizations are very aware of the advantages of critically reviewing old rules and testing new ones. Every year, rule changes are made in sports at all levels, ranging from minor technical adjustments to major overhauls. As a result, what amount to new variations of baseball, football, and basketball are played each year. Some rule changes prove unpopular and are rescinded, but many are found to improve the game. Sometimes there is no clear consensus and varying rules survive, such as the conflicting designated hitter rules in baseball's two major leagues and the many rule differences between college and professional football. Often, one rule may not be better than another in any objective sense, but simply different—leading to interesting changes in strategy and tactics when the game is played.

In my years of experience as a player, reviewer, and inventor of games, I have created many game variations, and tested and collected rules for hundreds of others—far more than could fit in any one volume. In this book, I have attempted to present a selection of my favorite variations for as wide a variety of games as possible—board games ranging from Monopoly to checkers; games played with cards, dice, paper and pencil, or no equipment at all; and even outdoor games such as croquet.

Also, in an attempt to broaden the theme of "finding new uses for old game equipment," the book presents rules for a number of little-known games that can be played with equipment from other games that readers are likely already to have, such as playing cards or a checkers set, or equipment that can easily be improvised.

Finally, the book gives tips on how to go about changing game rules to suit your own tastes, to cure a flaw in a game, to alter the playing time or number of players, to allow a game to be played by mail even when it involves a random element such as rolling dice, or simply to provide a new form of entertainment.

I hope that the material in this book will provide you with countless hours of entertainment.

R. Wayne Schmittberger

CONTENTS

CHAPTER 1

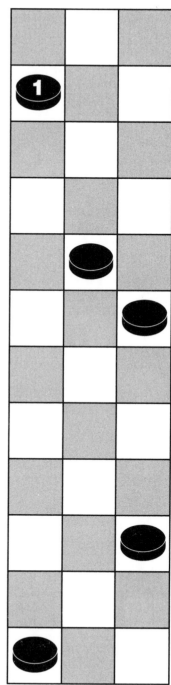

NEW TWISTS ON
OLD FAVORITES

Game players are often game inventors at heart. The more widely a game has been played, the more "house rules" players are likely to have invented for it. Even when they like a game—or, perhaps, *especially* when they like a game—many players cannot resist the urge to experiment with the rules in an attempt to improve, or at least vary, the play.

Each of the games discussed in this chapter has had deserved success in its basic version. At the same time, all of these games provide rich opportunities for experimentation. Many new and intriguing wrinkles can be added to each set of rules, without changing the elements of play that made them so successful in the first place.

No doubt the variations presented here are but a small fraction of the number of ways people have tried to play these games. They have been chosen because they are a representative sample of popular games, and because they are among my favorites. In this chapter, as in most of the book, it is assumed that readers are familiar with the basic rules of the games discussed.

MONOPOLY

Monopoly is often the first board game people think of at parties, at vacation houses, and on rainy days when they want to find a group activity everyone likes. But one thing about Monopoly has always bothered me. If you're unlucky (and, when it comes to rolling dice, who isn't?), you never seem to land on enough properties early in the game to have any kind of chance to survive later in the game. This is an especially big problem if you go last in a game with four or more players, since the properties you land on are likely to have been bought already.

Staggered Starts

One way to even out the chances is to adopt a "staggered start" setup. At the beginning of the game, the player who goes first (as determined by rolling the dice) places his token on Go, as usual. The player who goes second, however, places his token on Just Visiting. The third player's token starts on Free Parking, and the fourth player's token starts on the Go to Jail space. (That instruction is temporarily ignored.)

If there are five or six players, their tokens also start on Go to

Jail. This may not keep them from landing on properties that the fourth player just bought, but at least they'll still be likely to pass Go and collect $200 more quickly than the first three players.

A second way to even things up is to have everyone begin on Go, but to have the order of the turns decided by bidding instead of by dice roll. Anyone may begin the bidding by saying, for example, "I'll bid $20 for the right to go first." To expedite the process, the minimum bid should be $5, and each bid should be at least $5 more than the previous bid. Once no one wants to bid further, the highest bidder pays the bank the amount of the bid and then has the right to go first. The second position is auctioned off the same way, followed by the third, and so on. If at any time no one wants to bid, the standard dice-rolling method is used to determine the order of the remaining players.

After the playing order is completely worked out, players should rearrange themselves around the table in clockwise order according to the move order, so that the turn will pass to the left, as usual, throughout the game.

Auction Monopoly

For players who want every game of Monopoly to be a serious strategy challenge, there's an auction variation that has probably been invented independently many times. Here's my own form of it.

The game is played the same way as standard Monopoly, with one big difference: Whenever a player lands on an unowned property, *all* players may try to buy that property.

The player who lands on the property has the right to make the initial bid, and this bid must be at least equal to the mortgage value of the property. After that, bids pass in clockwise order around the table. In turn, a player may either "pass" or make a new bid that is at least $10 higher than the previous bid.

A player who passes is allowed to come into the bidding again later. When everyone has passed in succession, the property goes to the highest bidder.

Players may not bid more than they can afford to pay. Bidding more than the amount of cash you have is all right, provided you can make up the difference by mortgaging other properties you own. If no one wants to bid as much as the mortgage value, or if no one has enough money to do so, then the property remains unsold.

This is an extremely challenging game, although it can be slow going until the players get used to the auction process and develop a feel for how much to bid on various properties. The first time players try this variation, they often tend to bid too much too early, and then find they do not have enough cash to compete effectively on other properties. It can be very interesting to see what happens to the bidding on a property that someone needs to complete a monopoly.

Beyond Boardwalk and Park Place

A more elaborate auction version, with numerous twists, is presented in *Beyond Boardwalk and Park Place*, by Noel Gunther and Richard Hutton (Bantam Books, 1986). The book even includes a set of "Go" cards, which players draw when they land on Go.

Free Parking Jackpot

It's time to mention a popular variation of Monopoly that I *don't* recommend. A common house rule is to place money ordinarily paid to the bank as a penalty (e.g., as the result of drawing a bad Community Chest card or landing on Luxury Tax) on the Free Parking square instead. Then, a player who lands on Free Parking gets whatever money has accumulated there.

The problem with this rule is that, all too often, it causes the bank to go broke before anyone has won the game! The average cash flow to each player goes up just enough to sustain the player who has the second-best property holdings, while the player with the best properties ends up wealthy enough to barely notice landing on an opponent's Boardwalk with a hotel.

TRIVIAL PURSUIT

After initial success in Canada, Trivial Pursuit swept the United States in the early 1980s, generating more than half a billion dollars in sales in 1983 alone. More than a hundred other trivia games appeared soon after, attempting to capitalize on the craze. A few of these games were good, but most were pale imitations of the original. Today, several Trivial Pursuit editions and supplements are available.

Why did this trivia game achieve such success? Part of it was lucky timing. It was introduced just as the first video game boom was dying, and people were looking around for a new kind of home entertainment. Moreover, video games had accustomed people to spending $30 or more for a game; this made buyers willing to pay Trivial Pursuit's price, which at that time was extraordinarily high for any kind of board game.

But more important than timing was the quality of the game's questions: They are varied and lively and often offer players little hints, giving them a fighting chance to come up with a correct guess. The very popular TV quiz show *Jeopardy!* relies on a similar hint-within-a-question formula.

Still, it *is* possible to argue with success. Here are some new ways to play this popular game.

Trivial Pursuit with Challenges

Player interaction, which adds interest and excitement to almost any game, is minimal in Trivial Pursuit. One way to provide some is by introducing the possibility of challenges. Here's one way it can work.

When a player thinks an opponent's answer is incorrect, the player may say "Challenge." The player must then give the answer he believes is correct. Players then check the answer on the card.

If the original player was correct, the challenger loses a wedge, but gets to choose which one. If the challenger has no wedge, he loses his next turn and may not challenge again until he has taken another turn. The original player gains a wedge as usual if he is on a "category headquarters" space.

If the challenger is correct, he gains a wedge of the question's category, *even if the original player is not on a category headquarters space*. If the challenger already has a wedge of that color, he may instead take a wedge of his choice from the game box. If the challenger already has all six wedges, he may remove one wedge (challenger's choice) from the original player's token. If he has six wedges and the original player has none, nothing happens (and it was a mistake to have risked making a challenge).

If neither player's answer was correct, nothing happens and play passes to the next player as usual.

Only one player may challenge each question. If two or more players try to challenge, the privilege is given to the one who spoke first. If it's a tie, the player with the fewest wedges is given the chance to challenge; further ties are resolved by die roll.

Trivial Pursuit without the Board

Trivial Pursuit can be played any number of ways without the board, making the game more convenient to play while traveling. The following variations all work with any number of players, and can also work with cards from most other trivia games.

Boardless Game 1: Basic Trivia Cards

Players take turns reading questions aloud that the opponent (or the next player, if there are more than two) must answer. A die is rolled to determine which question on the card is asked (if a 1 is rolled, ask the first question; if a 2, ask the second question; etc.). Since two or three related questions are sometimes grouped on a single card, it is best to draw a new card after each question. Players play to an agreed total of correct answers, such as 10 for a short game or 20 for a long game.

If using a die is inconvenient, such as when the game is being played sitting on a couch or riding in a car, each player should rotate his question category each round—that is, answer the first question on the first card, the second question on the second card, and so on.

Boardless Game 2: Trivia Cards with Categories

This is played like Basic Trivia Cards, except that the goal is to answer one question correctly in each category. Players should use paper and pencil to keep track of who has correctly answered questions in which categories. When a player rolls a number that would give him a question in a category in which he already has given a correct answer, he tries to answer the question anyway. On an incorrect answer, his turn ends; but on a correct answer, he gets to choose to answer a question in any category he wishes. To win the game, a player with correct answers in all six categories must answer a question in a category of the opponent's choice.

Boardless Game 3: Going Out

Each player takes an equal number of cards—24 is a good choice—and places them, answer-side down, on the table in front of him. Each player in turn tries to get rid of as many of his cards as possible by answering questions correctly.

To begin the game, the first player reads the first question on his top card aloud, gives an answer, and turns the card over to check the answer. If his answer is correct, he discards that card and takes another turn, this time reading the second question on the next card in the pile. On each additional correct answer, the player discards, goes to the next card, and tries a question in the next category.

On an incorrect answer, a player discards the card, but his turn ends. When it is his turn again, he goes to the next category on the next card, just as he would have done on the previous turn if he had given a correct answer. After answering the last question on a card, a player's "next category" is the first category on the next card.

The winner is the first player to discard all of his cards. Since it is an advantage to go first, players may choose to allow "last licks" to players who have had one fewer turn than the first player to get rid of all his cards. If two or more players get rid of their last cards in the same round of play, the winner is determined as follows:

1. Players who answered their final card correctly win against players who did not.

2. Among players who still are tied, a "sudden death" phase takes place. Remaining players try to answer one question each; and if anyone answers a question correctly, then anyone who does not is eliminated. This procedure is repeated until there is only one survivor.

Boardless Game 4: Trivial Tic-Tac-Toe

This is a version for two players or two teams. Players draw a large tic-tac-toe grid on a sheet of paper. A stack of question cards from Trivial Pursuit (or any other trivia game) is placed on each space of the tic-tac-toe grid, question-side up. The grid should be large enough so that the cards do not fill the spaces completely, as shown in Diagram 1.1.

One team plays X, the other O. The first team, chosen at random, selects one of the nine piles and tries to answer a question on the topmost card. If, as with Trivial Pursuit, there is more than one question per card, a die is rolled to determine which one the player or team is to answer. (That is, on a throw of 1, the first question is answered, etc.)

On an incorrect answer, the player's turn ends, and the card is discarded. On a correct answer, the card is still discarded, but the player goes again, trying to answer a question on the next card down in the same pile.

Each time a player gives a correct answer, a small X or O (depending on the player's team) is written in the tic-tac-toe grid space from which the question card was drawn, as in Diagram 1.2.

The number of small Xs or Os needed to win a square varies with the square: Four are needed for the center square, three for each of the four corner squares, and two are needed for the squares in the middle of the edges. When a player gets enough Xs or Os in a space to win that square, the cards are removed from that square and a large X or O is drawn on it. When a player wins a square, his turn ends.

Diagram 1.1

To set up Trivial Tic-Tac-Toe, draw a tic-tac-toe grid on a sheet of paper. The grid should be large enough to accommodate nine piles of Trivial Pursuit cards.

Diagram 1.2

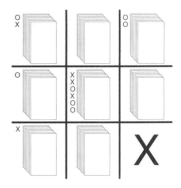

A player who correctly answers a question on a card gets to write a small X or O in the grid square from which the card was taken. When a player has enough Xs or Os to win a square, he removes the pile of cards from that square and draws a large X or O there, as X has done in the lower right corner of this grid.

CHINESE CHECKERS

A faster, more challenging variation on the old game of Chinese Checkers has become popular in France in recent years.

Super Chinese Checkers

The game is played in the usual way, except that the jumping rules are different. A piece may jump over another piece in the same line that lies *any* distance away, *provided that the piece that is jumped lies at the exact midpoint of the jump*. That is, the number of spaces the jumping piece moves before reaching the jumped piece must equal the number of spaces moved after passing it (see Diagram 1.3). Also, no other piece or pieces may lie within the line of the jump.

As usual, a jump onto an occupied space is prohibited. Multiple jumps of varying distances are allowed, as long as each single jump follows the new rule. Note that the conventional

Diagram 1.3

The Black piece marked with a star may make a triple jump to C as shown. (The Black piece may also stop at A or B, since jumps are always optional.) Note that pieces 1, 2, and 3 lie, as they must, at the exact midpoints of each jump. Once at C, the starred piece may not continue to Y or Z, since that would require jumping over both pieces marked X, and only one piece may be passed over in a single jump.

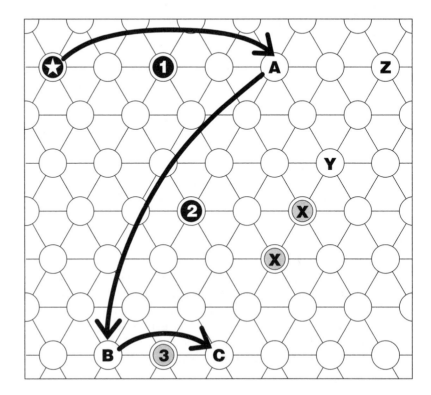

Chinese Checkers jump is still legal under the new rules; it just happens to be the shortest possible way to jump.

The new rules speed up play and add many interesting tactical possibilities. Compare to Halma and Mini-Halma in Chapter 7.

BOGGLE/BIG BOGGLE

Exponential Scoring

An ideal word game for a large group of people, since everyone can play at once, is Boggle, in which players attempt to find words that can be spelled by moving one letter at a time within a 4x4 array of letters that has been randomly generated by shaking some letter cubes. Even better is Big Boggle, which uses a 5x5 array of cubes.

For some players, writing down many short words within a brief time limit is tiring to the hand and is also less interesting than trying to find long words. Official Boggle rules do reward longer words with more points, but not really enough to make up for the extra time it usually takes to find those words.

A Big Boggle variation that works well is to count only words of five or more letters. As usual, a word also found by another player scores nothing. Words that only one player finds, however, score as follows:

Length	Points
5 letters	1
6 letters	2
7 letters	4
8 letters	8
9 letters	16
10 letters	32
11 letters	64
12 letters	128

Each additional letter doubles the word's point value. One thing this does is to make it possible for a player to come from far behind when the board contains common endings such as -IEST.

For regular Boggle, it may be better to make four letters the minimum, since five-letter words are sometimes hard to find on the smaller board. Four-letter words are then worth 1, five-letter words 2, six-letter words 4, seven-letter words 8, and so on.

JOTTO

This deductive word game was first marketed by Selchow & Righter in the 1950s. Each player thinks of a five-letter word containing no repeated letters and writes it on a piece of paper. Players try to be first to guess the other player's word and do so by saying one five-letter word out loud each turn. These words may not contain repeated letters. The opponent responds by stating how many letters in the guessed word are also in the secret word.

It is possible to get a response of "five" and still not have guessed the word. This would happen if you guessed an anagram of the word, such as LARGE when the answer was GLARE (or LAGER or REGAL). One possible strategy, therefore, is to choose a hidden word that has three or four anagrams. This can be effective, but it also tends to make it easier for the opponent to figure out what the set of letters is, since they will tend to be common ones.

Double Jotto

In a variation that adds more interaction, players must tell the opponents how many letters of their own words are contained in their guesses. For example, suppose Player A's secret word is PLAYS and Player B's word is GAMES. When Player A guesses MAZES, Player B will respond "four" as in normal Jotto; but at the same time, Player A must tell Player B that the guess has two letters in common with his own word. Therefore, players try to think of words that will uncover the information they want about the opponent's word while disclosing as little information as possible about their own word.

One-Lie Jotto

This variation is played the same way as regular Jotto, except that each player may lie once during the game. A player may lie in any fashion—for example, you can say "one" when you mean "four," or say "two" when you mean "none." It's completely up to you whether you make your lie early or late in the game, or not at all.

One-Lie Double Jotto

This is a combination of the two previous variations. A player may lie only once, and he may lie either when he is making a guess or when the opponent is guessing (but not both).

MASTERMIND

When you get good at MasterMind, you'll find that you will usually crack the four-peg color sequence code in either four or five tries. It really shouldn't take more than five, and you have to be pretty lucky to get it in three; so the chance of a tie is very high.

Harder Codes

One way to make the game more competitive is to allow the Codemaker to place fewer than the usual four colored pegs. A space left blank becomes, in essence, an additional possible color, and the Codebreaker must identify any blank spaces as part of the code.

For a time, a Super MasterMind version of the game was marketed, which had more peg colors and a five-hole code. Even without a Super MasterMind set, players can simulate the play. To increase the number of colors, players can paint a dot on top of some of the pegs, so that, for example, "blue" and "blue-dot" become two distinct "colors." To increase the width of the board, players can buy a second set and place the two boards side by side.

Variations with more colors or code positions may require more guesses than the number of rows provided in a set (and the same is true for some of the other variations described below). If this happens, another set can be used to expand the board's length, or players can use paper and pencil to keep track of guesses and answers.

The game on which MasterMind was based, best known as Bulls & Cows, was originally played with paper and pencil, and was also one of the earliest computer games. It involved guessing digits—10 "colors," essentially—in a code of whatever length the players felt like tackling. The Codemaker responded to guesses with numbers of bulls and cows, which correspond to the black and white pegs of MasterMind.

Interactive MasterMind

To reduce the element of luck, players can allow the Codemaker to change his code before responding to any guess. Thus, if the Codebreaker gets lucky and makes three correct guesses on his first turn of the game, the Codemaker may—before giving his response to the initial guess—alter the code in such a way as to make his response less revealing. He might, for example, change the code to one for which his correct response to the initial guess is one white peg and one black peg. As experience has shown, that's about as unrevealing a response as possible.

One important proviso: The Codemaker may never alter the code in such a way as to render any information he gave in earlier rounds incorrect. If he does, he loses the game.

Single White Pegs

A different way to complicate the game is to change the meaning of the white pegs, as suggested by British game inventor and puzzle expert David Wells. Whenever the Codemaker would place one or more white pegs under the ordinary rules of the game (indicating, for each white peg, one guess that is correct as to color but incorrect as to location), he instead places only one white peg. Thus, a white peg means that one *or more* pegs in the guess is correct in color but incorrect as to position.

Double Guesses

Another suggestion by Wells, and one that requires players to have a great intuitive grasp of probabilities in order to get the best possible scores, is to require the Codebreaker to place two rows of guesses at a time, before the Codemaker responds to either. The Codemaker then places pegs as usual in response to each guess. Since the guesser will not have had the advantage of knowing the results of one guess before making the second guess, he will generally have less information than in the basic game.

One-Lie MasterMind

Some players like to use a rule that allows the Codemaker to lie once in the game. This is a lot like One-Lie Jotto, described earlier. The Codemaker's lie can come at any time and may consist of putting down any response at all to the Codebreaker's guess. It takes a while to get the hang of playing against a slightly dishonest Codemaker, but it's a very rewarding experience when you do figure out the code.

Two-Lie MasterMind

Some players attempt a version in which the Codemaker may lie twice during the game. I don't recommend trying this unless you have a lot of time, and a pencil and a lot of scratch paper—but some hardcore logicians love it.

Double MasterMind

In this variation, two games are played simultaneously on different sets, with each player being the Codemaker in one game and the Codebreaker in the other. When making a guess, a player must tell the opponent how many white and black pegs the guess yields for his own code. This variation can be combined with the rules for One-Lie MasterMind, to create One-Lie Double MasterMind. (Compare to Double Jotto and One-Lie Double Jotto, above.)

Some other variations can be found in *The Official Master-Mind Handbook*, by Leslie H. Ault (Signet, 1976).

NERF PING PONG

Diagram 1.4

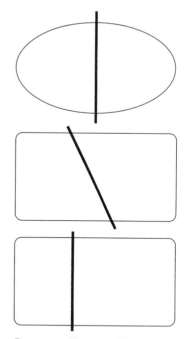

This game has a movable, adjustable-length "net"—actually a hard plastic barrier—that affords players the opportunity to change the game in ways that cannot easily be duplicated with a regular table tennis set or on a tennis court. These variations add interest to the game, and thus help make up for the fact that the Nerf balls do not bounce as high or spin nearly as much as regular Ping Pong balls.

Irregular Tables

Nerf Ping Pong is designed to be played on tables of varying size and shape. Tables shaped like a regular Ping Pong set work fine, but you may find it refreshing to try a round, oval, or square table.

Angled Net

To change the game even more, try turning the net at an angle. This creates both a short and deep fence for each player, varying the kinds of shots that are needed (Diagram 1.4). It's also possible to handicap the game by moving the net a little farther away from the better player. Two players can experiment with the net placement until they have it positioned in such a way that each player will win about half the time.

Because of its movable, adjustable-length plastic "net," Nerf Ping Pong lends itself to variations not possible with ordinary table tennis sets.

HEARTS

Few card games are played in as many different ways as hearts. It always seems that whenever new players get together for the first time, the session has to begin with a series of questions, such as: Are we playing with the jack or 10 of diamonds (as being worth –10)? Does the player with the low club, rather than the player to the left of the dealer, lead to the first trick? Are we always passing cards left, or does it vary (left, right, across, keep)? Can hearts be led before they're broken (i.e., discarded by someone)?

Sometimes a player may come up with a twist that is completely new to the other players. One such surprise I recall is hearing a player say, during the first hand, "But the way I have always played, whoever has the queen of spades has to play it at the first opportunity."

Attempts have been made to standardize the rules of hearts for tournament play; see *Win at Hearts* by Joseph D. Andrews and George S. Coffin (Dover, 1983). But still, many card game books give several alternative ways of playing hearts. Rather than repeat those here, I will confine myself to two versions that I think are unusual and particularly good.

Three-Handed "Shoot-the-Moon" Hearts

Most books will tell you that hearts is best for four players, whether played "cutthroat" (every man for himself) or in partnerships. But there is a three-handed version that I think is just as enjoyable.

All the cards are dealt out. The extra card goes to the player to the left of the dealer, and this player keeps this card throughout the hand. On the final trick, if you're on lead and have two cards while the other players each have one, you may lead either one. The extra card is taken by whoever wins the final trick.

Before the play, each player passes three cards, always to the player on his left. During the play, hearts may be led at any time—they do *not* have to be broken first. The player to the left of the dealer leads to the first trick.

Otherwise, Black Lady rules are in effect, with each heart counting 1, the queen of spades 13, and the jack of diamonds –10. Shooting the moon—capturing the queen of spades and all 13 hearts—is worth –26, or –36 if you get the jack of diamonds, too.

The effect of these rules is to give the player with the extra card a tremendous advantage, particularly in trying to shoot the moon. The other players know this, of course, but still are likely to hesitate in grabbing the queen of spades for themselves early in the hand—and that may be their last chance to stop the shoot. When no one can shoot, the extra card still gives that player a big advantage in employing the standard strategy of forcing out the queen of spades, making sure no one can shoot, and then trying to set up his own hand so that it can take the rest of the tricks, thus capturing the jack of diamonds.

What makes things fair, of course, is that all of the players take turns having the advantage of the extra card. Players should play a predetermined number of deals, divisible by three, so that each player has the extra card the same number of times. It is not uncommon in this game, by the way, for one or two players to have negative scores for an entire session.

Zero-Sum Hearts

Bridge expert Josh Parker devised a form of hearts in which the sum of the players' scores always adds up to zero. It often requires clever temporary teamwork by players to stop someone from getting too good a score on a hand.

Players can use whatever rules of passing cards and leading they prefer. Scoring, based on a four-player game and assuming that negative scores are good and positive scores are bad, is as follows:

1. Generally, hearts score 1 point each (just as in regular hearts), the queen of spades scores 11 (instead of 13), and there is no reward for taking the jack or 10 of diamonds.

2. If each player takes at least two hearts, or the queen of spades, the hand is thrown in and does not count.

3. When at least one player takes fewer than two hearts, players receive scores according to the following chart:

Result	Player(s) Score	Others Score
Player shoots the moon (takes all 13 hearts and the ♠Q)	-48	16 each
One player takes no hearts and does not take the ♠Q	-24	regular score
Two players take no hearts and do not take the ♠Q	-12 each	regular score
One player takes just 1 heart and does not take the ♠Q	-23	regular score
Two players take only 1 heart each and do not take the ♠Q	-11 each	regular score
Three players take only 1 heart each and do not take the ♠Q	-7 each	21

Note that when the chart requires players to receive their "regular score," the queen of spades should be counted as 11 points.

SCRABBLE BRAND CROSSWORD GAME

There's no better two-player word game than this 1940s invention of Alfred Butz, now published by Milton Bradley.

Scrabble with Other "Dictionaries"

Some players who love Scrabble, and who are very good at it, have one main complaint about the game: For serious play, it requires memorizing a particular dictionary of record. Many words are found in some dictionaries but not others, and most tournament players will know by heart, at a minimum, all the two-letter words and most of the three- and four-letter words found in *The Official Scrabble Players Dictionary* (Merriam-Webster).

This may seem unfair to those who feel that Scrabble should be a game of vocabulary, anagramming skill, and strategic word-play rather than a game of memory, but there is no other way to score the game objectively for serious purposes such as tournaments.

For casual play, though, players can have fun suspending the normal dictionary rules and instead choosing some other book as their source of words. I have known players to try such outlandish "dictionaries" as an unabridged atlas, the Bible, or the Manhattan telephone directory. Proper names are allowed in this variation, of course; all that matters is whether a word can be found in whatever book the players have agreed to use. When a word is challenged, the challenged player must find the word in the book—*anywhere* within the book—within a strict time limit, such as one minute—to avoid losing the challenge.

Replacing the Blanks

A popular variation is to allow any player to pick up a blank from the board and replace it with a tile from his rack, provided that the tile matches the letter the blank stands for. Because a blank will usually allow a player to get a "bingo"—a play using all seven tiles—within a few turns, this rule adds much more luck to the game, but it also tends to allow comebacks from greater deficits.

Incidentally, many players are unaware of just how easy it is to form a bingo when they have a blank in their rack. If you have a blank, concentrate on getting rid of high-point tiles and duplicates of any low-point tiles. Except when the board closes up late in the game, chances are good that you'll be able to find a playable bingo within two or three turns.

Bonus Category Scrabble

Some writers have suggested a Scrabble rule whereby players agree, before the game starts, on a special category, such as games or occupations. A player who forms a word that fits the category, regardless of the length of the word, earns a 25-point bonus. This is an interesting idea, but problems of interpretation can sometimes arise with this variation; for example, does "BONE" qualify as a "color"? Arguments can be avoided if players restrict themselves to categories with clearly defined members, such as state names, chemical elements, or months of the year. Alternatively, players can agree in advance on a reference source, such as a cookbook index for a list of foods, or ask an impartial third party to make rulings.

Toric (Wraparound) Scrabble

When playing Scrabble, nothing is more satisfying than finding a seven-letter word in your rack—and nothing is more frustrating than having nowhere to play it! This was one reason I started experimenting, some years ago, with changes in the board's geometry. The result was this variation and the next, both of which proved very popular with some of my regular Scrabble opponents.

A torus is the mathematical name for an object shaped like a doughnut. Can you picture how a Scrabble board would look if it were stretched to cover the surface of such an object?

First imagine bending the board into a cylinder; then imagine bending the cylinder to join its ends. The effect is a board in which the top is joined to the bottom, and the left edge to right edge, just as in video games that have a "wraparound" effect.

What this means in play is that, in addition to making all the ordinary plays, you can start a word near the right edge of the board and have it go beyond the edge, continuing on the same row at the left edge of the board. Or you can run a word off the bottom by having it continue down the top of the board in the same column.

This new board geometry makes it easier to fit a bingo on the board when you have one in your rack. Of course, normal rules and restrictions on word formation remain in effect.

Toric Scrabble has a variation is which words can be spelled either forward or backward, since direction doesn't seem too meaningful on the surface of a doughnut. In effect, this variation allows you to run words off the left edge and continue on the right, or off the top, continuing up from the bottom.

In either toric variation, there's a peculiar problem. All the triple word squares turn out to be adjacent to other triple word squares, making it too easy to run a word across two of them. This would happen, for example, with a word running across the upper right corner and continuing onto the upper left corner. In regular Scrabble, such "triple-triples," which multiply the value of the word by nine, are rare plays; and it seems wrong to make it so easy to score so many points in the toric game.

Fortunately, a simple rule fixes this flaw. If a word is played across two adjacent triple word squares, only one of them counts. If, on the other hand, a word is played on just one triple word square, its value is tripled, and the one left open is available for a future triple play.

One of the amusing results of playing Toric Scrabble is board positions that look not only illegal but totally ridiculous by conventional Scrabble standards. A word fragment or a single letter will be floating along an edge, seemingly unconnected to anything, when it is actually part of a word on the opposite edge. It's a great way to worry the kibitzers.

Spherical Scrabble

Another strange way to play Scrabble is on a spherical board. As in Toric Scrabble, the bending of the board is only in the players' imagination.

In Spherical Scrabble (Diagram 1.5), the right edge wraps around to connect to the left, just as in Toric Scrabble (above). At the top and bottom of the board, however, the various columns converge into "poles." If you think of the board as being stretched to fit on a globe, with the top row being the area closest to the North Pole and the bottom row being closest to the South Pole, you won't have much trouble remembering these rules.

First, the column of squares on the extreme right of the board is covered with masking tape or cardboard and is considered out of play. The purpose of this is to create an even number of columns.

A word may be played off the top of the board, reading upward; it then "crosses the pole" and starts to head south again *seven columns away from where it left the board*. If, in counting

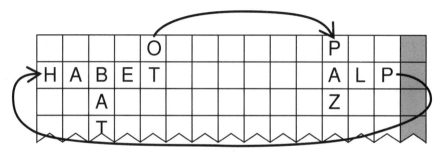

Diagram 1.5

In Spherical Scrabble, the right column of squares is out of play. A word may "cross the pole" by running off the top or bottom edge of the board and continuing seven columns away, as TOPAZ does here. Words may also run off the right edge and continue on the left, as ALPHABET does.

seven, you pass the right edge of the board, that's okay—just continue counting from the left column. Alternatively, count seven columns to the left—it should come out the same. Similarly, words may run off the bottom edge and then continue up from the bottom seven columns away from where they left. The special Toric Scrabble rule governing "adjacent" triple-word squares is in effect .

For a variation in which the luck of drawing tiles is completely eliminated, see Open Scrabble in Chapter 14.

CHESS

If you think of chess as a slow game, try this wild, rock 'em-sock 'em variation. It's my own invention and has proved popular enough that several postal tournaments have been held in NOST (an acronym for Knights of the Square Table, a postal game club to which I belong—see Chapter 14 for more information).

Extinction Chess

Most of the rules of chess apply, including the starting position and the movement powers of the pieces. The one change is the object of the game.

The concept of checkmate is abolished. Think of each kind of piece—king, queen, rook, bishop, knight, and pawn—as a different species of animal. Your job is to avoid the extinction of any of your species. That means you have to keep at least one of each kind of piece on the board at all times. If you don't, you lose.

From an offensive standpoint, this means you can still win, as in ordinary chess, by capturing the enemy king (although, technically, you'll have to complete the capture, instead of just playing to checkmate). But you can also win by capturing your opponent's queen, or both knights, or both bishops, or both rooks, or all eight pawns (that last one is pretty hard to do, though).

This means you can never offer a trade of queens, because as soon as your opponent takes your queen, the game is over (you just lost) before you can recapture. It also means that if one pair of knights, say, is exchanged, the other knight has to be protected just as hard as you would protect your king. And if your king and last remaining knight get attacked simultaneously by a piece you can't immediately capture, you lose.

As in chess, you may promote a pawn to any piece, but in this game you can even promote it to a king. With two kings on the board, you can afford to lose one of them (the same is true of two queens). But if you have to promote your last pawn to move it from an attacked square, you lose, since a pawn must promote to something. In practice, the game doesn't last long enough to worry about this rule.

Here's a sample game that shows some of the tactics. For an explanation of how to read algebraic chess notation, see Appendix A.

NOST Postal Tournament, 1988

White: Paul Yearout
Black: R. Wayne Schmittberger

1.e4 e6 2.b3 c5 3.Bb2 Nc6 4.Nf3 a6 5.d4 cd 6.Nd4 Qc7 7.Nc6 dc 8.Qg4 e5 9.Qg3 Bb4 (This is an indirect way of defending the e pawn. The problem with f6 is that it would expose the knight on g8 to attacks such as Bc4.) **10.c3 Bf8 11.Be2** (If White renews the threat on the e pawn with 11.c4, Black plays Bb4.) **Be6 12.0-0 0-0-0 13.Ba3 c5** (If 13....Ba3? White wins at once with 14.Qg7 Ne7 15.Qf6 Ng8 16.Qg5, dooming the knight.) **14.Bg4 Bg4 15.Qg4 Kb8 16.Rd1 b5 17.Rd5** (threatening Qd1) **b4 18.Bb2 Rd5 19.ed c4!** (Speed is important in opening lines of attack against White's knight and bishop, because Black's own knight and bishop are also vulnerable to White's queen.) **20.Qf3** (If 20.bc Qa5! creates an unstoppable threat of bc, followed by c2 after the bishop retreats.) **f6 21.d6 Qd6 22.bc e4 23.Qe2 Qe5 24.Qc2** (If 24.f4 Qa5! keeps a winning advantage because of the threat of bc.) **bc 25.Bc1 Ka8** (This prepares a quick forced win to which there is no defense.) **26.Be3** (See Diagram 1.6.) **Qb8 27.Resigns** (If 27.Nc3 Qe5 is "mate," since it skewers the knight and rook.)

Diagram 1.6

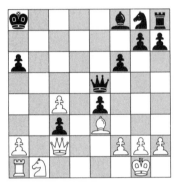

In this Extinction Chess position, whoever makes the next capture of a knight, bishop, rook, queen, or king will win. Black has a forced win with Qb8, attacking White's knight. If White responds Nc3, Black's queen returns to e5, skewering the knight and rook.

CHAPTER 2

FIXING A FLAW

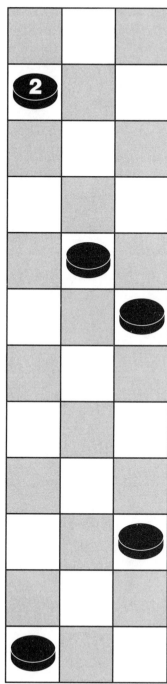

Some game variations arise not because players are ambitiously seeking new challenges, but because they find that a game isn't fun, or just doesn't work, when it's played according to the rules that come with it.

Even major game companies have published games that are unplayable. The problems with these games vary. Sometimes one side always wins. Sometimes the game goes on and on, never reaching a conclusion. Or it may be that an important rule is ambiguously stated or omitted, requiring players to fill in the gap.

If you've bought such a game, don't despair. Get creative and you may find a way to make a good game, or even a great game, out of the equipment you've purchased.

TABLUT: A CASE STUDY

Here's an example of a game with a flaw and how ways were found to cure it. As you will see, the methods used to fix this game have much broader application and can lead to the creation of whole new categories of games.

The game is taken not from the ranks of proprietary games, but from the large number of public-domain, traditional games handed down to us over the centuries. Some of these games are outstanding, but some are clearly lemons.

In some cases, the fault may lie with the sources reporting the rules of these games. Some subtle rule, crucial to the game player but overlooked by the casual historian, may have been left out. In other cases, though, the game may just have been bad from the start. It may never have been played enough for anyone to notice or to bother writing about how flawed it was. For most of these games, we'll probably never know the whole truth.

Swedish botanist Carolus Linnaeus (Carl von Linné), who is credited with establishing the modern system of botanical nomenclature, found a game being played as he traveled in Lapland in 1732 and reported the rules in his diary, *Lachesis Lapponica*. The game is called Tablut.

You can made a board yourself quite easily (for suggestions on improvising game boards, see Appendix B) and try it for yourself, as I did when I first saw its rules years ago. Or, you may find one of the commercial versions of the game that were produced in Europe (I know of at least two in the past two decades), or the version that was published in 1982, under the name Break Away, as part of Gabriel's Industries' Hi-Q line of games and puzzles.

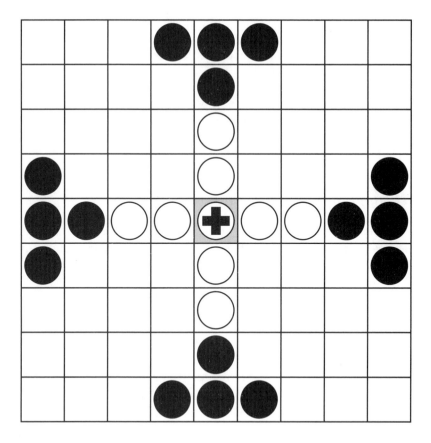

Diagram 2.1

In the opening position for Tablut, shown at left, the Swedes (White) are surrounded and outnumbered. They win if their king (the piece in the center, with the cross) reaches any square on the edge of the board.

Rules of Tablut (Linnaeus's Account)

The game simulates a battle between Swedes, represented by the light pieces (which we'll call White), and Muscovites, represented by the dark pieces (Black).

Pieces are set up as shown in Diagram 2.1. The center piece bearing a cross is the Swedish king. The Muscovites win if they capture the king, while the Swedes win if the king reaches any square on the edge of the board.

The rules are simple. Starting with Black, each player in turn moves one of his pieces. Pieces move any number of squares horizontally or vertically (like a rook in chess) and may not jump over or land on other pieces. No piece except the king may occupy the central square, known as the *konakis*, or throne, although pieces may pass over the throne when it is vacant.

A player captures an opposing piece, other than the king, by "sandwiching" that piece between two of his own pieces along any rank or file on the board. But if a piece puts itself into a sandwich

Diagram 2.2

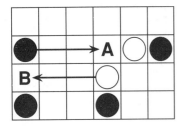

In this position, a Black move to A would simultaneously capture both White pieces, each of which would then be sandwiched between two Black pieces. But since a piece may safely move between opposing pieces, a White piece moving to B would not be captured.

by moving between two opposing pieces, it is not captured (see Diagram 2.2).

The king moves and captures like other pieces, but cannot itself be captured unless it is surrounded on all four sides, or on three sides by enemy pieces and the fourth side by the throne.

When the White player's king has a clear path to one board edge, he is supposed to announce "raichi" as a warning. When the path is clear to two edges, he says "tuichi"—the equivalent of checkmate, since it is impossible to block two paths at once.

Disappointment

The first time I played Tablut, I took both sides in a kind of solitaire experiment. I found I really liked the "feel" of the game. It was fun to try to escape with the outnumbered king. Clever sacrifices of the king's men would create paths into the open, where the king would soon find a way to reach the edge of the board. It also seemed to be an intriguing challenge to try to hem the king in with the opposing forces.

When the king finally escaped, seemingly by a whisker, the first time I played, I tried again and found that, after another brief but interesting struggle, the king escaped again. I continued to play many times, but disappointment gradually set in as I became convinced that, in a game between reasonably equal players, the king should always escape.

Here's a sample game, using an algebraic notation (captures are shown parenthetically; see Appendix A for a full explanation): **1.e2–g2 e4–h4 2.a4–e4 e6–h6(xh5) 3.a6–e6(xe7) d5–d7 4.d1–d5(xd4) d7–e7(xe6) 5.d9–d6 e7–c7 6.e8–e6 c7–e7(xe6) 7.d6–e6 e7–c7 8.d5–d7 e5–c5 9.g2–c2 c5–c6 10.b5–b6 c7–b7 11.d7–c7 c6–d6** and on move 12, the king will reach the edge at either d1 or d9.

Black can do somewhat better by attacking less directly, minimizing captures (the White pieces tend to impede their own king's escape), and trying to build walls a greater distance away from the king.

When Gabriel turned Tablut into Break Away, the company tried to balance the game by restricting the king to moves of one square at a time, and by requiring the king to reach either of two opposite ends of the board rather than any of the four edges. Such rule changes do make the game more balanced and are worth trying if you don't mind altering the historical rules of the game—but they don't work perfectly.

Indeed, it can be demonstrated mathematically that *in games with unequal forces and unequal objectives*—and Tablut is such a game—*it is impossible to create a perfect balance between the players*, unless a draw is the correct outcome. In Tablut, draws are not possible, except perhaps by repetition of moves—an event unlikely enough that the known rules don't cover it.

Thus, *no* tampering with the rules can create a version of Tablut that is perfectly fair for both players. Once players become sufficiently experienced with any new set of rules, they will find that one side or the other will still have a built-in advantage.

One Solution

Nevertheless, we can balance Tablut extremely closely, and without changing any of the game's rules of movement or capture. Two principles can be applied to "fix" Tablut: *bidding* and the *pie rule*. These ideas are important, because they can be applied to almost any game that favors the first player or the side with a particular objective.

For Tablut, bidding alone goes a long way toward correcting the game's flaw. The concept works this way. Suppose that in your first game of Tablut, the king escapes in 14 turns. You decide to play your next game with a bidding rule. Players take turns bidding for the right to play the king's side.

A bid amounts to a promise. Whoever promises, by making the lowest bid, to escape with his king in fewer turns, gets the right to play the king's side. But the king must escape within the promised number of moves, or the player loses the game.

Player A, having seen the results of the first game, might start the bidding at 15. Player B, confident that he can do at least as well as in the game before, bids 14. Player A thinks hard, but finally says 13, because he decides it will be easier to escape with the king in 13 moves than to defend for 14 moves. Player B feels the surrounding forces may have the edge, and bids no further. Then the game begins.

The right to make the first bid should alternate each game.

The Pie Rule

When players reach the point of agreeing on the best first bid, the pie rule can be employed to achieve an even finer balance. One player (chosen at random) begins by making one or more moves in the game's starting position—say, one move for the Black army and one move for the White army. He also states a bid that he thinks is as fair as possible. The opponent then gets to play whichever side he chooses, but must accept both the initial moves and the bid.

This balancing technique is the game equivalent of the old solution to the problem of how to divide a pie in half fairly: One person cuts the pie in half and the other person then chooses which piece to take. Note that if a bid seems to favor one side slightly, that side's initial move can be a relatively weak one in order to make the balance more exact.

The pie rule is a very effective way to balance games in which the first player has a significant advantage. Consider, for example, the connection game Hex (Diagram 2.3), which was independently invented by Piet Hein in 1942 and John Nash in 1948.

In Hex, two players, one White and the other Black, take turns placing a piece of their color on any empty board space. Once placed, a piece may never be moved or captured. One player tries to connect the top and bottom edges with a chain of pieces of his color, while the other player tries to build a chain of his color between the left and right edges. Chains may wind all over the board and may be any length. Draws are impossible; if one player's possible connecting paths have all been blocked, then the other player will necessarily have made his own winning connection.

Theoretically, the first player should win, unless he is handicapped in some way. It's fairly easy to prove this by a logical argument, which runs like this. If there were a winning strategy for the second player, then the first player could adopt it himself by pretending that the opponent had already made a move. After all, there is no way the absence of an opponent's stone can be disadvantageous. Therefore, there cannot be a winning strategy for the second player, and the first player should win—though no one has been able to show exactly how.

But theory is one thing, practice another. If a game is played

Diagram 2.3

In Hex, White tries to connect one pair of opposite edges (here, the left and right ones) with an unbroken path of White stones, while Black tries to connect the other two edges with a path of Black stones. In the game shown, White was restricted from placing his first move in the center, and so Black has played there.

Experienced players will prefer a larger board, such as one measuring 11 hexes on a side.

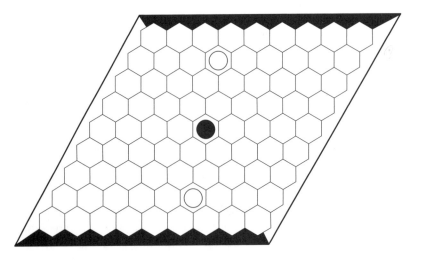

on a very large board, such as one with 19 hexes or more along each side, the first player's advantage is not very noticeable, and the second player's practical chances of winning are good. On a relatively small board, however, such as the 9x9 board in Diagram 2.3, the second player will find it hard to put up much of a fight if the first player is allowed to place his first stone near the center of the board.

To make the game closer, it's common for Hex players to add a restriction that the first move cannot be on or near the center hexagon, or on certain other important hexes; but figuring out just which hexes to forbid the first player isn't easy, particularly since board sizes vary. It's possible to go too far in restricting the first player, making the game too easy for the second player to win.

The pie rule solves the problem as perfectly as possible. If the rule in its simplest form is applied to Hex, one player places the first move and the other player chooses which side to take. If he takes the side that goes first, he must accept the first move placed by the other player as his own. The second player, therefore, becomes responsible for deciding whether or not a given first move leaves the advantage with the first player or shifts it to the second—and the first player has an incentive to make the second player's decision as close as possible.

Returning to theory for a moment, the pie rule shifts the winning advantage from the first player to the second player, since in principle, an omniscient second player would always know which side to take after seeing the first move. But there's no way to avoid giving *someone* a winning advantage in a game that cannot end in a draw—and the value of the pie rule is that it makes this advantage as small as possible.

A refinement can be made by having one player make additional moves, such as two for the first player and one for the second, before the other player makes a choice of colors. This greatly increases the number of possible starting positions. And the more positions players have to choose from, the more finely they can balance the game.

One possible objection to the pie rule method is that one player can make one or more opening moves to create a position he has analyzed in advance. This is not an important objection in most games. But in Renju, a two-player game in which players try to be the first to get five pieces of their color in a row, a more elaborate variation on the pie rule has been worked out to avoid this problem in serious competition. Players take turns making the first three moves (with certain restrictions as to where they may be made); after that, the player who went second has the option of switching sides, and there is still another wrinkle two moves later. For details and the rules of Renju, see Chapter 5.

A Different Solution

Another way to attempt to balance the players' chances in Tablut is to play a two-game match in which each player takes the king's side once. If the king escapes in both games, the winner of the match is the player whose king reached the edge of the board in fewer turns.

This approach is effective, but is not quite as fair as using the bidding rule. The reason is that the player who has the king in the second game knows what score he must beat and can play accordingly. If he needs to escape very quickly, he can take risks he might avoid if he had more time. His advantage is a lot like that of a home baseball team in the last of the ninth inning, when the team knows from the score whether its strategy should be to play for one run or many. Another difficulty with this approach is that it is a bit of a nuisance for the players to have to count moves, and errors are likely to be made.

Diagram 2.4

Hnefatafl, played by the Vikings in the tenth century, uses the same rules as Tablut, but the scale is larger and pieces are placed on intersections instead of squares. The board measures 19x19 lines, exactly the same as a go board.

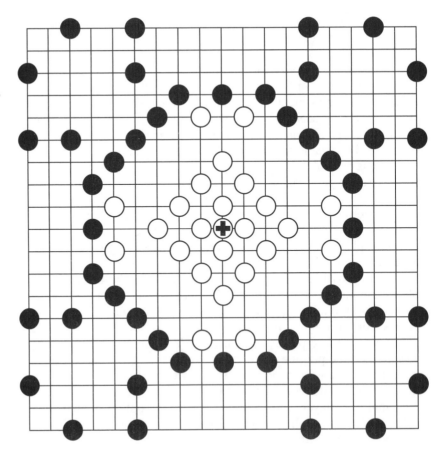

There is, however, a way to make the two-game match concept work very well, provided you have a second set: Play the two games simultaneously. This method will be explained and developed further in the next chapter.

HNEFATAFL, THE VIKING GAME

Possibly of Icelandic origin, the game of Hnefatafl is known to have been played by the Vikings in the tenth century. A forerunner of Tablut, it has the same rules, except that it is played with many more pieces on a larger board, which happens to be exactly the same size as a go board. One cosmetic difference that does not affect play is that the pieces occupy intersections instead of the squares and move along the lines. If you have a go set, you can use it to play the game. The opening setup is as shown in Diagram 2.4.

It is difficult to determine which side has the advantage in Hnefatafl. One cannot safely assume that it is the same as in Tablut, although that is certainly a possibility. But if you try the game and find that one side usually wins, you can balance it with the methods outlined for Tablut.

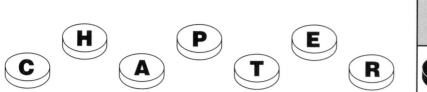

DOUBLING UP

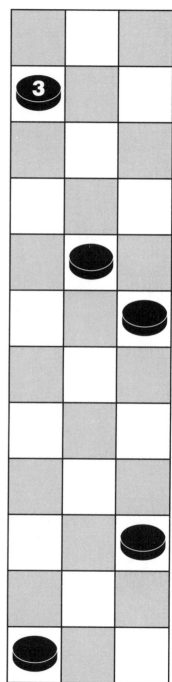

If someone gives you a board game you already own, think twice before going to the store to exchange it. It may be possible to put the two copies of the game together to form an entertaining new kind of game. After reading this chapter, you may even decide to start picking up extra copies of certain games at flea markets.

DUPLICATE BACKGAMMON

One way to make use of two copies of one game is to create a "duplicate" version, modeled loosely after Duplicate Bridge. In Duplicate Bridge, the same set of deals is played by many different partnerships and the results are compared. On each deal, for each partnership that you outscore (playing the same pair of hands), you earn one match point; and you earn half a point for each partnership whose result on a deal you tie. The winner is the partnership with the most match points—that is, the players that most consistently did the best with the cards they were dealt, regardless of whether those cards were good or bad.

As an example of how this principle can be applied to other games, let's create a game called "Duplicate Backgammon." Two backgammon boards are placed side by side. Each player plays White on one board and Black on the other.

To begin, either player throws the dice. Each player then uses that roll to move his White pieces—one player doing this on one board and the other player doing it simultaneously on the other board. The next dice roll is used by both Black armies. Thus, both players will be getting the same dice rolls throughout the game. This doesn't really eliminate the luck of the dice, because a roll may benefit one player's positions more than the other's; but it does reduce it somewhat.

The winner is the first player to win on *either* board.

In the opening, players may make the same "book" moves for a couple of turns, but play is likely to diverge fairly soon. If players are concerned that the opponent may copy them if they are first to reveal their play, they can place a screen between the boards and make their moves out of each others' views; or, one player can write down his planned moves, then reveal the writing after the opponent has moved on the board.

Doubling cubes are an unnecessary complication in Duplicate Backgammon. If players wish to use them, though, they should just have one cube in play to wager on the outcome of the two-game match. In view of how the match is won, it makes no sense to keep separate cubes going for the two games.

Double versions of other race games, such as Sorry! and Parcheesi, can be played in the same way. With Sorry!, of course, players share the move options of cards rather than dice rolls.

DUPLICATE AND SOLITAIRE SCRABBLE

For a while, Selchow & Righter, the original manufacturer of Scrabble, marketed a duplicate version of the game. In Duplicate Scrabble, each player has a pencil and a scoresheet depicting a miniature Scrabble board. At the start, a deck of cards depicting Scrabble letter tiles is shuffled, and seven cards are turned up. All players treat this set of cards as their "rack" of tiles for the first turn. Players simultaneously make plays by writing them on their scoresheets, following all Scrabble rules of word formation and scoring. After each play, all seven cards are discarded, and seven new ones are turned up. After the deck is exhausted, the player with the highest score on his board is the winner.

The same game can be played using one standard Scrabble set per player. With a single set, it makes an interesting solitaire game, the goal being to beat your own previous high score or some arbitrary point total.

In both Duplicate and Solitaire Scrabble, strategy is very different from that of the basic game. The key is to set yourself up for huge triple word scores and other big plays, since you never need to worry that an opponent will take your spot.

ADJUSTING THE BALANCE: DOUBLE TABLUT

Having two games of a kind also helps you balance games that favor one player. You'll recall from the last chapter that in Tablut, White should always win with reasonably good play. One suggestion to make the game fairer was to have players play a two-game match, switching colors after the first game. If White wins both games, the player who won more quickly (by reaching the edge of the board with his king in fewer turns) would be the winner. Two drawbacks to this method were mentioned: the advantage inherent in being the second player to have White, who then knows what score he has to beat, and the need for the cumbersome and error-prone procedure of counting moves.

But with two Tablut sets, both these difficulties can be avoided if the two games are played simultaneously. The sets are placed side by side, and each player plays White on one board and Black on the other. To begin, one player makes a move for Black; after that, each player's turn consists of making two moves, one on each board. The first player to escape with his king wins.

There's one slight problem with this. The player who was first to make a move with White has a one-move advantage. To make the game perfectly fair, a rule can be added that if the player who

Diagram 3.1

Player B

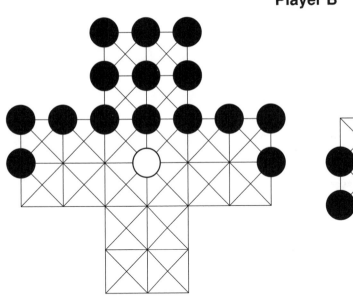
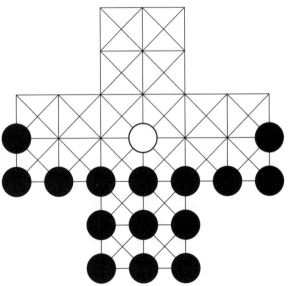

Player A

In the Scandinavian game of Fox and Geese, the fox (the White piece) can capture geese (Black pieces) by jumping over them, as in checkers, along any line. The geese may not capture, but simply move one point at a time along any line, in any direction except toward the side of the board where they began. The geese win if they surround the fox in such a way that the fox has no legal move; otherwise, the fox wins. Fox and Geese boards and

opening setups vary, and some forms of the game are played on a standard checkerboard.

With careful play, the geese should always win. But if two games are played at once, with each player taking the fox in one game and the geese in the other, each player's task becomes more complex: to win as quickly as possible with the geese while holding out as long as possible with the fox.

went first with White escapes with his king, the opponent can tie the match by escaping with his king on the very next move.

An alternative that avoids draws is to apply the pie rule: One player makes one or more moves (on one or both boards) and indicates, if it's not clear, which pair of armies is to move next. The other player then chooses which pair of armies to take. The player whose king reaches the edge of the board first wins, and the other player has no opportunity to tie.

The simultaneous two-game match is also very suitable for a four-player contest, with the players forming two teams of two. One member of each team plays White on one board, while his teammate plays Black on the other board. Players should decide in advance whether or not consultation is to be allowed between teammates. It probably should be, unless all the players have about equal skill at the game.

APPLYING THE IDEA

This simultaneous game idea can be used to balance any other game in which in which unequal forces battle, such as Fox and Geese (Diagram 3.1). The concept also provides an alternative to the pie rule in games in which one side (usually the first player) has an advantage. Examples are five-in-a-row games such as Renju and Pente, and connection games such as Hex. For example, two games of Hex (see page 26) could be played in which each player went first on a different board, and the winner would be the first player to complete a chain with his color on either board. The usual first-move restriction in Hex would not be needed, although the pie rule could still be applied, as explained above for Tablut, if the players wanted to balance the games more finely.

But there is another interesting use for the double game concept: Take a game that is already balanced, *deliberately unbalance it*, and then turn it into a double-game race for victory.

DOUBLE UNBALANCED CHESS

Take chess, for example. Set up two chessboards side by side and remove the two Black queens, as shown in Diagram 3.2. If players are even remotely close in ability, both White armies should prevail. The question is: Who can win more quickly with White and hold out longer with Black? This does make a fundamental change in the character of the game of chess, but so what? The purpose of the experiment is to create a new form of play.

Going a step further, there's no reason why the White sides even need to have kings in Diagram 3.2. Suppose you leave the Black queens on the board, remove the White kings, and replace the White kings with queens from another chess set, as shown in Diagram 3.3. Now Black will not be able to use the delaying tactic of checking the White king, but he does have an extra queen on defense.

In these chess games, as in Tablut or Hex, players may wish to use the pie rule to nullify the advantage of the player who makes the first move. On one board, a player might play a relatively slow move for White, such as pushing a pawn a single square; the other player would then get to choose whether to accept that move as his own or play the side that responds.

Pure strategy games are not the only ones that can be unbalanced and turned into double matches. Take two backgammon boards, for example, and alter the positions so that one side has already borne off some men, or has his men closer to home—then let players play the games simultaneously, with the winner being the first player to bear off all his men on either board. Strategy can

Diagram 3.2

Player B

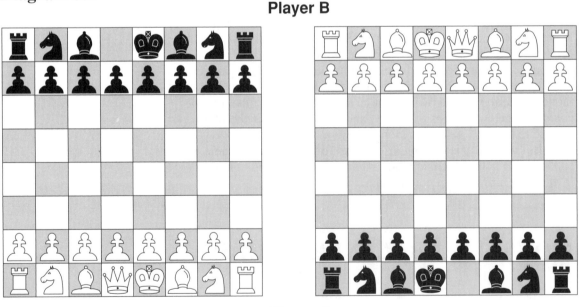

Player A

With an extra queen, White should win easily on both boards. The question is, which White will win *first*?

be very different from the regular game, since it may involve stalling tactics that would ordinarily be unsound.

EXPANDED DECKS

For some card games, such as poker, the number of players who may participate is limited by the size of the standard 52-card deck. By mixing two or more decks together, players can often increase the number of players who can take part. They may also change the game in interesting ways.

Typically, new rules must be worked out ahead of time to resolve some new situations. What happens in a trick-taking game, for instance, if two cards tie for highest, such as when both players play an ace of trumps to the same trick? The rule used in pinochle works well: The first player to play that card wins the trick.

In making up rules to cover these kinds of situations, two things should guide you: common sense and the spirit of the game. For example, in multideck poker, five of a kind clearly should outrank a straight flush, since this is the case in wild card poker varia-

Diagram 3.3

Player B

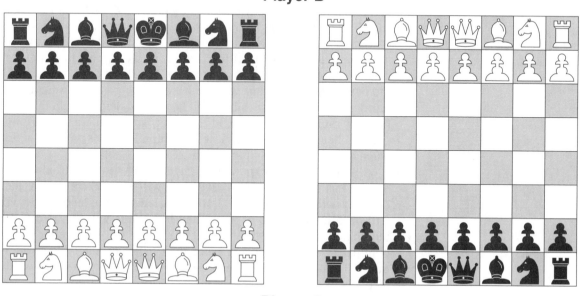

Player A

Who needs a king, anyway? Not White, who, with an extra queen, should never be in danger of checkmate.

tions (based on the relative probabilities of holding each hand). But should two aces of diamonds beat two aces of different suits? Probably not, since suits don't affect rank in any other situations— e.g., it is standard that a royal flush in spades and a royal flush in clubs are equal and share the pot .

Don't be disappointed if you have to experiment with various sets of rules before you find one that really suits you.

Six-Suited Bridge

When eight players are available for bridge, Team-of-Four is an excellent game. In Team-of-Four, there are two partnerships per team. The same deals are played at two different tables, with each team's members playing the North-South hands at one table and the East-West hands at the other. For each deal, scores are compared, and the difference is translated into international match points (IMPs) as a means of reducing the overall impact of high-scoring deals. But what do you do if you have six players?

One idea for the venturesome is to find two decks with matching backs. From one deck, remove the black cards and set them aside (they will not be used). Take the red cards in this deck and use a pen to mark their faces in some way, such as by putting an arrow through all the hearts and drawing a pair of diagonals through all the diamonds.

Now mix the 26 doctored cards in with the regular 52-card, unmarked deck. You now have a six-suited deck—let's call the new suits "valentines" and "kites." Divide players into two partnerships of three players each, and arrange everyone around a table in such a way that each player is sitting between two opponents. Shuffle, deal, and bid as usual. You must decide in advance, of course, how the new suits should rank and be scored. One possible system is to insert valentines and kites between hearts and diamonds in terms of bidding rank (i.e., in descending order, suits will rank notrump, spades, hearts, valentines, kites, diamonds, clubs) and to score valentines as a major suit and kites as a minor suit.

At first, bridge experts will have nearly as much trouble bidding in this game as novices. Everyone will have 13 cards, as usual, but they will be distributed among six suits. Voids and singletons will be common; suits of more than four cards will not. When the bidding ends, the player to the left of the declarer leads, after which both partners of the declarer place their hands on the table as dummies. Play proceeds as usual, except that the declarer has new kinds of plays available that cannot be made in normal bridge—such as leading a card from one hand, ruffing in another, and discarding a loser in a third. It's a lot of fun for those who like exploring unknown territory.

Other Six-Suited Card Games

If bridge is not your game, why not try the effect of using a six-suited deck—or a five-suited deck, an eight-suited deck, or anything else you feel like improvising—in a game of rummy, hearts, casino, cribbage, or other favorite card game? For some games, the result will be an amusing novelty, while in others, entire new strategies may open up.

A related idea is to combine two decks without marking any cards and simultaneously double the number of cards in each hand. If you're used to the usual American form of cribbage in which each player receives 6 cards and places 2 into the crib, try dealing each player 12 cards and placing 4 into a crib. There will be all kinds of new high-scoring combinations—so you should also double or triple the number of times you have to go around the cribbage board to win. Better suspend the Muggins rule for a while, too—counting up some of these hands will take some getting used to!

COMBINING GAMES

It's possible to combine two or more games to make a single, more complicated game. Here are two examples, after which you should have no trouble coming up with lots of additional ideas.

Chess-Checkers-Chinese Checkers

This is a combined game for two players. Side by side, set up one chess set, one checkers set, and one Chinese Checkers set. The Chinese Checkers game should be set up for two players.

Each player in turn makes a move on any one of the three boards. The object is to win at least two out of the three games.

This is a lot harder than playing each of these games consecutively, because you have to keep deciding which board is the most important one to play on next. If you let your opponent make two or three moves in a row on one of the boards, will you gain enough time to have a winning advantage on the other two boards?

And there's no reason that all three games have to be different. You could just as easily play three simultaneous games of checkers, or combine two chess games with one Chinese Checkers game.

You can also increase the number of games being combined to five or more. It's good to keep the number odd to reduce the likelihood that the match will end in a tie.

Backgammon-Parcheesi-Monopoly

Another idea is to combine three different games that rely on throwing a pair of dice, such as backgammon, Parcheesi, and Monopoly. Each turn, a player rolls the dice and then uses the roll to make a move on whichever board he chooses. Again, the object is to win a majority of the games being played.

Requiring players to choose a board *before* throwing the dice is not as interesting a way to play, because it reduces the amount of informed decision-making.

A twist on this idea is to have each player throw two, three, or even four dice each turn—players must decide on the number of dice in advance—and then allocate their throws among the three games however they wish. Players may need to invent rules to cover special situations; for example, if a player uses a pair of matching dice as doubles in the Monopoly game, thereby earning an extra throw, he may be required to play that extra throw on the Monopoly board.

CHANGING THE

NUMBER OF PLAYERS

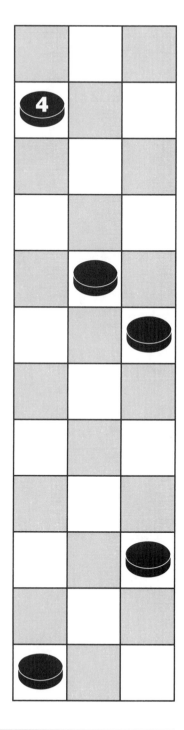

Some games, by their nature, are suitable only for two players, while other games require a minimum of three, four, or some larger number. But most games, regardless of what their rules may tell you, can be adapted to accommodate almost any number of players. There are several ways to accomplish this.

TEAM PLAY

When there are more players present than the maximum number allowable according to the rules of a chosen game, one surefire method to allow everyone to play is to form teams. A team may consist of any number of players, and teams need not all have the same number of players.

Teams can take the place of all or some of the players who usually play the game. In a game of chess, for example, two players might play Black as a team, consulting with each other about their moves, against a single person who plays White. Or, in a game of Trivial Pursuit, which comes with enough equipment for six players, nine players could take part by forming three teams of two, while the other three players play as individuals; or players might form three teams of three.

When players form teams to play a game, and when teams will perform the activities that are usually done by a single player, there are two basic ways for players on a team to cooperate:

1. Teammates take turns making their team's moves and decisions, without any consultation with one another.

2. Teammates consult and mutually agree about all their decisions. In this case, it is a good idea for a team to choose one player as the team captain, who will make the final decision whenever teammates disagree about what to do.

More complicated kinds of team interaction are possible, such as the chouette in backgammon described in Chapter 11.

ADDING EQUIPMENT

Many boxed games limit the number of players to whatever number can be accommodated by the amount of equipment included. Often, improvising additional equipment or mixing in equipment from an extra set will allow more people to play. For example, you can add a seventh player to Trivial Pursuit by using a small piece of cardboard as a token. As the game progresses, the player with the cardboard token can write on his token the names of categories for which he has earned wedges.

The only drawback, usually, is that the greater the number of players, the longer players must wait between turns. If this is a problem, it may be a better idea to form teams.

MULTIPLAYER GAMES FOR TWO: FROM CROQUET TO CHINESE CHECKERS

When a game is "for 2 to 4 players" or "for 2 to 6 players," the two-player version is sometimes less interesting than versions with more players. But when there is no element of hidden information in the game, there is no reason why two players cannot each play two or three roles at once to complicate and enliven the play.

Consider the backyard game of croquet, in which an important part of the strategy involves hitting other players' balls to gain extra turns. In a two-player game, opportunities to do this are very limited, and there may be relatively little interaction between the players during an entire game.

To spice things up, each player may play two or three balls, making the game feel like a four-player or six-player game. It's best if players select ball colors that allow them to play alternately, as governed by the sequence of colors shown on the game's stakes, but the game will work no matter what the order. Players may gain turns as usual by hitting any other ball, even if it is one of their own, provided the usual requirement is met that a ball must go through at least one wicket before it can hit the same ball again.

Strategy depends on how players decide to determine the winner. Here are three possibilities:

Variation 1. The first player to get one of his balls to the finish is the winner.

Variation 2. The first player to get all three of his balls to the finish wins.

Variation 3. Players continue until all six balls have reached the finish. The ball that finishes first earns its player 1 point, the ball that finishes second earns 2 points, and so on, and the player with the lowest total wins.

The choice of game variation 1, 2, or 3 above will greatly affect strategy. In the first variation, a player will typically sacrifice the position of one or two of his balls to help the third, while variation 2 places an emphasis on hindering the opponent's least-advanced ball. In the third variation, a player may need to shift between different strategies: It's all right to sacrifice one ball in order for your other two balls to finish first and third, but you have to avoid a sixth-place finish if your other balls only finish second and third.

Two players can play multiplayer versions of many other games with interesting results. In games such as Chinese Checkers, players will have to decide, as in the croquet game, whether the winner will be the first player to get all the pieces of one color home, all the pieces of all his colors home (this seems most in line with the spirit of Chinese Checkers), or the player who scores the most points according to some system.

THREE-PLAYER GAMES: THE "PETTY DIPLOMACY" PROBLEM

There's a problem that many game companies and inexperienced game inventors either are unaware of or have chosen to ignore. Certain kinds of three-player games—those of pure strategy, in which there is no hidden information or random moves—have serious inherent flaws. If a player starts to do well in the game, the other two players will be forced to team up against him. Even worse, in terms of the personal dilemma it can cause, a player who is doomed to lose will often be forced to choose arbitrarily between a move that will allow one opponent to win and a move that will allow the other opponent to win. The greater the amount of player interaction a game allows, the more obvious these flaws will become as the game progresses.

The "doing well means doing badly" paradox is clearly illustrated by three-player chess games. Many three-player chess games have been invented and marketed over the years, usually by people who thought they had come up with something very original—when in fact, the game not only wasn't new, it wasn't really even playable!

Let's imagine a three-player chess game with players known

as White, Black, and Red. If White and Black exchange rooks, then Red is effectively a rook ahead of each of them. But are things really so good for Red in this scenario? White and Black, now having the two smallest armies, will have to gang up on Red. Red will probably not survive, but he will have the chance to inflict more damage on one opponent than the other. In fact, the fate of White and Black will probably depend much less on how well they play as on which one Red feels kindlier toward.

But if it's bad to be doing well in a game, lest the others gang up on you, what kind of strategy should a player use? The only idea that makes any sense is to lie low. Try to look like you're losing, and most importantly, try to convince the other players that one of them—and most assuredly, not you—has the strongest position. This boils down to a kind of low-level diplomacy game, which is not what chess—or any pure strategy game—is supposed to be about.

What should three players do, then, when they want to play a pure strategy game together? The only fully satisfactory answer is for one player to compete solo against a team consisting of the other two. If the game is one that can accommodate four players, one player can play two of the sides and the others can play one side each.

The best way to play three-handed Chinese Checkers, for example, is to have one player control two colors while the other players, who act as a team, control one color each. The side that gets all the pieces of both its colors home first is the winner. Whether or not the two teammates are allowed to consult during the game is something the players should decide in advance

I have seen some very clever attempts to solve the petty diplomacy problem. The best one was a three-player hexagonal shogi (Japanese chess) variant invented by Tanigasaki Jisuke around 1930. As in regular shogi, captured pieces become the property of the capturer, which means that piece exchanges do not in themselves cause any player to gain too big an advantage or disadvantage.

The inventor carefully defined situations in which two players were considered to be simultaneously attacking a third. When such a situation arises—here's the essence of the trick—the game automatically transforms into a two-team game, with two players teamed up against the remaining player.

The player who is left to fend for himself immediately gains numerous advantages. For example, his king immediately promotes to a very powerful piece, which can win the game at once by reaching the "Pleasure Garden" at the center of the board. Thus, the game requires players to keep calculating, constantly and carefully, whether an alliance can succeed.

LIMITATIONS ON IMPROVISATIONS

Some games don't lend themselves well to altering the number of players. If key information needs to be kept secret, as in Clue, or if trading is an essential element of the play, as in Haggle or Super Babel (see Chapter 9), not much can be done to reduce the number of players.

But if trading is only one element of a game, as in Avalon Hill's outstanding game Civilization, two players may be able to work out a way to play, say, three nations each. The problem is, how do players simulate arms' length deals between their own nations? Often, it will be to a player's advantage to let one of his own nations give an unreasonably good deal to one of his other nations, and then to repay the favor on a later turn—something that is unlikely to happen in a game with six independent players.

Players can handle this in a variety of ways. One possibility is to allow such one-player deals without limit; after all, both players should be able to use them to the same advantage. Another choice, which allows the game to develop along more normal lines, is to place restrictions on such trades. A player might be limited to a single trade between one pair of his nations per turn and/or be required always to exchange equal numbers of cards in a trade between two of his nations.

A more complex variation is to give each player the power to veto the opponent's "trades with himself" a limited number of times (five, for example) throughout the game. Each veto, when exercised, would forbid all such trades for one turn. A promise not to veto a particular trade can then become an additional element of the normal trade-good bartering between the players: "I'll let you make your trade if you let me make mine."

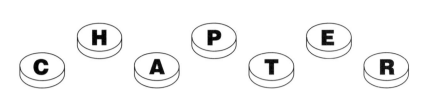

CHAPTER

MORE VARIATIONS

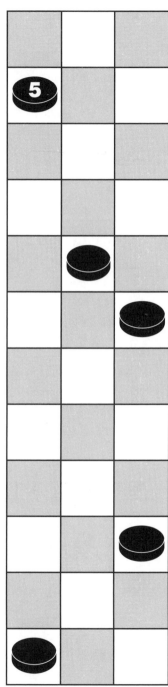

Like Chapter 1, this chapter offers variations on a number of well-known games. The difference is that most of the games in this chapter are more complicated.

Mah-Jongg

Mah-jongg is often described as rummy in which tiles are used instead of cards, but there's really much more to it. In the Shanghai version, which is just one of several forms of the game, a player can go out with many different kinds of hands, each of which is worth a different number of points. The point values of hands vary widely. In theory, the harder a hand is to get, the more it's worth. But in practice, some hands seem to be overvalued and others undervalued.

Adjustable Scoring

To make the scoring system fairer, and thus reduce the luck element in the game, players can try to keep track of how many points each kind of hand was responsible for during a session. Before a new session, players should add a point to the value of each hand that never came up in the previous session and offset this by subtracting one or two points from the value of each of the two or three kinds of hands that scored the most. If players keep doing this, eventually all the hands will be scoring about the same number of points each session.

This "supply-and-demand" method of adjusting point values also works with the card game Mhing, which is based on the Shanghai style of mah-jongg. It can also be applied to any other game that uses a similar mechanism.

Risk

Few games have had as many variations developed and written about as Parker Brothers' Risk. Though a very enjoyable game of world conquest, its very simplicity seems to make players feel they can improve the game by adding some extra rules. Here are a few examples.

Risk with Retreats

The first Risk variation I ever tried was created by my father, Robert A. Schmittberger. It offers additional strategic possibilities and became our usual way of playing the game.

Rules are as in basic Risk, with one important difference: When a territory is attacked, the defender has the option of retreating his forces to any adjacent territory that he already occupies. The retreating option may be exercised either before a battle begins or any time during a battle (i.e., between sets of dice rolls).

When a defender retreats, the attacking player loses one army. The attacker must then advance at least one army (he may advance more if he wishes) into the vacated territory. Since no territory may ever be left unoccupied under standard Risk rules, use of the retreating rule means that an attacking force may never consist of fewer than three armies, unless the defender has nowhere to retreat. With just two attacking armies, if the defender were to retreat, the attacker would be unable to both give up an army and occupy both his original and newly conquered territories.

Nuclear Risk

This version was suggested by Ross A. Kohler and was described in *Games* magazine (August 1985). Upon a roll of double 4, double 5, or double 6 by any player, the top card of the Risk deck is drawn. The country shown on that card has suffered a nuclear accident, wiping out all of its armies in that country. A coin is used to mark that country for future reference, and any armies moving into that country are halved (due to radiation) for the rest of the game. Countries that have been nuked no longer count toward control of continents.

Tactical Nuclear Risk

Kohler also suggested a more strategic rule in which a player, instead of taking his normal turn, may play a single Risk card from his hand, thereby "nuking" the country shown on that card. The effect on the country is the same as in Nuclear Risk.

Since such a move effectively puts the player two Risk cards behind (the one played, plus the one not earned as a result of having given up a normal turn), a more lively variation might be to allow players to carry out one nuking in addition to taking their normal turns.

One effect of this rule is to discourage players from concentrating a lot of armies in a single territory unless that territory's Risk card is in their hand or has already been played.

Simultaneous Risk with Bombardments

One of my more successful board game creations may have been Ozymandia, a Risk-like game that was an attempt to reduce the concept of simultaneous movement to its bare essentials. The game appeared in *Games* magazine (September 1981) and had very favorable feedback both from readers and game-playing acquaintances..

The Ozymandia board was small and simple, with just 18 territories in all (actually 9 territories and 9 capital cities, as shown in Diagram 5.1). Later, though, it occurred to me that the game's movement and combat rules could be applied to Risk to make the two-player form of the game more strategic. Here's how it works:

1. To start, players each take 40 armies and alternately place them on the board, either in empty territories or in territories they already occupy. After this placement phase is over, players move simultaneously for the rest of the game, which requires a pencil and paper to keep everyone honest and to avoid arguments. Before the movement phase of each turn, both players add new armies as in regular Risk.

2. Players are restricted to one of two kinds of moves: *con-*

Diagram 5.1

A schematic drawing of the original Ozymandia board is shown at right. The straight lines connect areas that are adjacent for movement purposes. Each player starts with nine armies, placed as shown.

Provinces (large circles) are adjacent to their capital cities (small circles). For each city a player controls at the start of a turn, one new army is entered either in the city or the adjacent province (but not in the latter if it is enemy-occupied). The winner is the first player to occupy any five cities at the start of his turn.

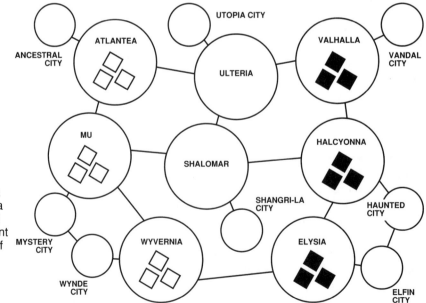

centration and *dispersal*. Specifically, they may either move armies *into* one territory or *out of* one territory. See Diagram 5.2.

When moving into a territory, armies may come in any desired numbers from any combination of adjacent territories; when moving out of a territory, any kind of dispersal pattern is allowable (although, of course, armies may only move into adjacent territories). Players need not move if they do not wish to and may always leave some or all armies in a territory unmoved. It is also permissible for players to leave a territory unoccupied.

3. All moves must be written down, allowing players to compare notes for verification purposes after each move. If opposing armies end up in the same territory or try to switch territories with each other, combat occurs and must be resolved before the next turn. Combat is resolved as follows:

a. The smaller force is completely eliminated.

b. The larger force loses the same number of armies as the weaker force, less the difference between the sizes of the two forces. For example, if seven armies attack four, the four are wiped out and the seven armies lose just one (because one is equal to four—the number lost by the weaker side—minus three—the numerical advantage of the stronger side, as determined by subtracting four from seven). Note that a force with at least two-to-one superiority wipes out a defender without losing any armies at all.

c. If both forces are equal, one defending army survives. The defending force is the one that was in the territory first. (If no one was there first, both sides are completely wiped out.)

d. When opponents try to switch territories, combat occurs on the border before the move is completed. Surviving forces then complete their move and, if necessary, have a new battle with any unmoved enemy forces that remain in the destination territory.

4. Three times during the game, each player may bombard one area (shades of Nuclear Risk). This is done in addition to a player's normal move and is written down along with the rest of the move (e.g., "Bomb Kamchatka"). Bombardment effects are figured out after all movement and combat for the turn are concluded. The effect is simple: Half of all armies in the territory are eliminated. This is true even if the armies belong to the player who did the bombardment, as can occasionally happen when a player expects the opponent to attack a particular place but doesn't want to waste time withdrawing his armies from it. If the number of armies in a bombarded territory is odd, the extra army survives.

Diagram 5.2

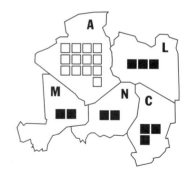

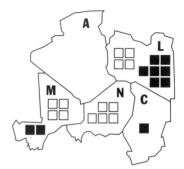

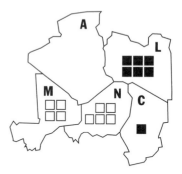

In the position shown at the top, White decides to make a "dispersal" move by sending armies from country A into countries L, N, and M, while Black makes a "concentration" move from N and C into L (keeping one army in C).

The result, before combat, is shown in the second position. The position after combat is shown at the bottom.

The winner is the first player to occupy 12 points' worth of continents. Alternatively, players may agree on some other goal, such as the occupation of a certain number of territories.

PENTE

Keryo Pente

Diagram 5.3

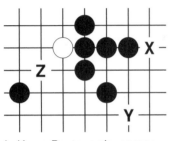

In Keryo Pente, a player may capture lines of three connected pieces, as White can do here with a play at X, as well as pairs of pieces, as White can do here at Y. In both Pente and Keryo Pente, White may safely play at Z, even though that creates a pair of White pieces surrounded on both ends. Creating three pieces in a row between two opposing pieces is also safe.

A popular game in the 1980s was Pente, a slight modification of the Japanese game of Ninuki-Renju. In Pente (as well as Ninuki-Renju), two players alternately place pieces (or "stones") of their color on the board, on the intersections of lines, trying to get five pieces of their color in a row horizontally, vertically, or diagonally.

A player can also win by capturing five pairs of opposing pieces. Only a pair of adjacent pieces can be captured. To capture a pair, the opponent must "sandwich" it between two of his own pieces by occupying the two points on either side of the pair, along the same line (Diagram 5.3). A player may, however, safely place a piece so as to create a pair lying between opposing pieces; in other words, you only get to make a capture if you create the sandwich position yourself.

The simplest way to escape from a threatened capture is to extend your pair of pieces into a line of three, blocking the point where your opponent would have to play to make the capture. But in Keryo Pente, a game variation suggested by former Pente champion Rollie Tesh, a player may capture not only a pair but also a line of three in a row, using the same method of surrounding the pieces at their end points. The object of Keryo Pente is to form five in a row (as in Pente) or to capture 15 pieces (instead of the 10 needed in Pente).

Pente sets are also ideal for playing five-in-a-row games without captures, as described in Chapter 5.

BRIDGE

Contract bridge (as distinguished from the older auction bridge) is a fine example of a game in which several variations successfully coexist. Rubber, Duplicate (see page 32), Team-of-Four (see page 38), Board-a-Match, and offshoots such as Duplicate with IMPs scoring all are played by many of the game's top players. The only real difference among all these forms of the game is in the scoring. But among top players, slight scoring differences can lead to big differences in how a hand is played and even in what bidding systems players decide to use.

When playing a three notrump contract in Rubber Bridge or Team-of-Four, for example, a player's first duty is to make his contract if at all possible, without worrying about making overtricks unless and until the contract is safe. But in Duplicate Bridge, making three notrump will be worth zero if all the other players bid it and make more overtricks than you do, so it is sometimes correct to risk failing in a contract in order to try for an extra trick.

Complete rules for these games will not be presented here, as they are available in many sources. (For information, contact the American Contract Bridge League, 2200 Democrat Road, P.O. Box 161192, Memphis, TN 38186.) One variant worth describing, though, is Chicago, which is a popular alternative to Rubber Bridge among Duplicate players when only four players are available.

Chicago

Chicago is a four-player game, like Rubber Bridge, but it lasts only four hands. If players have time for additional rounds, they cut for new partnerships after each set of four deals.

Vulnerability has nothing to do with who has won games, as it does in Rubber Bridge, but instead is predetermined, as in Duplicate. In the first deal, neither side is vulnerable; in the second and third deals, the dealer's side is vulnerable and the nondealer's side is not vulnerable; and on final deal, both sides are vulnerable. The deal rotates as usual, so that after the four games are played, each player will have dealt once (except that if a deal is passed out, it is redealt by the same player).

Bonuses for scoring a game are as in Duplicate. A team earns a 300-point bonus for a nonvulnerable game and 500 points for a vulnerable game. Slam bonuses, penalties, and other scores are also as in Duplicate, except for part scores.

Part scores earned by a team in different deals in the same four-deal round may be combined to score a game, provided they add up to at least 100; if this happens, the game bonus is determined by the vulnerability of the deal in which the game is completed. If a part score gives one side a game, no part scores previously earned by either side may count toward a game for the rest of the round. A part score that is earned on the final deal earns a bonus of 100 points, provided it is not used to make a game in conjunction with a previous part score.

Some Duplicate players play a simplified form of Chicago.

Rules are the same as described above, except that part scores may not be carried over from one hand to the next; that is, each deal is completely independent. Part scores simply receive a bonus of 50 points, as in Duplicate. Instead of ending after four deals, the game goes on as long as time allows, sometimes with the same partnerships, but ends with a number of deals that is a multiple of four.

Compensation Bridge

This outstanding, recently invented alternative to Chicago originated in Kharkov, Ukraine, and was developed further by players in Moscow. Alan Truscott described it in his bridge column in *The New York Times* in December 1991.

Vulnerability varies as in Chicago, and hands are scored as in Duplicate Bridge, with one major adjustment: After each deal, the partnership that held fewer high-card points is given compensation as described below.

High-card points are determined by the standard method used in most bidding systems. Each ace is worth 4 points, each king 3, each queen 2, and each jack 1, giving the deck a total of 40 high-card points. To facilitate verification of how many high-card points each player held, cards played during a deal should be kept in front of their owners, as in Duplicate play, rather than mixed together in tricks.

After each deal, a special bonus is given to the partnership that held fewer high-card points. (Alternatively, the bonus can be subtracted from the other partnership's score.) The bonus is equal to the score that the partnership with the greater number of high-card points should typically have expected to earn on such a hand, as detailed in the following table:

Partnership's Total High-Card Points	Expectation If Vulnerable	Expectation If Not Vulnerable
20	0	0
21	50	50
22	70	70
23	110	110
24	200	290
25	300	440
26	350	520
27	400	630
28	430	630
29	460	660

Partnership's Total High-Card Points	Expectation If Vulnerable	Expectation If Not Vulnerable
30	490	690
31	600	900
32	700	1,050
33	900	1,350
34	1,000	1,500
35	1,100	1,650
36	1,200	1,800
37-40	1,300	1,950

Suppose, for example, a partnership with a combined 16 high-card points bids one notrump and is down two, not vulnerable. Their penalty is 100 points, but since their opponents held 24 high-card points, they receive compensation of either 200 points (if their opponents were not vulnerable) or 290 points (if their opponents were vulnerable). In order to have come out ahead on the deal, the opponents would have to have doubled the one notrump contract.

The table is based on a computer analysis of thousands of deals. While it does not eliminate luck from the game, it does go a long way toward reducing it.

POKER

The term "poker" is often used to refer to an entire class of different games, the acceptability of which may vary from one circle of poker players to another. Since rules for scores of poker variations can be found in many books, I will limit myself to a brief discussion of poker variants, and the presentation of one relatively little-known example that is among my favorites.

Dealer's Choice

Poker can vary in such elements as the number of cards dealt (as in Five-Card Stud or Seven-Card Stud), the mechanics of play (Draw Poker, Indian Poker), wild cards (Deuces Wild, Baseball, Follow the Queen), and the object of the game (Lowball, High-Low). It is common for players to agree to "Dealer's Choice," in which the dealer will decide what kind of game to play and will describe the rules if necessary.

If you're playing poker for money, unfamiliarity with different variations can cost you more than you realize. And if you're not playing for money, you would probably have more fun playing something else!

Take a game like Chicago—Seven-Card Stud in which the high spade in the hole splits the pot with the high hand. The high spade rule sounds harmless and even rather silly, but how many players fully appreciate the betting implications of the fact that the high hand will only get half the usual return from the pot? And how many have a good feel for whether, say, aces up and a queen of spades in the hole is worth a call when two other players have raised? Or, playing Five-Card Draw with deuces wild, how many players know how likely a straight is to win? Chances are that the dealer who chose the game has played it a lot and will have an advantage that goes beyond the dealer's usual advantage from betting in the last position.

Poker is difficult enough—in many ways, it's more complex than bridge—and players need to make use of every advantage they can find. One way to improve your odds in dealer's choice games is to pick a game, when you're the dealer, that gives you as big an edge as possible. The following game is a good example, as well as being a lot of fun.

Push

This game is essentially Six-Card Stud High-Low, with an optional replace at the end, plus a peculiar "push" rule.

One card is dealt face down to each player. The next card is dealt face up and offered to the first player to the left of the dealer. That player has two options: keep the card or "push" it to the next player (the player to his left). A player who chooses to push a card must pay something to the pot for the privilege; an amount equal to the ante is a reasonable price for the players to fix.

When a card is pushed, the next player who gets it has the same options: keep it or pay to push it again. If the card gets around to the dealer and the dealer elects to push it, it goes to a discard pile instead of being offered to the next player.

Once a pushed card is accepted by a player, the dealer immediately deals each of the players who pushed it a new card, face up, which the players must accept. Then the deal continues, picking up with the player to the right of the player who accepted the pushed card. Throughout the entire game, every player receiving an up card has the option of keeping it or paying to push it.

Each player's second, third, fourth, and fifth cards are dealt face up and thus are subject to being pushed. As usual in stud poker, there is a round of betting after each set of up cards is dealt.

A sixth card is dealt to each player face down. Like the first face-down card, it may not be pushed. After another round of betting, each player may pay the pot to replace one card. Replacing a face-up card typically costs as much as the maximum allowable bet, and replacing a face-down card costs double.

Players then simultaneously declare (by hiding and then revealing zero, one, or two chips in their fist) whether they are going to try for the high hand, the low hand, or both. In most circles that play this game, straights and flushes "swing both ways," so that A-2-3-4-5 is both a straight and a perfect low.

The final round of betting begins with the highest hand showing among the declared highs, unless only one player declares low, in which case that player bets first. After the showdown, the high and low hands split the pot. Normally, a player who declares both high and low must win both ways to win at all, but players can follow whatever house rules they like for this situation.

Pots in this game get very large, and players tend to fold less than in most stud games. You'll find that the pushing option makes

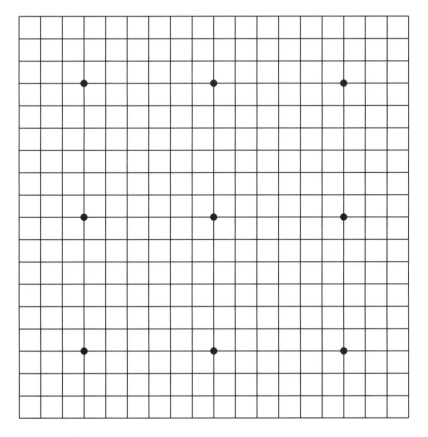

Diagram 5.4

A go board is empty at the start of play. The nine small dots are known as the "star points." These are just like any other points for play purposes, but they act as visual guides to the players. They are also the points on which handicap stones are traditionally placed.

it easier to collect unusually good hands, both high and low. I once had to fold a hand showing four jacks after a player who was aiming for a low hand pushed a fourth king to one of the other players! I was lucky, though, that all his kings were showing—I'm not sure I could have folded four jacks facing three kings.

Go

To many, go is the quintessential pure strategy game. Invented in China somewhere between two thousand and four thousand years ago, it has far greater depth than chess, yet it has simpler rules. Moreover, go's rules are based on such simple geometric principles that former world chess champion Emanuel Lasker is once said to have remarked that although chess is probably confined to Earth, if there is intelligent life on other planets, surely they know go.

Go is played professionally in the Far East and has a strong amateur following all around the world. In the United States, information about clubs and tournaments can be obtained from the American Go Association, P.O. Box 397, Old Chelsea Station, New York, NY 10113-0397.

Chinese versus Japanese Rules

Rules for go vary in minor ways in different countries. The most important versions are generally known as the Japanese rules, which are given in most English language go books, and Chinese rules. Chinese rules are much easier to state and much easier for a beginner to understand. Following are the basic Chinese rules, with a few explanations of how they differ from the Japanese ones. Familiarity with these rules will help the reader learn some of the other games presented later in this book.

1. Two players—one with a set of black stones and the other with a set of white stones—play on a board of 19 horizontal lines and 19 vertical lines. When the game starts, the board is empty (see Diagram 5.4 on page 57).

2. Beginning with Black, each player in turn places a stone on any empty intersection on the board. Once placed, a stone may not be moved (however, it may be removed if it is captured).

3. After placing a stone, a player captures—and removes from the board—any opposing *stone* or *solidly connected group of*

Diagram 5.5

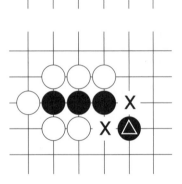

In the position at the top, White needs only to occupy the point X to eliminate the Black stone's last liberty, thereby capturing it and removing it from the board. In the bottom position, if White were to occupy both points marked X, the three unmarked Black stones would be captured. The Black stone marked with a triangle is not "solidly connected" to the other three stones, although go players would refer to it as being part of the same "group."

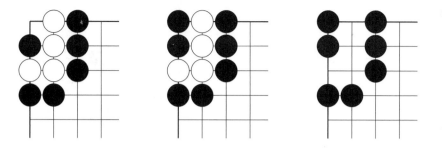

stones that is "surrounded," meaning that it is no longer orthogonally adjacent to at least one empty intersection. (An empty intersection adjacent to a group is known as a "liberty.") More than one opposing stone or group may be captured simultaneously.

> *Definition:* A "solidly connected" group is one in which all stones can trace a path to one another along the lines of the board, without skipping any intersections; stones that touch only diagonally are not connected (see Diagram 5.5).

4. If no opposing stones are captured, the player looks to see whether any of his own stones are surrounded by the opponent. If so, his own stone or stones are removed.

> *Note:* This situation could not occur under Japanese rules, which prohibit "suicide" moves; but the difference is of little practical importance, because suicide moves are useful only in situations that occur very rarely.

If a stone placement simultaneously causes groups belonging to both players to be surrounded, as in Diagram 5.6, the group belonging to the player who made the move survives and the opponent's group is captured. This rule is the same under both Chinese and Japanese rules.

5. A move may not be made if it recreates a prior board position. This is known as the ko rule—or, more precisely, as the "superko" rule, since it prohibits not only local repetitions (such as the one shown in Diagram 5.7), as the Japanese ko rule does, but global repetitions as well. This takes care of situations in which there are multiple local, repetitious situations around the board.

6. Instead of placing a stone, a player may pass. A player who passes may resume play on a later turn.

7. When both players pass in succession, the game is over and the winner is the player with the most "territory." A player's territory is equal to the sum of the points he occupies and the empty points surrounded by his stones, or by his stones and the board edge.

Diagram 5.6

In the first of these three positions, if Black plays on the upper left corner of the board, his group of two stones and White's group of four stones will simultaneously be deprived of their last liberties, as shown in the center figure. Since Black was the player who made the move, his stones survive and White's stones die, resulting in the position at right.

Diagram 5.7

At right, if White plays at X, one Black stone will be captured, resulting in the position shown at far right. If Black were then to recapture at Y, the previous position would recur, leading to a repetition of position. The ko rule disallows Black's immediate recapture.

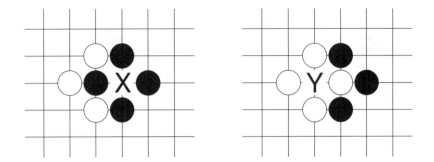

Diagram 5.8

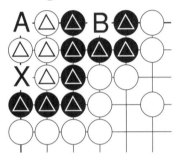

Neither of the marked groups can capture the other. If White occupies point X, Black will capture at A; while if Black occupies X, White will capture at B. A local standoff of this kind is known as a seki. When the game is scored, point X does not count as territory for either player.

Diagram 5.9

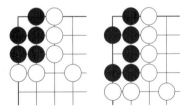

The surrounded Black group on the left is doomed because it has only one eye. The Black group on the right, however, can never be captured, since it has two eyes.

Note: Under Japanese rules, occupied points do not count as territory, but captured stones are worth one point each to the capturer. When both players make the same number of non-passing moves in a game, the rules turn out to be equivalent in all but some unusual positions.

8. It is possible for a point to be under neither player's control at the end of a game. In Diagram 5.8, neither side can safely play at the point marked X, which therefore will remain unoccupied and neutral. If White occupies X, Black will be able to capture the marked White stones by playing at A; if Black occupies X, White will capture the marked Black stones by playing at B. Such a local stalemate is known as a *seki*.

9. Since the first player has an advantage, the second player has some extra points, known as *komi*, added to his score. The most common value for komi in Japanese professional games is now 5.5 points (the fraction avoids ties). But when a recent tournament was held in Taiwan with a komi of 7.5 points, some professional players still preferred going first. No one can say for sure what the fairest value of komi is, but one study, based on an analysis of thousands of professional games, concluded that the advantage of going first is equal to exactly 7 points.

The beginning of a professional game is illustrated in Diagram 5.11. A discussion of tactics and strategy is beyond the scope of this book, but a vast literature exists, including dozens of books currently in print in English, most of which are published by Ishi Press International, 76 Bonaventura Drive, San Jose, CA 95134.

One thing beginning players do need to be aware of is the concept of "eyes." The Black group shown in the first position in Diagram 5.9 encloses a single vacant point, known as an eye. If White plays on this point, the Black group will be captured. In fact, White need not hurry to make this capture: There's nothing Black can do to save his group, since a Black play on the vacant point would be suicide, taking away the group's last liberty.

Now consider the second position in Diagram 5.9. Black's

group surrounds two points, and the points are separated by Black stones. White can never capture this group. Because a White play on either point would be suicide, White can never occupy both of Black's "eyes" simultaneously.

The principle to remember is that a group with one eye dies if it becomes surrounded, while a group with two or more eyes survives. But when you count a group's eyes, be careful. In Diagram 5.10, Black has surrounded two points instead of one, but he still has only one eye. Because the points are adjacent, White can reduce them to a single point. First, White plays on one of the vacant points, threatening to capture the Black group by playing on the other point. Black is helpless because, if he captures the white stone, the position will revert to the first position in Diagram 5.9.

In deciding whether a vacant area within a group constitutes one eye or two, what matters is whether the player who owns the group can forcibly divide it into two separate areas each containing at least one vacant point. Sometimes an attacker can reduce as many as six or seven vacant points to a single eye, whereas a straight line of four vacant points can always be split into two eyes.

Diagram 5.10

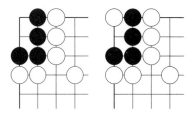

Although the Black group in the position at left surrounds two vacant points, it has only one eye. White can capture the group by playing on either interior vacant point, as shown. If Black plays on the other point to capture the White stone, the resulting position will be the same as the first part of Diagram 5.9, when Black is about to be captured.

Diagram 5.11

Shown here are the first 50 moves of a professional go game (Ishida Yoshio, Black, vs. Rin Kai Ho, White; 1971 Honinbo Championship, Game 6).

Early in the game, players typically sketch out territory first in the corners, where territory is easiest to make, and then along the sides. Complicated fights often break out in corners, such as in the upper left here. Moves 4 through 33 are just one of many variations of the onadare joseki (large avalanche corner opening). Note that the players do not bother to capture stones 9 or 18, since other moves are far more valuable at this stage of the game.

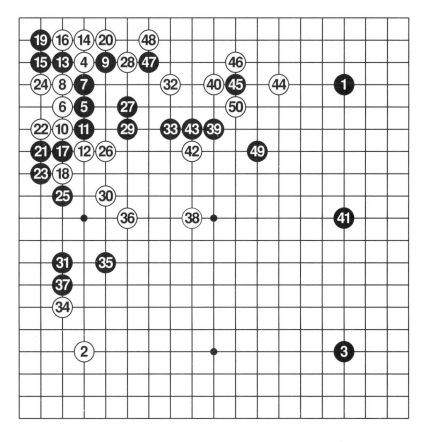

Diagram 5.12

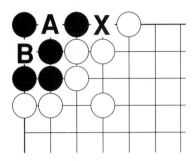

Black may seem to have two eyes, but point A is really a "false eye" that White will be able to occupy once either player occupies the point marked X. A "ko fight" (as will be described in Chapter 15) may delay things, but White will inevitably occupy A, after which a play at B will capture the Black group.

Beginning players also need to beware of "false eyes," which resemble true eyes but are missing a solid connection somewhere. In Diagram 5.12, point A is not an eye for Black, because White can play there once point X is filled by either player. Since the Black group has only one true eye, it is doomed.

Other Board Sizes

The simplest way to vary go is to change the size of the board. Smaller boards, most often 9x9 or 13x13, are commonly found in postal play, computer tournaments, and games by novices who are trying to develop a feel for the game before investing the time it takes to play a game on the standard 19x19 board.

Occasionally, professionals have experimented with larger boards such as 21x21 and 23x23. If 19x19 go theory ever reaches a point at which top players seem to feel the game holds too few secrets, then a switch to a larger board—with no other rule changes—will open up whole new worlds for players to conquer.

Other Board Geometries

Both Cylindrical Go, in which players imagine that one pair of opposite board edges are adjacent, and Toric Go, in which players imagine that each pair of opposite board edges is adjacent (compare Toric Scrabble in Chapter 1), have been tried and even played postally by NOST. Neither game is as good as the basic game.

Indeed, at high levels of play, it would seem that Toric Go should always result in a tie because neither player should be able to form a group with two eyes. Typically, each player should end up with one large group, both groups will share common liberties, and both players will be forced to pass when each of their groups has just two liberties left. In other words, Toric Go is one big seki.

Diagram 5.13

In Tetromino Go, a player may place up to four stones per turn, provided they are placed on adjacent points in one of these basic patterns. Rotations or reflections of these patterns are also allowed.

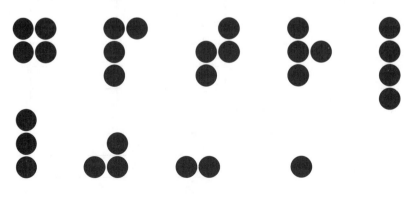

Double-Move Go

If each player is allowed to make two moves per turn, an interesting offshoot develops in which many tactics change. For example, a group needs three eyes to be permanently safe.

Omino Go

Around 1980, I had an idea that might be viewed as an extension of Double-Move Go. I wondered what would happen if, each turn, players were allowed to occupy a line segment instead of a point. The variation I eventually settled on could be called "Tetromino Go," because each player, in turn, is allowed to play up to four solidly connected pieces at once. Being allowed to play just two adjacent pieces would make it Domino Go, five would be Pentomino Go—and these variations turn out to be interesting, too.

Specifically, a player may play up to four stones in a turn, provided they form one of the shapes shown in Diagram 5.13, or any shape that can be obtained by rotating and/or reflecting one of those shapes.

There is no komi. Instead, Black is restricted to playing no more than two pieces on his first turn. After that, each player may play up to four. The winner is determined by Chinese scoring methods: Occupied points and surrounded points count 1 point each, but captured stones do not earn any points.

Instead of using a go set, I usually play on a homemade square board of 225 squares, with one-inch square tiles as pieces. This creates nice visual patterns and makes the "omino" theme more apparent, as shown in Diagram 5.14.

The game takes much less time to play than go, and its tactics are very different. A variation I thought of at the time, but have not spent much time trying, is to give each player a different set of allowable shapes to play. Each player also is permitted to play a single piece at any time, since that often becomes necessary to close off borders in the endgame, as well as to make captures. Actually, this idea could lead to a wealth of variations, and players could have fun trying to discover which shapes do best against which other shapes.

One-Capture Go with No Passing

A common go tactic is to sacrifice one or more stones in order to gain time to build a wall around the opposing forces that are capturing the sacrificed stones. Later, this wall is used as a base from which to launch attacks on other stones and, ultimately, to make more territory than the amount sacrificed. This tactic becomes impossible in a variation known as One-Capture Go; but, in return for giving up this tactic, players get a game with the excitement and tension of a sudden-death overtime period in hockey.

Rules are as in go, with two differences: (1) players may not pass, and (2) the first player to capture a stone wins.

One big difference between this game and go is that a single eye of two or more spaces is just as good as two eyes. The opponent no longer can reduce a two-point eye to one point by placing one of his own stones in the eye, as in Diagram 5.10, since the capture of that single stone would end the game.

Nevertheless, the opening strategy of the game is much like that of ordinary go. Players try to stake out territory with loosely spaced stones, first in corners (the easiest place to make territory, since the board edges help), then along the sides (the next easiest place to make territory), and last in the center.

The reason for the similarity to ordinary go is that, because of the no-passing rule, the basic strategy still must be to form territory.

Diagram 5.14

A completed game of Omino Go, using a 15x15 board and square tiles, is shown. The players could have ended the game after move 44, but continued with a fruitless invasion (move 45, correctly answered by playing 46 to make two eyes) and the completion of some captures. (Move 47 captures the pieces placed on move 6, and moves 48, 50, and 52 capture 45. The Black player passes on moves 49 and 51. Black may not recapture 52 by playing at 45 because of the ko rule.)

The game ends in a 113–111 win for the second player (the lighter color). The square to the right of 43 does not belong to anyone; if either player occupies it, the opponent will be able to capture an entire group—Black by playing between 34 and 2, and Gray by playing inside 37.

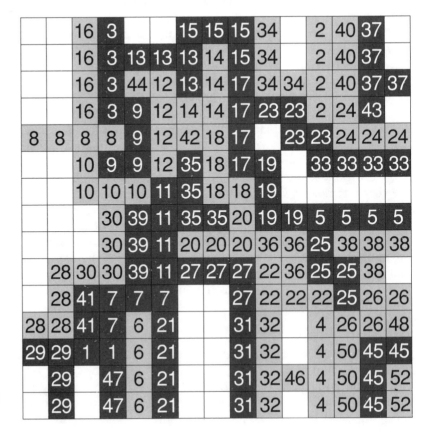

If an endgame is reached in which the board's territory has all been divided up, players will have to begin to use their moves to fill in their own territory, since a stone placed in the opponent's territory will usually be captured quickly.

Eventually, one player will run out of safe moves in his own territory and must fill in one of his group's next-to-last eyes, allowing the opponent to make a winning capture, as in Diagram 5.15. Generally, the player who stakes out more territory will be the last one to run out of safe moves—although there are complicating factors such as the number of groups a player has (each of which must maintain two vacant internal points as long as possible) and the shape of the remaining spaces within each group (which can sometimes be left vulnerable to an opponent's invasion).

Diagram 5.15

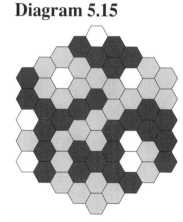

In this game of One-Capture Go on a hexagonal grid, the player who moves next will lose, since he must reduce one of his groups to a single liberty.

One-Capture Go on Other Grids

Because there are no captures in One-Capture Go prior to the end of the game, it makes a good paper-and-pencil game. Instead of placing stones on points, players use colored pencils or crayons of different colors to fill in squares.

Playing with paper and pencil makes it easy to try the game on other grids. Hexagonal grids work especially well, since it is relatively hard to capture a stone on them, requiring six stones instead of the four stones needed in regular go (anywhere except on the

Diagram 5.16

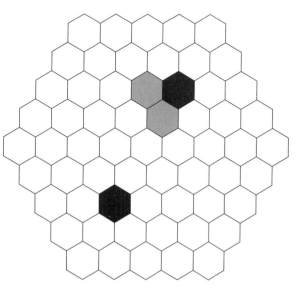

Two of an infinite number of possible boards for One-Capture Go are shown early in the game.

Diagram 5.17

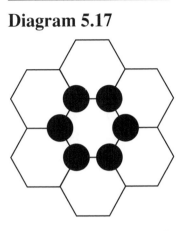

In Rosette, a hexagonal ring of six stones, as shown, is impervious to capture, even when completely surrounded by the opponent's stones. The same is true of any group containing a rosette.

Diagram 5.18

This grid is used for both Hexago and Rosette. In Hexago, stones are placed on the spaces; in Rosette, they are placed on the points where the lines intersect.

edge of the board, that is). Diagram 5.16 shows two possible grids; several others are given in Chapter 8.

Hexago and Rosette

The idea of playing "regular" go—that is, go played for territory, with unlimited captures—on other grids is not new. In 1972, Stephen Wynn came up with Hexago, which is played on a grid of 127 hexagons (Diagram 5.18). Stones are placed on the spaces rather than on the intersections; otherwise, the rules of go apply.

In 1975, Mark Berger created Rosette, played on the same grid as Hexago, but with smaller stones that are placed on the inter-sections of the hexagonal grid's lines. Because of the difficulty of forming two eyes in Rosette, a special rule was added to make sur-vival of groups easier. The rule makes permanently safe any group containing a "rosette," which is defined as a ring of six points sur-rounding a hexagon (Diagram 5.17). Rosettes also play a role in the games of Lotus and Medusa, which can be found in Chapter 7.

Nearly any kind of grid makes a playable go-type game. But square and hexagonal grids are particularly good because of their regularity, which allows players to learn tactics and develop percep-tions that are applicable to any region of the board.

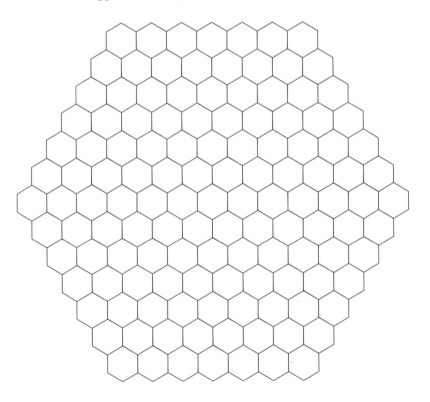

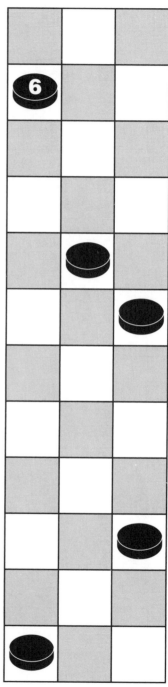

CHAPTER 6

HANDICAPPING

Handicaps are prevalent in games as well as in sports such as golf, yacht racing, and harness racing. Many game players, however, don't like the idea of receiving a handicap against a stronger player. They feel that victory is meaningless unless the fight is fair.

This argument may sound admirable, but it overlooks the two main reasons for playing games: to have a good time and to improve one's ability by learning more about the game. In playing many games, both of these ends can be better served by means of a handicap system. Using such a system requires that players modify the way they think about competition.

No game is better suited to handicapping than the Oriental game of go described in the last chapter. Because the game is so "deep"—that is, it can be played on so many different skill levels—a formal handicap system was developed centuries ago. Unequal players can play games that are interesting to both and that both have a chance to win, and yet the character of the game is unchanged.

Go players everywhere accept the handicap system and the ranking system that goes with it. Among amateurs, the stronger player gives the weaker player as many stones' handicap as the difference in their ranks. (Professional ranks are much closer together and require much smaller handicaps, if any.) Thus, if an amateur 1-kyu player (akin to a brown belt in karate) plays a 5-kyu player (four ranks lower), the 5-kyu player receives a four-stone handicap, and can place four stones of his color on the board at the start of play. Under Japanese rules, handicap stones must be placed on specific points (the nine "star points" highlighted in Diagram 5.4), but it would be hard for the player to improve on the required points even if he had the option.

With a one-rank difference, the weaker player takes Black without giving White a komi. In principle, a player should win exactly two out of three nonhandicap games against a player who is one rank below him.

Handicaps are not fixed, and therein lies the secret of the system's success. For two go players playing a series of games with one another, the question becomes not simply one of winning or losing, but rather of the weaker player's trying to reduce the handicap and the stronger player's trying to maintain or increase it.

THE KADOBAN CONCEPT

The system works this way: If either player wins three games in a row at a certain handicap level, the handicap changes by one stone. For example, if the weaker player wins three in a row at a handicap of four stones, the next three games are played at three stones. If at three stones he loses three in a row, the handicap goes back to four.

When one player has won two in a row at a certain handicap, the third game is known as a *kadoban* game and will decide whether or not the handicap changes.

Another Oriental game with a beautifully effective handicap system is shogi, a chesslike strategy game that is even more popular in Japan than go. Like go players, shogi players can become wealthy celebrities in Japan, earning hundreds of thousands of dollars a year in tournament prizes and commercial endorsements.

In shogi, like chess, the object is to checkmate the opposing king. The game is played on a 9x9 board with 20 pieces per side (actually 9 pawns and 11 other pieces).

Most of the pieces move quite differently from chess pieces, but the game's biggest difference is its "drop" rule: In shogi, pieces are captured just as in chess, but a captured piece becomes the property of the player who captured it, who may use any later turn to drop it back onto the board, on any vacant square (subject to a few minor restrictions), where it immediately becomes part of his army.

Since they must be able to switch sides unobtrusively, shogi pieces are all a single color. Ownership of pieces is indicated by the direction in which they point, which is away from their owner and toward the opponent. They are also flat, so that they can be flipped over to reveal their promoted values (see Diagram 6.1).

It is difficult to handicap Western chess without changing the nature of the game. If one player removes a piece at the start, the other player can adopt the unnatural strategy of exchanging pieces at every opportunity in order to simplify into a winning endgame. In shogi, however, every exchange *complicates* a position by giving the exchanged pieces more mobility than they had before; they're still in the game, and now they can be dropped anywhere!

As a result, when a shogi player gives a handicap by removing one or more pieces from his side at the start of a game (these pieces are removed from play, not given to the opponent to drop), he is giving up much less than a chess player might think. An elaborate handicap system has been worked out for shogi, just as it has in go, and it is observed throughout Japan. For information about shogi, the best English language book is *Shogi for Beginners* by John Fairbairn (Ishi Press, 1984).

Not all games lend themselves so easily to handicaps as go and shogi. If our goal is to create a handicap system that is adjustable (i.e., has at least several levels) and that does not markedly alter the character of the game we are handicapping, what are some of the ways players can balance their winning chances in other board games? Let's look at a few examples.

Diagram 6.1

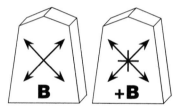

Shogi pieces are pointed, allowing ownership to be determined by the direction they face. They are also flat so that they can be flipped over to reveal their promoted value.

Shown here are the front and back of a bishop from a Westernized shogi set in which movement powers are illustrated on the pieces. (When promoted, a bishop gains the ability to move one step orthogonally.) On Japanese sets, only the names of the pieces appear, written with Japanese characters.

TRIVIAL PURSUIT WITH HANDICAPS

No doubt many readers of this book have played Trivial Pursuit more than once. Some of you may play it on a regular basis. If so, here's a way to even things up if some of the players seem to win a lot more often than the others.

Each time a player wins a game of Trivial Pursuit within a circle of players, he gets a handicap point. He carries this handicap point with him from one session to the next. One player in the group should be assigned to keep track of these points.

Before a game begins, a player must choose one category to become a "handicap category" for each handicap point he has. Thus, a player with three handicap points must choose three handicap categories. When that player lands on the headquarters space of one of his handicap categories, he must answer *two questions in a row*, instead of one question, to earn a wedge of that category's color.

If a player has more than six handicap points, so that all categories are handicap categories for him, he must name some categories as "double handicaps" —which means he must answer *three* consecutive questions correctly to earn a wedge on those categories' headquarters.

If all players in a game have handicap points, they all subtract enough points from their total so that at least one player has a total of zero handicap points. Then they choose their handicap categories and begin play as usual.

When players have played enough games to achieve accurate handicaps, this system should give everyone an equal chance to win. In addition to winning, each player will have a secondary objective of trying to increase his handicap points.

DICTIONARY ODDS

If you're in a big city coffee house and a local hustler offers to play you Scrabble for a few cents a point, watch out. When Scrabble is played with challenges, a strong player can defeat an average player by *hundreds* of points in a single game. One reason for the strong player's success is familiarity with the dictionary of record, which today is usually *The Official Scrabble Players Dictionary.* Unless the average player knows all the two- and three-letter words in the dictionary, most of the unusual short words containing the high-point letters, and a great deal more, he will stand very little chance against the hustler.

But if the hustler is in a charitable mood, he may agree to play at "dictionary odds." That means that although he cannot look at the dictionary during play, except to find one of his own words if it's challenged, his opponent may consult it at will throughout the game. The hustler may still win, but not by the kind of margin he can get when the normal challenge rule is in effect.

Dictionary Odds may also be an equitable handicap for other word games.

Takebacks

For pure strategy games, such as chess and go, when there is a great difference in skill between the players, an interesting handicapping method is to allow the weaker player to take back his most recent move. There is one restriction, though: He cannot take back a move more than once per turn. Thus, if the weaker player makes a move, then decides he doesn't like it after seeing the opponent's response, he can take it back. But if he doesn't like the way things go after his substituted move, he's stuck with it.

Chess Handicaps

Many kinds of handicaps have been tried in chess over the years. The most common is for the stronger player to remove a pawn or a piece, such as a knight, before the game starts. Usually, whoever gives the material handicap gets to play White and go first. "Pawn and move," however, is a popular handicap in which one player plays Black and gives up his f pawn (his king's bishop's pawn). "Pawn and two moves" is similar, except that the White player gets to make two moves at the start instead of one.

An interesting handicap is "rook versus pawn and move." White removes his queen's rook and Black removes his f pawn, as shown in Diagram 6.2. The extra rook is not worth as much as it

Diagram 6.2

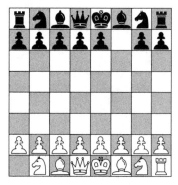

The handicap of rook versus pawn and move is less one-sided than it appears, since the absence of the f pawn creates exploitable weaknesses near Black's king.

might seem in this setup, because White has many attacking opportunities against the weakened Black kingside.

Still another classic chess handicap is the "ringed piece." Before the game begins, the weaker player chooses one of the stronger player's pieces or pawns, and the stronger player must use that piece or pawn to deliver checkmate—or lose the game!

IN GENERAL

Some games can be handicapped by giving one player extra moves (go or Hex), points (bridge), more money (Monopoly), more armies (Risk), extra guesses (Clue), more time (Speed Chess), a lesser goal to achieve (fewer pieces to get home or a shorter distance to travel in a race game such as Chinese Checkers or backgammon), or other advantages related to the game itself. Players will need to experiment with a game until they find a handicap level at which everyone wins about the same number of games.

CHAPTER

NEW WAYS TO USE GAME EQUIPMENT

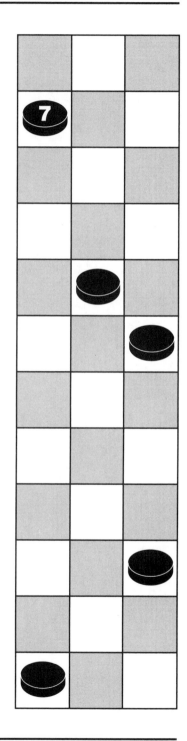

Sometimes the distinction between a game variation and a new game is fuzzy. Since this book, in its broadest sense, is about new ways to play with game equipment, I have taken the liberty of eliminating the distinction entirely in order to present rules for some interesting games that can be played with equipment found in games you are likely already to own or that you can easily improvise.

Playing Cards: Eleusis

Eleusis was invented in 1956 by Robert Abbott, who revised the rules from 1973 to 1976. It is a game played with cards, and yet it uses cards in a completely original way, making it appropriate for this chapter's theme.

The game is for four to eight players. It is possible for three to play, but in such a game no player can become Prophet. More than eight can play, but a group of this size might prefer to split into two games.

Enough cards should be on hand so that the stock does not run out. To start, shuffle together two 52-card decks to form the stock. If, after a play, the stock is down to four or fewer cards, immediately add another 52-card deck. However, don't add the extra deck until it is needed. Three decks will normally be enough for a game.

Object. A game consists of one or more rounds (hands of play). A different player is chosen as dealer of each new round. How to choose the dealer is explained later under "Miscellaneous Rules."

All plays are made to a central layout that grows as the round progresses. An example is shown in Diagram 7.1. A layout consists of a horizontal *mainline* of cards that follow a certain pattern. Below this are vertical *sidelines* of cards that are exceptions to the pattern.

Players score points by getting rid of the cards in their hands. In most cases, they get rid of cards by playing the ones that are accepted on the mainline of the layout. Players also score (and normally score higher) by acting as Prophet.

The dealer of a round does not play a hand that round. His score is based on the scores of the other players.

The Secret Rule. Each round has a different rule that determines which cards are accepted on the mainline and which are rejected. At the beginning of a round, no player knows this rule.

The secret rule is devised by the dealer of the round. He does not reveal his rule, but, when a card—or string of cards—is played, he says whether it is accepted or rejected. Cards that are accepted are added to the right of the mainline. Cards that are rejected are placed below the mainline.

Players attempt to figure out the rule by observing the pattern that emerges on the layout. The closer a player gets to understanding the rule, the better he is able to play.

Here are some examples of rules. In all of these rules, "last card" refers to the last card accepted on the mainline or, if no card has yet been accepted, it refers to the "starter" card.

- If the last card was a spade, play a heart; if the last card was a heart, play a diamond; if the last was a diamond, play a club; and if the last was a club, play a spade.

- The card played must be one point higher or one point lower than the last card.

  Note: When numbers are involved in a rule, ace is usually 1, jack is 11, queen is 12, and king is 13.

- If the last card was black, play a card higher than or equal to that card; if the last was red, play lower or equal.

- If the last card is an odd-numbered card (ace, 3, 5, etc.), play a black card; if the last card is even, play a red card. (This was the rule used in the round that created the sample layout in Diagram 7.1.)

The dealer should write his rule on a piece of paper that is put aside to be examined later. Before the play begins, the dealer may, if he wishes, give a hint about his rule. Once play begins, however, no hints should be given.

Diagram 7.1

This sample layout for Eleusis shows a game in progress. Players attempt to deduce the dealer's secret rule that determines whether a card may be placed on the mainline. If a player tries to play a card that does not conform to the rule, the dealer tells him to place the card on a sideline.

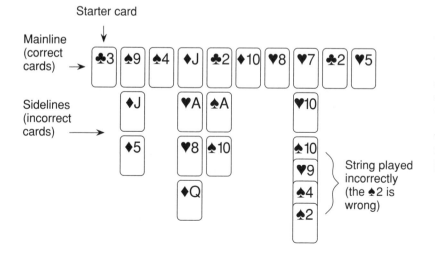

Starter card

Mainline (correct cards) →

Sidelines (incorrect cards) →

String played incorrectly (the ♠2 is wrong)

The Deal. Normally, the stock contains two 52-card decks, but, if another deck has been added during a previous round, it is retained as part of the stock. The dealer shuffles the stock and deals 14 cards to each player, taking no cards himself. He then places one card face up. This "starter" card is the first card of the mainline.

The Play. The player who goes first is chosen by this randomizing method: The dealer starts with the player on his left and counts clockwise around the circle of players, excluding himself from the count. He continues, going around more than once if necessary, until the count equals the number of the starter card. At this point he stops, and the player he stops at goes first.

In his turn, a player must play one card, play a string of cards, or declare that he has no play. After his play, the turn passes clockwise.

Playing One Card. To make a play of a single card, the player takes the card from his hand and shows it to the dealer. The dealer then says "right" or "wrong," depending on whether the card is playable at that point under his secret rule. If "right," the card is put on the layout to the right of the last mainline card. If "wrong," the card is put below the last card played (it either starts a sideline or continues one) and the dealer gives the player two cards from the stock. Thus a right play will decrease a player's hand by one card and a wrong play will cause a net increase of one card.

Playing a String of Cards. A string consists of two, three, or four cards which, if all are correct, will extend the mainline pattern. To play a string, the player takes the cards from his hand, overlaps them slightly to indicate their order, and shows them to the dealer.

A string of, say, three cards is the same as three consecutive plays of a single card each. The dealer calls this string right only if all three cards would be right. If one or more of the cards in the string are wrong, the dealer declares the entire string wrong. He does not reveal which individual cards are wrong.

Here is an example. Suppose the dealer is using the first of the sample rules given above. This rule produces the simple mainline pattern spade-heart-diamond-club-spade-etc. If the last mainline card is a ♥7, a player could show a ♦3-♣Q string and it would be called right. But if he showed the same two cards in reverse order (♣Q-♦3), the string would be called wrong.

When a string is called right, it is placed to the right of the last mainline card. Thus a correct string of four cards would look the same as four correct plays of a single card each. If a string is called wrong, its cards remain overlapped and the entire string is placed below the last card played (see Diagram 7.1). The overlapping is necessary to retain information that these cards were played as a string and to show the order that the player gave to the string.

For a string played wrong, the player is given cards from the stock equal to twice the number of cards in the string.

Declaring No Play. A player has the option of declaring that he has no correct card to play. He shows his hand to everyone, and the dealer says whether the player is right or not.

If the player is right—he really could not have played—and if his hand is down to four cards or fewer, his cards are put back in the stock, and the round ends at that point.

If the player is right, and if he has five or more cards, his cards are counted and then put on the bottom of the stock. He is dealt a fresh hand from the top of the stock, but he is dealt four cards less than the number he held previously.

If the player was wrong—he really had one or more cards that could have been correct—the dealer takes one of the correct cards and puts it on the layout to the right of the last mainline card. The player keeps the rest of the cards in his hand and is dealt five more cards from the stock.

A player who thinks he has no correct play, but who has little notion of the secret rule, should realize that the odds are against his using this option successfully. He would do better to play a single card, even one he suspects will be wrong.

Becoming Prophet. Once a player thinks he's discovered the secret rule, he has the opportunity to prove it, and score higher, by predicting how the dealer will speak—in other words, he becomes a *Prophet*. He will call "right" or "wrong" when others play, and he will take over all the dealer's normal functions.

A player becomes a Prophet simply by declaring himself one. However, he can make this declaration only if (1) he has just played (right or wrong) and the next player has not yet played, (2) no other Prophet exists, (3) there are at least two other players still in the round (that is, two besides himself and the dealer), and (4) he has not been Prophet before in the round.

When a player declares himself Prophet, he puts a marker on the layout on the last card he played. This records the point at which he became Prophet. A chess king or any object of similar size can be used. The Prophet keeps his hand but plays no more cards from it unless he is overthrown.

Acting as Prophet. After a player has declared himself Prophet, the turn continues clockwise around the other players. The Prophet does not take a turn.

When a player plays a single card, the Prophet says "right" if he thinks the card is playable at that point under the dealer's secret rule, or he says "wrong" if he thinks the card is not playable. The dealer now says whether the Prophet made the correct call. If the dealer says "correct," the Prophet completes the play, putting the card on the mainline or sideline and giving the player cards from the stock if his play was wrong. If the dealer says the Prophet is incorrect, the Prophet is overthrown.

The turn on which the Prophet is overthrown is completed by the dealer according to special rules. If a card—or a string of cards—was played, the dealer puts it in the proper place on the layout, either on the mainline or the sideline. The player of the card or string is not, however, given any penalty cards, even if his play was wrong.

This is an exception to the normal procedure, but it has a purpose. It makes it more likely that a player will attempt an unusual play, even a deliberately wrong play, in hopes of overthrowing the Prophet.

Things get complicated when there is a Prophet and a player declares he has no play. There are also special rules here when a Prophet is overthrown. Let's look at each case separately.

- In the first case, the player declares he has no play, the Prophet says he is right, and the dealer says the Prophet is correct. The procedure described in the section "Declaring No Play" is now followed: The player either gets rid of his cards or is dealt a smaller hand.

- In the second case, the player declares no play, the Prophet says he is right, but the dealer says, "No, he is wrong." The Prophet is now overthrown. The dealer takes one correct card from the player's hand and puts it on the mainline. The player is not, however, given any penalty cards.

- In the third case, the player declares no play, the Prophet says "wrong," but the dealer says, "No, the player was right." The Prophet is overthrown and the player either gets rid of his cards or is dealt a smaller hand.

- In the last case, the player declares no play, the Prophet says "wrong," and the dealer says the Prophet is correct. The Prophet now must pick one correct card from the hand and play it on the mainline. If he does this right, he then deals the player the five penalty cards. But it's possible for the Prophet to slip up here and not pick a correct card. If this happens, the dealer steps in, overthrowing the Prophet. The card the Prophet picked is put back in the player's hand, and the dealer picks a card that actually is correct. This card is put on the mainline. The player (that is, the one who originally declared no play) is not given any penalty cards.

After a Prophet Is Overthrown. When a Prophet is overthrown, he is given five cards from the stock as a penalty. He adds these cards to his original hand and resumes his normal turn. He cannot become Prophet again during that round. The Prophet's marker is removed from the layout.

The player who just played can now declare himself Prophet, as long as his declaration does not violate any of the rules listed in "Becoming Prophet." Or, on a subsequent turn, another player might become Prophet.

Expulsion. After a round has lasted for a certain time (see below), players may be expelled from the round when they make incorrect plays. An incorrect play is either a card or string played incorrectly or an incorrect declaration of no play.

A player is expelled if he makes an incorrect play, there is no Prophet, and there were 30 or more cards on the layout before his play. Or, a player is expelled if he makes an incorrect play, there *is* a Prophet, and there were 20 or more cards following the Prophet's marker before his play. However, no one is expelled during a turn in which a Prophet is overthrown.

When expelled, a player makes no further play for that round (and he cannot become Prophet). He is, however, given the penalty cards for his last incorrect play and retains his hand for scoring at the end.

Players should know when expulsion is possible by keeping a count of the cards on the layout. It's helpful to use markers, such as a white chess pawn or checker on every tenth card of the layout if there is no Prophet. If there is a Prophet, also place a black pawn or checker on every tenth card following the Prophet's marker. If the Prophet is overthrown, the black markers are removed, along with the Prophet's marker. Notice that a round can go in and out of a phase in which players can be expelled. For example, suppose there are 35 cards on the layout and there is no Prophet. Smith plays incorrectly and is expelled. Jones now plays correctly and declares himself Prophet. Brown now plays incorrectly. Brown is not expelled, because there are not 20 cards following the Prophet's marker, even though there are more than 30 cards on the layout.

Scoring. When one player gets rid of all his cards, the round ends. It also ends if all players (or all players besides the Prophet) have been expelled.

The players, including any who were expelled during the round, now receive scores based on the number of cards in their hands. The Prophet, if there was one at the end, receives a score based on the cards in his hand plus a bonus for successfully remaining Prophet until the end of the round.

First, the greatest number of cards in any one hand, including the Prophet's, is determined. This is called the "high count." Each player, including the Prophet, then scores this high count *minus* the number of cards in his own hand. If a player got rid of all his cards, he also receives a 4-point bonus.

Next, the Prophet's bonus is calculated and added to this score. This bonus is one point for every card played correctly after he became Prophet plus two points for every card played incorrectly after he became Prophet.

Finally, the dealer's score is figured. The dealer is given a score equal to the highest score in the round, with the following exception: If there is a Prophet, count the number of cards (mainline and sideline) that precede the Prophet's marker and multiply this number by two. If the resulting number is smaller than the highest score, the dealer scores that smaller number.

The scores are added to those for any previous rounds. The players now decide whether there is time for another round. If not, the game ends at that point.

At the end, 10 points are added to the score of any player who has not acted as dealer. This is to compensate for the fact that the dealer's score for a round is usually higher than the average score for that round.

If there is time to play another round, a new dealer is chosen from among those who have not yet been dealer. The game also ends if every player has been dealer—but, unfortunately, such a game would take the better part of a day.

Here is an example of the way a round is scored. The layout at the end of the round is shown in Diagram 7.2. (Can you figure out its secret rule?)

Smith is dealer. The round ended when Jones got rid of all his cards. Brown was Prophet at the end; he had 9 cards in his hand. Robinson was expelled when he mistakenly played the ♠10 near the end. His hand consists of 14 cards. Adams has 17 cards in his hand.

The high count is 17. Adams scores zero (17 minus 17). Robinson scores 3 (17 minus 14). Jones scores 21 (17 minus 0 plus the 4-point bonus for getting rid of all his cards). Brown scores 8 for the cards in his hand (17 minus 9) plus the Prophet's bonus of 34 (12 mainline and 11 sideline cards follow the Prophet's marker). Therefore, Brown's score is 42.

The highest score for the round is 42. Two times the number of cards that precede the Prophet's marker is 50. The dealer, Smith, scores the smaller of these two numbers, which is 42.

The secret rule in the layout in Diagram 7.2, by the way, was this: "If the last card is lower than the previous card, play a card higher than the last card; otherwise play lower. The first card played is correct unless it is equal to the starter card."

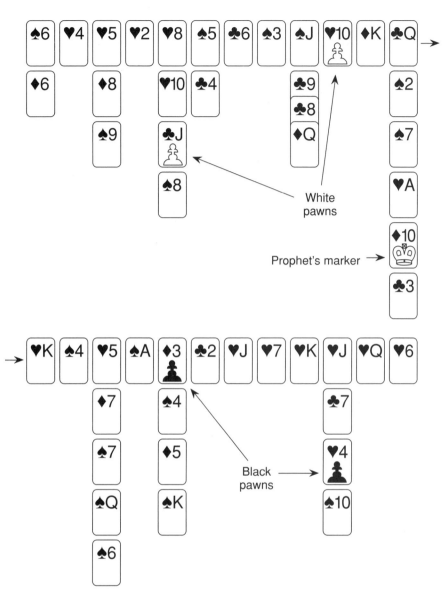

Diagram 7.2

This is a typical layout at the end of a round. Even when playing on the floor, players may find it convenient, for space reasons, to jump the mainline from one row to another. Here, the ♣Q is followed by the ♥K. White pawns are used to mark every tenth card from the start, while Black pawns are used to mark every tenth card after the Prophet's marker.

White pawns

Prophet's marker →

Black pawns

Miscellaneous Rules. Because of the size of the layout, the game normally must be played on the floor. But it is possible to play at a large table with miniature cards. When the mainline of the layout progresses too far to the right, it can be continued below on the left, as in Diagram 7.2.

Following are some additional rules:

- The dealer is usually chosen informally—in most cases, the first player who thinks he's formulated a good rule becomes the dealer. If the group consists of both experienced and inexperienced players, the dealer of the first round should be one of the experienced players.

- If all players in the group are experienced, they may prefer a more formal method of choosing the dealer. The following method can be used: Each player who has not yet been dealer draws a card from the stock. The player who draws the highest card is dealer. The cards are ranked king down to ace, and cards of the same number are ranked as in bridge: spades high, then hearts, diamonds, and clubs. If a player draws a card identical to one drawn by another player, he draws again.

- There's a certain disadvantage in following an experienced player in the playing order. Therefore, it's a good idea for players to change their order of seating after a round. If the players prefer a formal method of randomizing the seating, this can be used: If a player obtained a card during the formal drawing for dealer, he keeps that card; if not, he draws a card from the stock. The players then form a circle in such a way that the player with the highest card sits to the left of the dealer, followed by the player with the second highest card, and so on.

- Sometimes a dealer will formulate a rather rigid secret rule under which the starter card is incorrect. When this happens, he should exchange the starter card for another in the stock. But, before he does this, he should use the original starter card to count around the players to determine who goes first, as described above in "The Play."

Strategy of the Dealer. Ideally, the rule made up by the dealer should be neither too simple nor too complicated. A rule of medium difficulty will score more points for the dealer and, more importantly, will make the round more interesting for all the players.

It takes experience to judge the complexity of a rule. In general, it can be noted that more restrictive rules (ones that allow about one-fourth of the cards to be played at any one time) are easier to discover than less restrictive rules (ones that allow half or more of the cards to be played at any time). Beginning dealers have a tendency to underestimate the complexity of their rules and should be wary of this.

Discussing Eleusis in his "Mathematical Games" column in *Scientific American*, Martin Gardner pointed out that the strategy of the game is essentially the scientific method. Players formulate and test hypotheses about the dealer's secret rule in the same way that scientists try to discover laws of nature. For this reason, experienced players sometimes jokingly refer to their turn to be dealer as their "turn to be God"—which makes the term "Prophet" particularly apt.

Two other games that use cards in novel ways—as objects to be traded—are described in Chapter 9.

SCRABBLE: ANAGRAMS

Scrabble Crossword Game comes with 100 letter tiles that are ideal for playing Anagrams. Anagrams achieved peak popularity several decades ago, but it richly deserves a comeback. If Scrabble is the best word game for two players, Anagrams may be the best for three or four. Tiles or cards from games other than Scrabble can be used instead, of course; the important thing is to have a good-sized selection of letters that are distributed with roughly the same frequency as they are in English (or whatever language you're playing in). No numbers are needed on the tiles; if Scrabble tiles are used, the numbers are ignored.

Tiles are mixed and placed face down on the table or floor. One player begins by turning tiles face up, one at a time, until a player—who may be the one turning over the tiles—calls out a word that he sees can be made from the exposed tiles. The player who called out the word takes the tiles needed to spell it and places them in front of him, rearranging the tiles as necessary to spell out the word in order. Players resume turning over tiles one at a time, calling out words when they see a way to spell them.

Once you've made a word, however, don't feel too secure—the other players may steal it! If a player sees a way to form a new word that uses *at least* one tile from the pile plus *all* the tiles of a word in front of a player, the player may call out the new word, take the tile(s) from the pile as well as the tiles in the word previously formed, and make the new word in front of himself. For example, a player could take an A and an N from the pile and steal the word GAMES by forming the word MANAGES. Later, though, the word MANAGES might be stolen by someone who notices that by adding the letters HIMPS, the word can be rearranged to form GAMESMANSHIP.

To steal a word, it is not enough to add an -S, -ER, or other suffix, or to add a prefix such as RE-. The root word must be changed or the steal cannot be made.

A player may "steal" his own word, thereby lengthening it and making it harder for the opponents to steal. If you have the word TEAMING, for example, you should look hard for a chance to "upgrade" it. But don't just add an S to form STEAMING, which needs only an R to be stolen as STREAMING or MASTERING. Look for something longer, such as adding DEZ to form MAGNE-TIZED.

The game ends when all the tiles have been taken from the pile or when no one can use any of the remaining tiles. The player with the most tiles in the words in front of him is the winner.

As in most word games, players should agree in advance on what kinds of words are acceptable. Usually, any uncapitalized words in a designated dictionary of record are acceptable, other than abbreviations or words containing hyphens.

MANCALA SETS: THE GLASS BEAD GAME

Mancala games, played by moving pebbles, seeds, or other small objects around a series of pits, are played in many parts of Africa, Asia, and South America. Laurence Russ's book *Mancala Games* (Reference Publications, 1984) gives rules for more than 100 known forms of mancala, and no doubt there are many more that have been played but never catalogued.

Most of these games date back centuries, yet they display a mathematical complexity that makes them a challenge even for computers to play well. But many players find them to be somewhat dry. Each turn, the only choice a player has is to select one of his pits and pick up all the pebbles in it; then he mechanically "sows" those pebbles, by dropping one pebble into each of the other pits, moving in a predetermined direction around the board, until all the pebbles have been sown.

Christiaan Freeling, a Dutch game inventor, has created a

Diagram 7.3

The opening setup for The Glass Bead Game is shown on a board with two rows of five pits, plus one large storehouse at each end. The game's rules can also be extended to boards of other sizes.

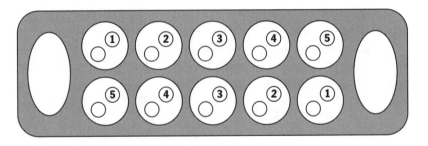

mancala-type game that may make you want to forget all the previous ones you've seen. Instead of having only five or six possible moves per turn, as in most mancalas, players sometimes have *hundreds* of choices. That's because in The Glass Bead Game—named for the fictitious game in Hermann Hesse's novel *Magister Ludi*—not all pebbles are equal. As a result, the order in which players sow their pieces around the board makes a difference.

The game is played on a 2x5 mancala board with two collecting pits at the ends, as shown in Diagram 7.3. Most commercially sold mancala boards are 2x6; one of these can be used if two pits are covered up. The board can also be improvised from cups or an egg carton.

Also needed are 20 "beads," consisting of 10 white or clear-colored beads, known as "stones," and a variety of colored beads, known as "gems," as follows: two reds, worth 1 point each; two oranges, worth 2 points each; two yellows, worth 3 points each; two greens, worth 4 points each; and two blues, worth 5 points each. (Other colors may be substituted.) Marbles or large colored beads work well, but players can use any small objects of different colors. They can even use pieces of cardboard, some unnumbered (the stones) and others numbered 1 through 5 (the gems).

At the start, players set up the pieces as shown in Diagram 7.3. Each player controls the set of pits on his own side of the board, as well as the storehouse to his right. In turn, each player chooses one of the pits on his side of the board, picks up all the beads in it, and sows them, one at a time, into the other pits around the board, moving in a counterclockwise direction. Beads are not sown into the storehouses. See Diagram 7.4.

While sowing, a player is free to choose which beads are placed in which pits. No pit may receive more than one bead, unless there are enough beads to go around the board more than once. No pits are skipped, except that if the pit whose contents are moved contains more than nine beads, the original pit is skipped. Thus the tenth bead is sown into the same pit as the first, and any additional beads continue to be sown counterclockwise, as usual.

If the last bead sown is a *stone* that goes into a pit on the

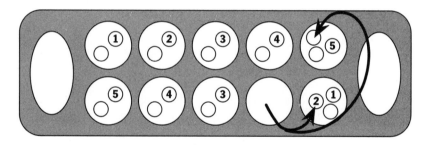

Diagram 7.4

In turn, players pick up all the beads in any pit on their own side of the board and sow them counterclockwise, one bead per pit, skipping over the storehouses. Shown here is a possible opening move.

Diagram 7.5

In the position at the top, the player sitting on the far side of the board can make a "direct capture" of two gems by sowing the contents of pit d. The 2-gem must be dropped into pit e, and the stones into pits A and B. This captures the 1-gem and 4-gem in those pits, leaving the position shown at the bottom.

If the player on the near side of the board now sows pit D by dropping the 1-gem into pit E and stones into pits a, b, and c, an "indirect capture" results when the last stone lands in pit c. The player may then take any gem from the opponent's side of the board (in this case, either the 2 in e or the 4 in b) and place it in his storehouse. The stones dropped into pits a and b do not bring about additional captures because a player may not mix direct and indirect captures in a single turn.

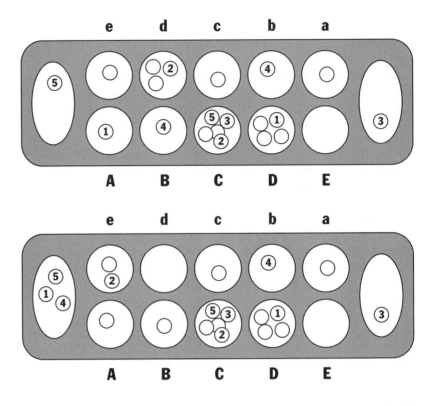

opponent's side of the board, *and* if that opponent's pit contained *exactly one* bead before the stone was placed there, the player making the move makes a capture. It makes no difference whether the single bead in the opponent's pit got there because the opponent left it there or because it was sown by the moving player as part of the same turn (in a move that involved enough beads to go all the way around the board).

What is captured depends on what the single bead in the opponent's pit is:

- If the bead is a gem, it is captured, which means it is placed in the player's storehouse. This is known as a "direct capture."

- If the bead is a stone, the player gets to capture any gem from any pit on the opponent's side of the board. The player places the captured gem in his storehouse. This is known as an "indirect capture."

- If the bead is a stone, but the opponent has no gems anywhere on his side of the board, the player gets to take a gem of his choice from the opponent's storehouse and place it into his own storehouse. (This is also an "indirect capture.") Thus, gems in a storehouse are never completely safe until the game is over. If the opponent's storehouse has no gems, either, no capture is made.

Multiple captures may be made in a single turn. If the last two or more beads sown are stones, and if each of these stones falls into an opponent's pit containing exactly one bead, then a capture may be made for each such stone—provided that all the captures are of the same type (direct or indirect). Diagram 7.5 shows an example.

If a player has no beads in any of his pits, the opponent *must* sow at least one bead onto his side, *unless* all the gems have been captured. If all the gems have been captured, a player may leave the opponent with no move, and this causes the game to end.

A player wins when all of the gems have been captured, he has 15 or more points in gems in his storehouse, it is the opponent's turn, and the opponent has no legal move. But a player *loses* if he has fewer than 15 points in gems *and* his opponent has no legal move.

As in many mancalas, a good tactic is to accumulate many beads in your rightmost pit (pit E or e in the diagrams). Such a "house," if it grows large enough before it has to be played, will allow you to make a move that wraps more than once around the board, usually giving you a nice multiple capture.

Note. The same rules can be used to play a longer game with a 2x6 mancala set, using two more pieces for each player in the opening setup. Each player puts one extra stone and one purple gem in his extra pit; the purples are worth 6. The object then is to have at least 21 points and run the opponent out of moves. Or, the game can be shortened by playing on a board as small as 2x3, in which case the colored beads are valued 1, 2, and 3, and the key point total is 6. Despite the small board size, a 2x3 Glass Bead Game is far from trivial.

CHECKERS SETS

Halma

The original inspiration for Chinese Checkers, Halma originated in Victorian England. It can be played on four checkerboards placed together, on an improvised board, or on a go board (in which case the outer ring of squares is ignored). Diagram 7.6 shows the board and starting position.

Halma is played the same way as Chinese Checkers, except that the board grid is square rather than hexagonal. This makes the play more complicated because pieces can move in eight direc-

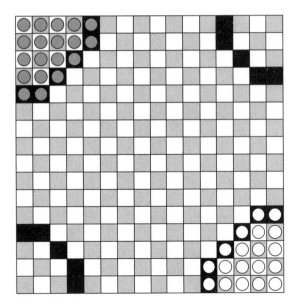
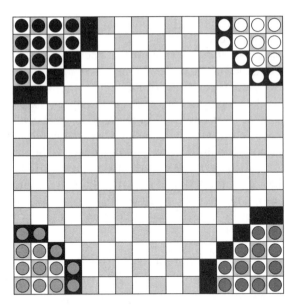

Diagram 7.6

A Halma board can be improvised by placing four checkerboards together or by drawing rules on a piece of paper. Setups are shown for two players (left) and four players (right). Interesting variations are possible when two players use the four-player setup, with each player controlling two colors.

tions—that is, along any horizontal, vertical, or diagonal line—instead of only six.

Pieces may move one square in any direction onto an empty square, or jump over an adjacent piece, no matter who that piece belongs to, landing on the square immediately beyond. The landing square must be vacant or the jump may not be made. A piece may make more than one jump, in any direction or combination of directions, as part of the same turn (see Diagram 7.7). Jumps are never compulsory, and pieces are never captured during the game.

The game can be played by two players, in which case each player has 19 pieces, or by four players, in which case each player has 13. The object is to get all of your pieces to the opponent's starting area, which is diagonally opposite your own starting position. The first player to achieve this wins.

Diagram 7.7

The piece marked with a triangle may move to any of the squares marked X, jump to either of the squares marked Y, or make a double jump to a square marked Z (via the upper right Y square). A triple jump to A is also possible, as shown on the right. A jump to B is not allowed, since two adjacent pieces may not be jumped.

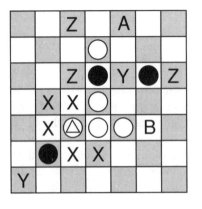
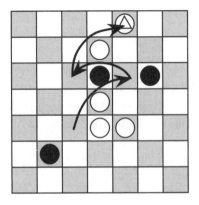

While the original rules did not make this explicit, a player should not be allowed to block his opponent's victory by leaving one or more pieces in his home area indefinitely. Thus, it is necessary to add a rule that a player wins any time, other than at the very start of the game, when the starting area diagonally across from his own starting area is full of pieces, regardless of who owns those pieces.

The rules of Super Chinese Checkers" (see Chapter 1) can be applied to Halma, making a game of "Super Halma." This speeds up the game and makes the tactics more complex.

Mini-Halma

An ordinary checkers set can be used to play a smaller, faster version of Halma. All the rules of Halma apply; the opening setup is as shown in Diagram 7.8.

Salta

Invented around 1901, this game is something like Halma, except that each piece must be moved to a specific location within the opponent's starting area, as determined by the numbers on the

Diagram 7.8

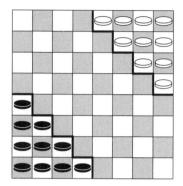

The rules of Halma can be applied to a standard checkerboard, using this opening setup. Players may use thin tape to mark the borders of the starting areas.

Diagram 7.9

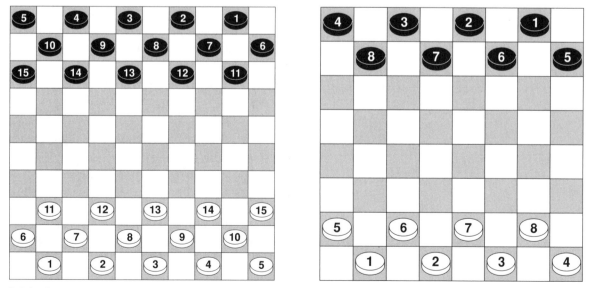

Originally played on a 100-square board, Salta can easily be adapted to an 8x8 checkerboard for shorter games.

pieces (see Diagram 7.9). For example, White must try to get his number 1 piece to the square where Black's number 1 piece started, and vice versa. The first player to get all his pieces to the correct locations on the other side wins.

Pieces may move one square diagonally, either forward or backward; or a piece may make a single diagonal jump—no multiple jumps are allowed in this game—over an adjacent piece, whether friendly or enemy, onto the square beyond, which must be vacant for the jump to occur. If a jump is available, a player is required to take it. Jumped pieces are not captured.

The original Salta, which could last well over 100 moves, was played with 15 pieces per player on a 10x10 board. A shorter version can be played with an ordinary checkers set, requiring that players mark eight checkers each with numbers as shown on the 8x8 board in Diagram 7.9. One easy way to do this is with circular self-sticking labels, which can be found in most stationery stores.

Fields of Action

Contemporary American game inventor Sid Sackson, whose many well-known games include Acquire, Can't Stop, Focus (also marketed as Domination), and Sleuth, was inspired by Claude Souci's outstanding game Lines of Action (for rules, see Sackson's *A Gamut of Games*, Castle Books, 1969) to create this interesting strategy game using an ordinary 8x8 checkerboard.

Before play, each set of checkers is numbered from 1 to 12 (as in Salta, stick-on labels work well). At the start, the pieces are set up as shown in Diagram 7.10. Once they become familiar with the game, players may wish to experiment with other setups.

Rules are as follows:

1. Starting with White, each player in turn moves one of his pieces either horizontally, vertically, or diagonally (eight possible directions of movement).

2. A moving piece may pass over any number of other pieces belonging to either or both players.

3. A player does not have a choice of how far to move a piece: A piece must always move exactly as many squares as the number of pieces that were adjacent to the piece when it started its move (see the second position in Diagram 7.10). Pieces are considered "adjacent" if they occupy one of the eight squares surrounding the piece, and both players' pieces count in figuring out the total.

4. A piece may not end its move on a piece of the same color.

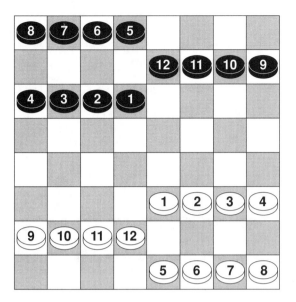
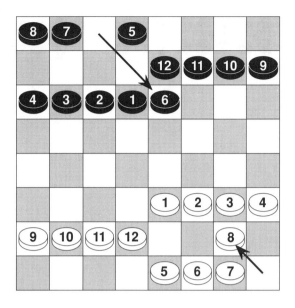

5. A piece may end its move on an opponent's piece. If this happens, the opponent's piece is captured and removed from play.

6. A special rule governs pieces that are "isolated," that is, that have no pieces adjacent to them. An isolated piece may move any number of squares in any direction, provided that it does not make a capture and that it ends its move adjacent to at least two pieces (regardless of who owns them).

7. A player wins in one of two ways:

   a. By capturing five pieces that form a numerical sequence, such as 4-5-6-7-8 (the order in which the pieces were captured does not matter).

   b. By making a move that leaves the opponent with no legal move to play. (The isolated-piece rule often comes into play here.)

Epaminondas and Crossings

Crossings, an invention of Robert Abbott's that originally appeared in *A Gamut of Games*, is an intriguing game that can be played with an ordinary checkers set. But like many inventors, he was not fully satisfied with his creation. Eventually, he transformed it into a game he published himself, called Epaminondas. The game is named for a Theban general who used phalanx strategy to defeat the Spartans in 371 B.C.

Epaminondas differs from Crossings in two ways: The captur-

Diagram 7.10

The normal starting position for Fields of Action is shown at left. Once players become experienced, they may wish to experiment with other setups.

In the position on the right, each player has made one move, White with his 8 piece and Black with his 6 piece. Captures are already being threatened. White's 8 piece, which is now adjacent to five pieces, may capture Black's 10 piece; while Black's 6 piece can capture White's 1 or 4 piece. Black's 12 piece can also capture White's 1 piece.

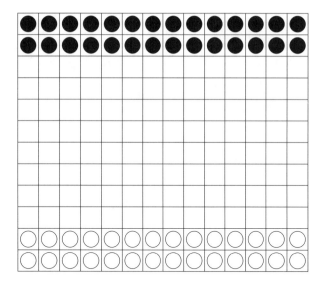

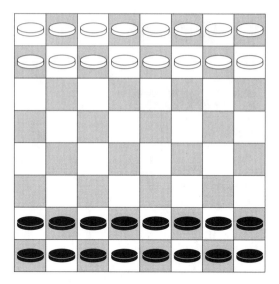

Diagram 7.11

The rules of Epaminondas (set up as shown at left) can be adapted for use on a checkerboard, as shown in the setup on the right.

Diagram 7.12

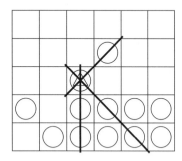

A piece may belong to more than one phalanx. The piece marked with a triangle is part of a three-piece vertical phalanx, a three-piece diagonal phalanx, and a two-piece diagonal phalanx, along the lines shown. Horizontally, it is essentially a "phalanx" of one.

ing rule gives more impetus to the offense, and the scale of play is greater, with a larger board and more pieces. But Epaminondas rules can be used on an 8x8 board, thereby creating a game that might be called "Neo-Crossings."

The game is for two players, known as White and Black. Each player begins with 16 checkers of his color, set up as shown in Diagram 7.11. White moves first, after which turns alternate.

Each player, in turn, moves either a single piece or a "phalanx" of his color. A *phalanx* is defined as an unbroken line of two or more pieces of the same color, all lying along any horizontal, vertical, or diagonal line. Under this definition, a piece may belong to more than one phalanx (see Diagram 7.12).

A single piece may move one space in any horizontal, vertical, or diagonal direction (like a king in chess). A phalanx may move, as a unit, any number of squares less than or equal to the number of pieces in the phalanx. Thus, a phalanx of two pieces may move one or two squares; a phalanx of three pieces may move one, two, or three squares; and so on. When pieces in a phalanx move, all of them must move the same distance and direction, and they may only move along the line that defines the phalanx (see Diagram 7.13).

A player may "split up" a phalanx and move just part of it, provided the pieces that move form an unbroken line and that the number of pieces moved is equal to or greater than the number of spaces moved (see Diagram 7.14).

A phalanx may not move over or through friendly pieces, but the "head" piece of a phalanx may land on either a single opposing piece or the first piece of a *smaller* opposing phalanx. If the opposing phalanx is greater than or equal in size to the moving phalanx, the capturing move cannot be made. In determining phalanx size, only its length along the line of movement is considered, and only pieces that make the move are counted (see Diagram 7.15).

When the head of a phalanx lands on the head of an opposing phalanx, the entire opposing phalanx is captured. (This is the key rule change from the original Crossings; in that game, only the piece landed on was captured.) Capturing moves are never compulsory.

A player wins if, at the start of his turn, he has more pieces on the row farthest from him than the opponent has on the row farthest from him. Stated differently, this means that when a player gets one of his pieces to the other side of the board, he will win unless the opponent either captures this piece immediately or gets (or already has) one of his own pieces on the last rank. If both players have an equal number of pieces on the ranks farthest from them, the game continues (see Diagram 7.16).

There is one other rule. It turns out that if the second player mimics the first by making moves that are symmetrical with respect to the center point of the board (that is, a play on the left is mirrored by an opposing play made in the opposite direction on the right), the game will always end in a draw. To eliminate this strategy, the following rule is added: A player may not move a piece onto the row farthest from him if the move would create a pattern of left-to-right symmetry (symmetry about the center point).

Other board sizes will also work well, no doubt. The reason for preferring a board that is wider than it is deep is to make the diagonals more equal in value to the orthogonal lines of movement.

OTHELLO SETS

Reversi

When the board game Othello became popular in the early 1980s (then published by Gabriel), you may recall that a host of virtually identical games was published by other companies. Did you wonder how they got away with it? The reason is the game of Reversi, a public-domain game invented in Victorian England. Except for some minor technicalities, the only difference between Reversi and Othello is the opening setup. Thus, if you own an Othello set, you can play Reversi, and vice versa.

In both games, two white pieces and two black pieces are

Diagram 7.13

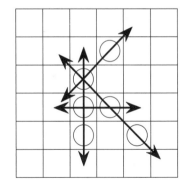

A phalanx moves as a unit, along the line that defines the phalanx, in either direction. The arrows indicate possible movement directions for the two- and three-piece phalanxes in the diagram.

Diagram 7.14

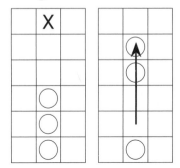

A player may split up a phalanx by moving just part of it. The maximum number of squares the moving pieces can go is equal to the number of pieces that move. At left, the three-piece phalanx can move as far as the square marked X; but if only two pieces of the phalanx move, they may advance no more than two squares, as shown at right.

Diagram 7.15

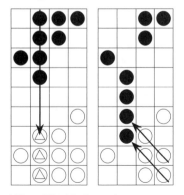

When Black's four-piece phalanx runs head on into the marked White phalanx, all three pieces in the White phalanx are captured. The head of the Black phalanx must stop on the square where it encountered the first White piece, leaving the position shown at right. White now may make a recapture along either of the two diagonals shown.

Diagram 7.16

In this position, Black has just moved a third piece to his last row (White's first row). White has no way to capture any of these pieces. To prolong the game, therefore, White must immediately move a third piece to the last row, to one of the spaces marked X. But Black's four-piece phalanx (marked with triangles) will then be able to capture at least two of White's three last-row pieces, giving Black the victory.

placed on the four center squares of the board. In Othello, the colors must crisscross. In Reversi, players begin by alternately placing pieces in the four center squares however they wish, leading to two possible configurations (apart from rotations or reflections, which do not meaningfully change the play), as shown in Diagram 7.17.

After the first four pieces are on the board, each player in turn must capture at least one opposing piece per turn, by sandwiching an opposing piece—or an unbroken line of opposing pieces—between two of his own pieces along any row, column, or diagonal. Captured pieces flip over to become the color of the capturing player.

Paradoxically, the best strategy is to *avoid* capturing any more pieces than necessary throughout most of the game. This restricts the opponent's choices, and often forces him to let you win key squares, such as corners, late in the game.

Modern Ming-Mang

British game historian R. C. Bell, in his *Discovering Old Board Games* (Shire Publications, 1973), gives fragmentary information about a Tibetan game he calls Ming-Mang. But, in fact, that term is used in Tibet as a general term for any board game and often refers

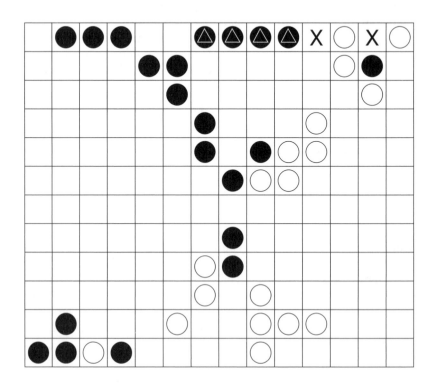

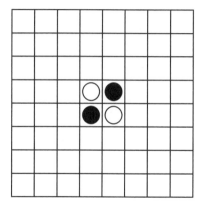
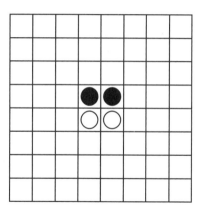

Diagram 7.17

Othello uses only the opening setup shown at the far left. In the century-old game of Reversi, either of these two opening patterns is possible.

An interesting variation is to place a marker on one square before the game. Throughout the game, the marked space is treated like a hole in the board. No piece may be placed there, and a line of pieces that is interrupted by the marked square cannot be captured along that line.

to a local version of go. The opening setup described by Bell is the one shown on the large board in Diagram 7.18.

The form of capture in the game Bell described was unusual: When a player surrounds a solid line of opposing pieces on both ends, all the pieces in that line turn to his color. This is the same rule as in Reversi or Othello, but I had never seen it in a game in which pieces, rather than just being placed on the board, could move around. ("Custodian captures," in which pieces surrounded on both ends are *removed*, however, are found in a number of old

Diagram 7.18

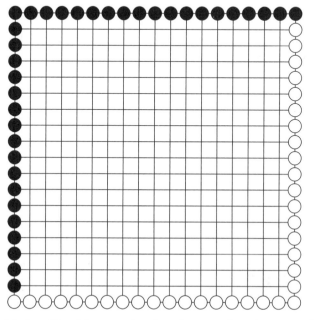
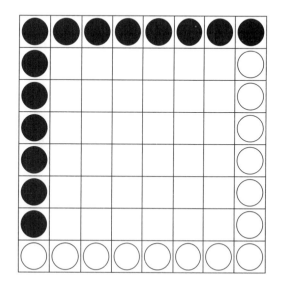

Modern Ming-Mang can be played on a go board or on an Othello or Reversi set, with the initial positions shown.

Diagram 7.19

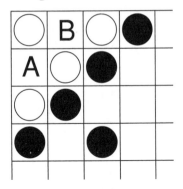

Under the fragmentary rules provided by R. C. Bell, there is nothing to stop one player from setting up an impregnable fortress to assure a draw. Here, all White has to do is to move the piece in the corner back and forth to A or B, and Black will have no way of capturing any of White's pieces.

games, including the Egyptian game Seega, the Roman game Ludus Latrunculorum, and, as seen in Chapter 2, Tablut.)

Although Bell explained setup, movement, and capture, he said nothing about the game's object. A little experimentation convinced me that if the rules given were correct, the object could not have been to capture all the opposing pieces, because it is very easy to arrange a few pieces in a corner in such a way that they can never be captured (see Diagram 7.19).

Possibly, a rule was omitted that would allow capture of corner pieces. But in trying to make the game playable within Bell's rule framework, I took a different approach. Since Bell described the game as being played on a go board, I decided to change the object of the game so that it was the same as in go: to capture the most territory. Piece captures occurred as in Bell's rules, but now they were merely a means to an end.

It's often a good idea to start small with new games, so I recommend you first try this game on an 8x8 board. This means playing on the squares rather than the intersections, but it makes no difference in the play.

Checkers equipment can be used for the game, but it's more convenient to use an Othello or Reversi set. That way, you can perform captures by flipping pieces over to change their colors, rather than having to replace white pieces with black, or black with white, as you must if you use a go set. Once you get used to the game and start to feel limited by the 8x8 board, you can try playing on a larger board.

Here, then, are my rules:

1. Players set up their pieces as shown in Diagram 7.18. Color is determined in any random fashion.

2. Starting with Black, each player in turn moves one of his pieces any number of squares in any horizontal or vertical direction. A piece may not land on or jump over an occupied square.

3. When a player moves a piece so as to sandwich an oppos-

Diagram 7.20

A player captures an opposing piece by "sandwiching" it between his own pieces in any row or column. At left, Black moves to the square marked X, capturing one White piece. Instead of being removed from the board, captured pieces change color, as shown in the position at right.

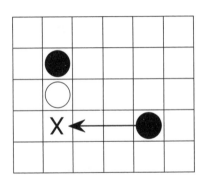

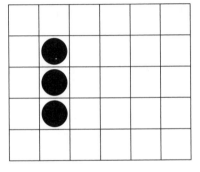

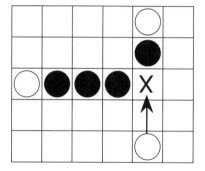 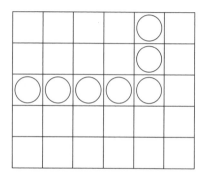

Diagram 7.21

An unbroken line of pieces may be captured in the same way shown in the previous diagram. At left, White moves to X to sandwich the line of three Black pieces between two White pieces. The result is shown at right. Note that White's move also captures a fourth Black piece.

Diagram 7.22

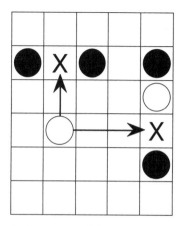

A piece may safely place itself into a sandwiched position. Here, White can move to either X square without being captured.

ing piece between the moving piece and another piece of the moving player's color, along any horizontal or vertical (not diagonal) line, the opposing piece is captured (see Diagram 7.20). A captured piece is removed from play and is replaced with a piece (from off the board) belonging to the player who made the capturing move. (If a Reversi or Othello set is being used, the captured piece is simply flipped over.)

4. A solidly connected row of pieces is captured in the same way as a single piece: by being sandwiched. All pieces in the row change to the opponent's color. Captures may be made in more than one direction simultaneously (see Diagram 7.21).

5. Pieces that have changed color become the opponent's and can be moved like any of the opponent's other pieces.

6. A player may safely move his piece between enemy pieces or in such a way as to create a line that is sandwiched between opposing pieces (see Diagram 7.22). In other words, for a capture to take effect, the capturing player must be the one who creates the sandwich position.

7. A player wins when his pieces have securely walled off more than half the board. To be "secure," a wall must be constructed in such a way that there is no possibility that the opponent can ever capture any part of it in the future (assuming, of course, that the player with the wall leaves it where it is). The amount of territory walled off is the sum of the total number of squares occupied by the wall plus the number of empty squares within the wall, including empty squares surrounded by the wall or lying between the wall and the edge of the board.

In Diagram 7.23, White has two impregnable walls that occupy or surround 35 squares out of a total of 64 squares on the board. White has won. In Diagram 7.24, however, the game is not over. Even though White's area is free of Black pieces, his wall is still subject to attack due to the strategic placement of Black pieces along the top and bottom edges. If Black moves the piece marked

Diagram 7.23

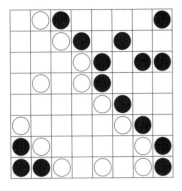

Since neither player can make further progress, the game ends. White occupies or surrounds a total of 35 squares, and so wins 35-29.

Diagram 7.24

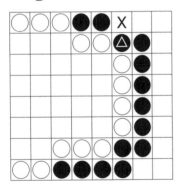

The players' walls of pieces may look secure, but this game is far from over. When Black moves the marked piece to X, he will be threatening to return to the vacated square to capture four White pieces. White has no good defense.

with a triangle to the square marked X, he will be threatening to return immediately to the square he just vacated, capturing four of White's pieces. With best play, in fact, Black should be able to push White back just far enough to win the game.

8. A player may not make a move that brings about a repetition of a previous position, unless it was a different player's turn when that position existed. (This rule avoids draws by repetition of moves.)

9. A player may pass rather than move. If both players pass in succession, the game is over and the player with the most territory wins.

10. If neither player can safely occupy a square, that square is not counted in either player's area. Also, in determining whether a player has walled off more than half the board, the square is not counted as part of the total board area.

In Diagram 7.25, White cannot occupy the square marked X without opening a gap in his wall. Black can move a piece to X, but will be forced to retreat when White slides his marked piece two squares to the right, threatening to return and make a capture. Unless Black can find a way to use the rule against repetitions to his advantage, White will win by a score of 32 to 31.

11. The advantage of going first is significant when the game is played on an 8x8 board. (On large boards, such as a go board, the advantage is less noticeable.) When playing on an 8x8 board, therefore, Black should not be allowed to move a piece more than two squares on the first turn of the game. Alternatively, players can balance the game by using the pie rule.

CHESS SETS

Racing Kings

V. R. Parton, an Englishman who created numerous chess and checkers variants in the mid-twentieth century, created this offbeat game, which has proved popular in NOST postal play. The opening setup is shown in Diagram 7.26.

1. The object of the game is to be the first player to reach the last rank with his king. Since White has the advantage of moving first, Black gets a draw if he can move his king to the last rank immediately after White does.

2. Pieces move exactly as they do in chess.

3. Checks are illegal. Not only is a king forbidden to move into check, but *it is illegal for a player to check the opposing king.* (Compare Checkless Chess in Chapter 13.)

The most common opening move is 1.Bd4. This virtually forces the symmetrical reply Be4, which seems to lead to equality. For this reason, some players try 1.Kg3.

It may be tempting to take a bishop with a knight in the opening position, but experience has shown that the slight material gain is less important than the help the exchange gives the opponent in developing his pieces.

Dodo Chess

Parton also invented a simpler version of Racing Kings. The rules are the same, but the opening setup is as shown in Diagram 7.26.

Modern Chaturanga

Backgammon and chess lovers will find a worthy and intriguing challenge in this updated version of an old Indian game of skill and chance that was described in a 1283 Castilian manuscript. The game is designed for four players, but can be played perfectly well by two (each taking a pair of allied armies) or three (with one

Diagram 7.25

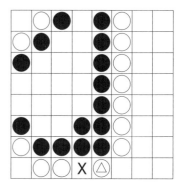

White is leading 32 to 31, but what about the square marked X? If Black occupies it, White can slide the marked piece two squares to the right, threatening to return and make a capture. Black has several possible continuations, but, because of the rule against repetitions, he cannot do better than leave the position as is.

Diagram 7.26

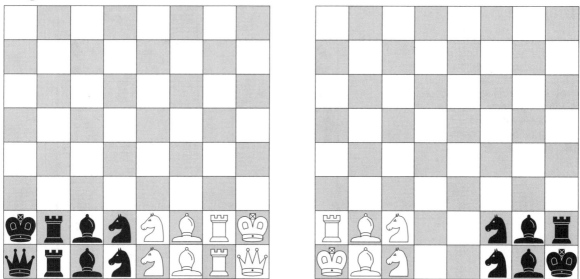

Starting positions are shown for Racing Kings (left) and the simplified variation Dodo Chess (right).

player taking two allied armies and the other players each taking one of the remaining armies).

Ideally, players should use two chess sets of different designs or sizes. It is possible to use a single set, however, by using queens as extra kings and by marking half the pieces of each color with tape or string to distinguish them from their colleagues.

The opening setup is shown in Diagram 7.27. The starting square of each raja (king) is known as a "throne" and should be permanently marked in some way, such as by placing a checker or a piece of paper there.

Pieces move as follows:

Modern Piece	Translation of Sanskrit Name	How the Piece Moves
king	raja	like a chess king
rook	elephant	like a chess rook
knight	horse	like a chess knight
bishop	ship	two squares diagonally, jumping over the intervening square if necessary
pawn	soldier	like a chess pawn, but without a two-square initial move option

Diagram 7.27

In the four-player form of Chaturanga, Red and Green are allied against Yellow and Black. With its dice-controlled movement and its point-scoring system, the game has features that should appeal to backgammon and chess players alike.

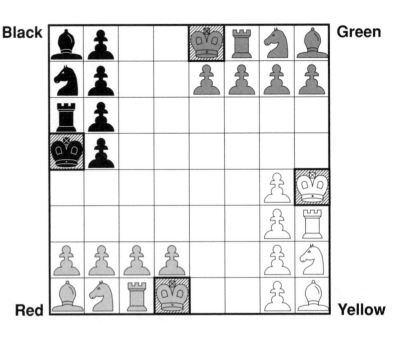

In Diagram 7.27, Red pawns move up the board, Black pawns move from left to right, Green pawns move down the board, and Yellow pawns move right to left.

Rules are as follows:

1. Red and Green are allied against Yellow and Black. When there are more than two players in the game, consultation between allies is permitted.

2. Turns pass counterclockwise around the table, in the order Red, Yellow, Green, Black.

3. A player rolls two dice each turn. (The original game used four-sided dice—this is one of the "updates.") The numbers rolled indicate which piece or pieces he may move that turn, as follows:

Die Roll	Piece(s) That May Move
1	ship (bishop)
2	horse (knight)
3,4	elephant (rook)
5,6	raja or soldier (king or pawn)

A player may make one move for each die roll, may make just one move, or may choose not to move at all. On a roll of 2-3, for example, a player may move his horse, his elephant, or both (in either order). The dice may *not* be added together; thus, with a roll of 2-3, a player may not move a raja or soldier.

On a roll of doubles, or a roll of 3-4 or 5-6, a player may choose to move the appropriate piece twice, which can have a devastating effect on the opponent's position.

4. As in chess, a player captures an opponent's piece by landing on it. As usual, a player may not move a piece to a square occupied by one of his own pieces. Rajas *may* move into check.

5. On reaching the far side of the board, a soldier promotes to its owner's choice of any piece previously lost by its side. If all that army's pieces are still on the board, the soldier must remain on the last rank, immobile, until a piece is captured, at which time the promotion is made at once.

6. When a raja is captured, its army—but not its ally's army—becomes immobile. Immobile pieces may be captured by anyone, even by their ally. The immobile army may come back to life, however. If the allied raja reaches the captured raja's throne, he assumes command of the immobile forces and uses them as if they were his own. The army without the raja, however, does not regain its separate turn unless its raja reenters the game. This can happen in one of two ways:

a. A soldier may be promoted to a raja. (This can only happen when the allied raja has assumed command, as explained above, to allow the soldier to move again.)

b. An exchange of captured rajas may occur. *This may only happen once in a game.* When each team has lost one raja, the player that captured the second raja has the option of demanding an exchange of captured rajas. Such a demand must be made immediately after the capture of the second raja (delay of even one turn forfeits the right)—and if it is, the opponent may not refuse. If the exchange is made, both owners get back their captured rajas and regain their turns. Before moving any pieces, however, they must roll a 5 or 6 to get their raja back on the board (in which case they can use the other part of their roll to move something else, or to move the raja again). *A raja may be reentered on any vacant square on the board* (when a 5 or 6 is rolled)—*even on an opposing throne!*

In deciding whether or not to trade rajas, a player should take careful note of which thrones are vacant, as well as the order in which the rajas will return. The first one to reenter, after all, stands one chance in nine of throwing a roll that will allow a double raja move (5-5, 5-6, or 6-6), which will allow him to reenter next to the last enemy raja and then capture it, ending the game.

7. The game is played for points. Since both teams may earn points in a game, it is recommended that players play a series of games—either a predetermined number of games, or as many games as it takes for one side to reach a predetermined point total. Teams earn points as follows:

a. One point for having the last surviving raja on the board (this is known as *chaturaji*);

b. One point for each opposing raja's throne that it has occupied with a raja at any point during the game (*sinhasana*)—but occupying the same throne more than once does not gain additional points;

c. One point for capturing an opposing raja with a raja.

Note that when a raja captures a raja on its throne, two points are earned: one for the capture and one for the throne. Percentagewise, it is a good idea to advance your raja to within two squares of an opposing raja still on its throne. Even though such a move gives your opponent the first chance to gain a point by capturing your raja with his, you stand to gain twice as much as your opponent if you get one of the double-move rolls first.

8. *Optional rules:* To make the game closer to the original, but at the cost of making the game slightly more complicated, players may wish to add the following rules. These are based on the description of the game in the Sanskrit poem *Bhavishya Purana*, which can be found translated into English in Edward Falkener's *Games Ancient and Oriental and How to Play Them* (Dover, 1961).

a. If the four ships come together in a square, the ship completing the square captures the other three (even its ally's). The fourth ship is then known as *vrihannauka* ("the great ship").

b. If a raja loses all its pieces before being captured, the game is a draw and neither side earns any points.

c. A soldier may promote only when at least two soldiers of its own army have already been captured.

d. A soldier may only promote on a file where its elephant or horse started, and it must promote to the piece that began the game in the file where the promotion occurs.

e. There is an exception to the previous rule. When a player is left with only a raja, a ship, and one soldier, that soldier may promote on any square of the far side of the board, and to any piece—even to an extra raja.

Variation Without Dice

Chaturanga can be played as a pure strategy game in which the object is to eliminate both opposing rajas rather than to score points. Each army in turn moves a single piece, as in chess, instead of throwing the dice. There are no exchanges of captured rajas; but other rules, including the immobilization of pieces whose raja has been captured, are as in the dice version.

Although pieces are relatively weak, tactics are complicated immensely by the need for players to take into account the order of movement of the different armies.

3D CHESS SETS

Did you ever buy one of the many different three-dimensional chess games on the market that use three 8x8 boards? If you played it, did you find some serious problems, such as being unable to mate a king even when you were three queens ahead?

Commercial three-dimensional chess sets come with many different rules, most of which have one thing in common: They're very bad. They attempt to extend two-dimensional movement into three dimensions without taking into account the differences between plane and solid geometry or the problems humans have in visualizing some kinds of three-dimensional moves.

While I don't claim to have come up with the perfect set of three-dimensional chess rules, here are two games you may enjoy more than the ones that came with your set. If you don't own a 3D chess set, you can still try these games by placing three chessboards side by side and imagining that they are stacked on top of one another.

3D Hook-Move Chess

An extra set of pawns is needed for each player (checkers may be substituted). Set the White pieces up as usual on Level 1 (the bottom level), the Black pieces on Level 3 (the top level), and the extra pawns on the first and last ranks of Level 2, as shown in Diagram 7.28.

The "board" is really an 8x8x3 parallelepiped. It can be thought of as comprising three parallel 8x8 planes, or eight parallel 8x3 planes running in a vertical direction, or eight parallel 8x3 planes running in a horizontal direction. Each of these planes (all of which are parallel to some pair of opposite faces of the 8x8x3 parallelepiped) is called a "plane of movement." In a turn, a piece's move must lie entirely within a single plane of movement, whether on an 8x8 or an 8x3 plane.

Here's how pieces move. *Within any plane of movement:*

- A rook makes either an ordinary rook move or two perpendicular rook moves of any length.
- A bishop makes either an ordinary bishop move or two perpendicular bishop moves of any length.

Diagram 7.28

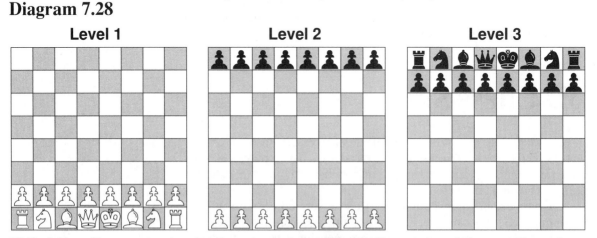

3D Hook-Move Chess can be played on three standard chessboards, with one extra set of pawns. The center board (Level 2) is turned 90° to keep squares on 3D diagonals the same color.

- A queen makes any move that the rook or the bishop in this game could make. Thus, a queen may make two perpendicular rook moves or two perpendicular bishop moves, but not a combined rook and bishop move in the same turn.

- A knight jumps—over other pieces, if necessary—to any square that lies one or two squares away. This includes the standard knight move as well as any move that a standard queen could reach by moving one or two squares.

- A king moves like a standard chess king.

- A pawn moves like a standard chess pawn, but only toward the end of the board where the opponent starts. A pawn may capture one square diagonally toward the opponent's starting area *in any plane of movement*. Thus, a pawn must always stay on its original 8x8 level unless it makes a capture. A pawn promotes on the last rank of any of the three 8x8 planes.

Diagram 7.29 illustrates how the pieces move (except queens, which simply can make any move that a rook or bishop can make

Diagram 7.29

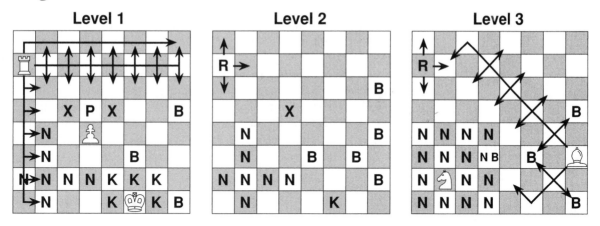

A rook may make a normal move, or may make a pair of perpendicular moves in a single turn. The two moves may be of any lengths, but both must be made on the same 8x8 board or 8x3 plane. Some of the rook's possible moves are shown above left. In addition, the rook can travel up one or two levels to one of the squares marked R, then make another rook move from there. Or, it may move along the a file of Level 1 and then move directly upward to Level 2 or 3 (a possibility not shown in the diagram).

Bishops may also make two perpendicular moves within a plane parallel to a board face. The squares

marked B can be reached by traveling within an 8x3 plane; for example, the bishop can go from h3 on Level 3 to g3 on Level 2 to f3 on Level 1, and then make a perpendicular move to e3 of Level 2 or d3 of Level 3. A queen may make any move that a rook or bishop may make.

A knight's power is extended in a different way; here, it can jump to any square marked N. The pawn may capture at any of the three squares marked X, or advance one square as usual to P.

The king may move to any of the squares marked K.

in this game). A rook, bishop, or queen must stop on any square on which it makes a capture. If a piece used only one standard move to reach the capturing square, it still may not take the second leg of its move that turn.

The effect of these rules is to allow a king and rook to mate a king, just as in standard chess, because, on an empty board, a hooking rook cuts off planes in the same way that a standard rook cuts off ranks and files in standard chess. Far from being a modern invention, this piece, known as a *hook mover*, is found in some large variants of shogi invented in medieval Japan and was probably the invention of Buddhist monks. As far as I know, though, this game is the first to make use of the piece in three dimensions, where it seems to function ideally in terms of both the power and the clarity of its move.

Parallel Worlds Chess

This game requires three boards and two sets of chessmen. As shown in Diagram 7.30, the boards on Levels 1 and 3 are set up as usual, and the Level 2 board begins empty.

Each player, in turn, may make one, two, or three moves with his pieces. The only exception is that on the first turn of the game, White may not make more than two moves. This rule reduces the advantage of going first.

There are two restrictions: All the moves a player makes in a single turn must be made with different pieces, and all the pieces moved must *end* their moves on different levels. More than one move may begin on the same level, however. Thus, in a single turn,

Diagram 7.30

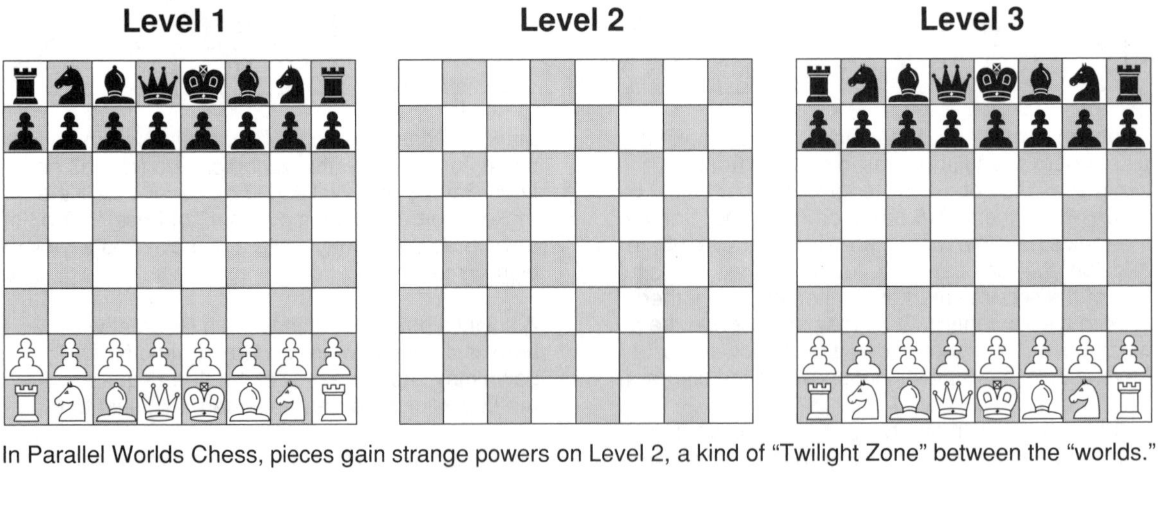

Level 1	Level 2	Level 3

In Parallel Worlds Chess, pieces gain strange powers on Level 2, a kind of "Twilight Zone" between the "worlds."

a player may at most make one move that ends on Level 1, one move that ends on Level 2, and one move that ends on Level 3.

On Levels 1 and 3, moves, captures, and pawn promotions are the same as in orthodox chess.

On Level 2, however, which can be thought of as some kind of interdimensional "Twilight Zone," some strange rules apply:

1. All pieces and pawns move like queens (which also means they may not jump over other pieces).

2. No captures are allowed.

3. Pawns may move to the eighth rank, but do not promote.

Kings must always remain on the levels on which they start. All other pieces and pawns, however, may move straight up or down one level, provided that the square to which they are moving is empty. This means that no captures may be made by a piece as it moves to a new level.

A pawn may move to Level 2, then on a later turn move back to Level 2's first rank, and still later transfer back to the first rank of Level 1 or 3. A pawn on the first rank of Level 1 or 3 may advance only one square; then, when it is on the second rank, it regains its two-step option.

The object of the game is to be the first to *capture either* opposing king.

The game is very wild. A player may maneuver both his queens to Level 1 to launch an all-out assault there, while his opponent does the same thing on Level 3; thus, each player will have a two-queen advantage on a different board (compare to Double Unbalanced Chess in Chapter 3). In such situations, one common tactic is to promote pawns sacrificially on the board where you have a disadvantage, so that the opponent must waste time capturing them instead of proceeding with a mating attack.

For a slightly tamer version, players may prohibit pawns from moving directly from Level 2 to the eighth rank of Level 1 or 3 (although drops on the seventh rank can be nearly as severe). If players find the game too lengthy for their tastes, they may enjoy trying the game on smaller boards, using fewer pieces.

RECTANGULAR GRIDS

Many good games are played on large grids. Grids that are square or rectangular are easy to improvise, as described in Appendix B. But it's also possible to buy a premade large grid that that comes with a large supply of black and white pieces—that is, a go set.

Diagram 7.31

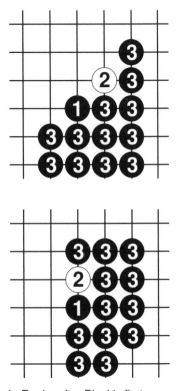

In Renju, after Black's first move (1) is placed at the center of the board, White must reply with move 2 either "indirectly" with a diagonal play, shown at the top, or "directly" with an orthogonal "attachment," shown at the bottom. In each diagram, Black's third move must be at one of the points marked 3. Reflections and rotations of these positions are also acceptable openings.

Go sets come in many sizes and are made by many manufacturers. Pieces may be plastic, glass, or seashell and slate. The game of Hnefatafl described in Chapter 2 can be played on a go board; so can many of the games that follow.

Five-in-a-Row

Also known as Go-Moku, Go Bang, or Spoil Five, this two-player game is often played on a go board, although a 15x15 board—the size of a Pente board—is the official one. One player takes the white stones, the other the black stones. The rules are very simple:

1. Black begins by placing a stone on the center point of the board.

2. White then places a stone anywhere on the board.

3. Black then places a stone anywhere except in the 5x5 area in the center of the board. That is, Black's second stone must be at least three intersections away from the center point occupied by his first stone.

4. Once placed, no stone may be moved or captured.

5. The first player to get exactly five stones of his color in a row—horizontally, vertically, or diagonally—with no empty points or opposing stones intervening, wins. Lines of six or more in a row do not win.

6. The game is a draw if neither player gets five in a row by the time the board is full.

The first player has an advantage in this game, but you can play a long time before you are good enough for this to become a problem. Players who want a more equal and somewhat more complex challenge will prefer the game of Renju.

Renju

Played professionally in Japan, and popular in Europe and Russia, Renju is an outstanding game. It is similar to Five-in-a-Row, but with these differences:

1. A board of 15 lines by 15 lines is used. The reason is that a larger board tends to favor the first player (Black) too much, while a smaller board results in too many draws.

2. One player is randomly chosen to be the "tentative Black" player, who puts a black stone on the board's center point.

3. The other player, known as "tentative White," places a white

stone on one of the eight intersections adjacent to the black stone.

4. The tentative Black player then adds the next stone, and in so doing must form one of the 24 patterns shown in Diagram 7.31 (or a rotation or mirror image of one of them).

5. The tentative White player now has the option of switching sides and becoming Black or of remaining White.

6. Whichever player is now White places a white stone anywhere on the board.

7. For the next move (the fifth move in the game), Black suggests two different choices—which must not be equivalent to each other by virtue of symmetry—by placing two black stones on the board. White chooses one of these two black stones and removes it.

8. White now makes a move anywhere on the board.

9. For the rest of the game, the players take turns placing one stone of their color on the board. White may place stones anywhere, without restriction. Black's choices, however, are subject to certain restrictions, known as "prohibited moves":

   a. Black may not make an "overline," which is six or more stones of his color in an unbroken line. (White may make an overline—and if he does, he wins, since he has then made five in a row.)

   b. Black may not make a "double four," which is a move that simultaneously makes two "fours." A "four" is a set of four stones of one color in a row—not necessarily an unbroken row—that can become a five-in-a-row with the addition of a single stone.

   c. Black may not make a "double three," which is a move that simultaneously makes two "threes." A "three" is defined as three stones in a line that, with the addition of one stone, can become a "free four." A "free four" is defined as a "four" that can become a five in two different ways—that is, an unbroken row of four that has a vacant point at each end.

   Note that Black may make a move that simultaneously creates a three and a four, which is in fact the usual way for Black to win. Diagram 7.32 shows some examples of threes and fours.

10. Black wins if he makes five in a row. White wins if he makes five or more in a row. White also wins if Black makes a prohibited move—unless the prohibited move gives Black five in a row, in which case Black wins.

Diagram 7.32

An addition of a Black stone at point X would illegally create two "threes," one diagonally and the other horizontally. The horizontal line is a three even though it is broken, since the addition of one more stone (to the left of X) will make it a four with two open ends.

Black may not play at Y, either, since that would form two fours. But a play at Z is allowed, because it forms only one three that can become a "free four." That's because once Black has played at Z and A, a Black play at B would form an illegal overline. Thus, the horizontal four threatened by Black's play at Z will only be open on one end.

White may make two threes, two fours, or an overline without restriction.

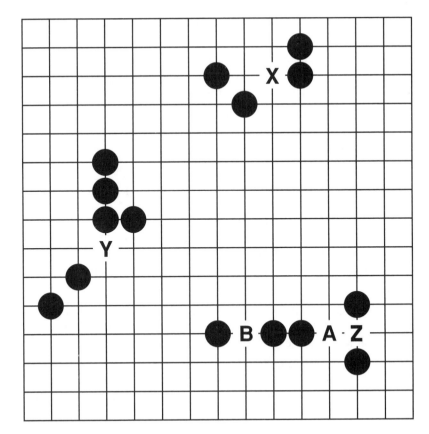

Renju's rules are an excellent example of how far serious players are willing to go to fine-tune the rules of a game to balance both sides' chances. The rules given are those of the Sweden-based Renju International Federation, and they have been used in international competition. Older, but slightly less complicated rules may be found in the excellent book on Renju strategy, *Five-in-a-Row (Renju)* by two Japanese professional players, Goro Sakata and Wataru Ikawa (Ishi Press, 1981).

Toric Renju

The game of Renju (as well as Five-in-a-Row) can be played on a board having the wraparound geometry of a torus. A line of five may extend off one board edge and continue on the opposite edge. (Compare to Toric Scrabble in Chapter 1.)

One effect of this rule is that the board has no real center, so it makes no difference where the first move is made.

Conspirators

Conspirators is an eighteenth-century French game, best for two players, played on a grid of 17 horizontal and 17 vertical lines. A go board works well, as shown in Diagram 7.33, since players can simply ignore the outermost line around the board.

At the start, 39 intersections around the edge of the board are designated as "shelters" by placing coins on them.

One player takes 20 white pieces, the other player 20 black pieces. To start, each player in turn places one of his pieces on the board on any vacant intersection within or along the edge of the shaded area.

After all the pieces are placed, players take turns moving one piece per turn, trying to get all their pieces into shelters. Pieces move as in Halma (see page 87): They may either make a simple move one point in any direction (horizontally, vertically, or diagonally) onto an empty intersection, or they may make a jump over an adjacent piece belonging to either player, in any horizontal, vertical, or diagonal direction, onto an empty intersection. A piece

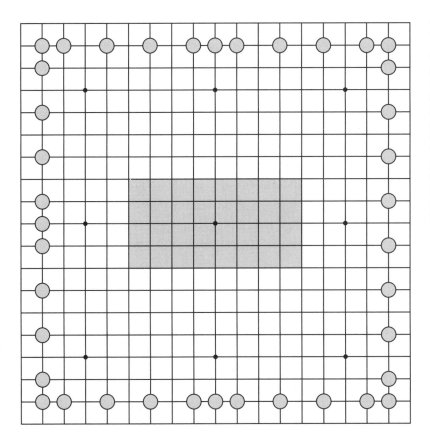

Diagram 7.33

Conspirators can be played on a go board as shown. Coins can be used to represent the shelters (the circled points). To be faithful to the game's original rules, players should keep the edge of the go board out of play; but the game will not be changed much if players decide to allow moves to be made there. Relocating the shelters is another way to vary the play.

may make a series of jumps in any direction or combination of directions in a single turn. Jumped pieces may belong to either player and are never captured.

Only one piece may occupy a shelter, and so there are not quite enough shelters to go around. The player who is stuck with the piece that does not reach a shelter is the loser. Think of the game as a strategic Musical Chairs.

Philosopher's Football

Also known as Phutball, this game's rules first appeared in *Winning Ways for Your Mathematical Plays,* by Elwyn R. Berlekamp, John H. Conway, and Richard K. Guy (Academic Press, 1982), an incomparable work in the field of mathematical analysis of game situations. The two-volume set is by no means all dry or difficult mathematics; it is readable and witty, and it also contains rules for many intriguing games, most of which can be played with pencil and paper or other easily improvised equipment.

Philosopher's Football can be played on a go board or, as presented in the book, on a 15-line-by-19-line board (a go board with four lines covered up). The only other equipment needed is one black stone and a reasonably large supply of white stones. If you don't have go stones, a dime and a roll of pennies will do nicely.

Here are the rules:

1. To start, the black stone is placed on the intersection in the center of the board. Players sit at opposite ends of the board, where the edges constitute "goal lines." The object is to maneuver the black piece, which symbolizes the "ball," onto or across the goal line on the opponent's side of the board.

2. Each player, in turn, may do one of two things:

   a. Place a white stone on any empty intersection; or

   b. Move the ball by jumping over one or more white pieces. Jumped pieces are captured and immediately removed from play.

3. Jumping rules are as follows:

   a. The ball may make a single jump in any horizontal, vertical, or diagonal direction. A jump may be of any length, provided that every intersection jumped over is occupied by a white piece, and that the ball stops on the first unoccupied point in its line of movement.

   b. If the ball jumps to an intersection from which it can make another single jump, in the same direction or in a new direction, it may do so, all as part of the same turn. These extra jumps are always optional, as is making a jump in the first place. Since jumped pieces are removed immediately, it is impossible for a piece to be jumped more than once in a turn.

c. The ball may be jumped onto a sideline point. A player may also jump the ball onto his own goal line (although he must also jump it off again as part of the same turn, or lose the game). A player may win by jumping a ball over a piece on the opponent's goal line, even though there is no intersection there for the ball to land on.

Diagrams 7.34 and 7.35 show the first few moves of a game. The book's authors call this opening "standard," but there seems little doubt that there are good alternatives to some of these moves.

In Diagram 7.34, the player making the odd-numbered moves (let's call him "Odd") is trying to get the ball to the goal line on the right, while the other player ("Even") is trying to move the ball left. Odd begins by placing a white stone immediately to the right of the ball's starting position in the center, and Even replies by starting a chain in the other direction.

Experience has shown that it is good to delay making a jumping move as long as possible and to concentrate instead on building a chain of white stones toward your goal line. Still, after Odd places stone 5, Even gets worried and jumps pieces 2 and 4, which are removed from the board. Odd uses his next two turns to rebuild

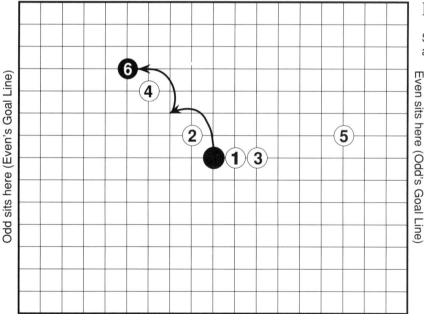

Diagram 7.34

Shown is a typical opening in a game of Phutball.

this part of the chain, as shown in Diagram 7.35, while Even places a stone at 8 and then jumps it on his next turn.

Odd's move 11 is an advanced play. If it were placed at 8 instead, Even could place a stone at A, after which an Odd jump of the ball from 10 to B would make it hard for Odd to make use of the rest of his chain. Odd 11 is also good because it prepares to answer an Even threat such as C with a jump over 11 and 7, giving Odd a good position. Even sees this and plays 12, a strong move, after which an Odd jump of 11 and 7 could be answered by an Even play at 7, threatening a jump over both 7 and 12.

After 12, Even threatens a play at C, after which he could make a triple jump of 11, 12, and C to get close to the goal while eliminating part of Odd's chain to the other side. Also, if Odd now places a stone at D, Even can make the 11-7 jump himself, after which any connection that Odd makes with his old chain will also help Even get the ball back to his edge by jumping 9, D, and 12.

At this point, the game is still close; Odd's chain means that the ball is not as far from his goal line as it may appear.

One important tactical tip provided in *Winning Ways* is that, most of the time, a stone that is a knight's move away from the ball is useless.

The book also points out that the game can be handicapped in an elegant way by moving the starting position of the ball closer to the goal line being defended by the stronger player.

Diagram 7.35

After a dozen moves, the ball is close to Even's goal line, but Odd has built a chain of well-placed stones that make the two players' chances in the game about equal.

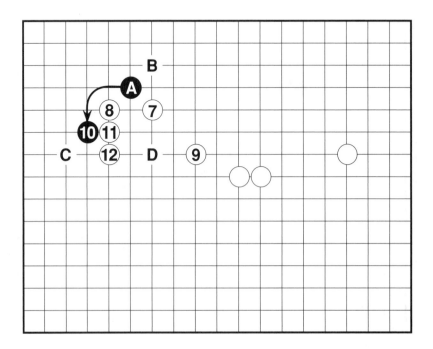

Hexagonal and Other Grids

Hexade

This game and the next one are companion games. Both were created by Christiaan Freeling; both are two-player games, played on a hexagonal-shaped grid of hexagons, with eight hexagons along an edge; and both use the principle of winning by reaching any of three different objectives.

In Hexade, the board (shown in Diagram 7.36) is initially empty. Players take turns placing one stone of their color on any vacant hexagon, with just one restriction: On his second turn of the game, the player who went first must place his second stone at least three spaces away from his first stone.

Diagram 7.36

Hexade is played on a board of 169 cells. Examples of the three kinds of winning formations, each of which consists of a pattern of six stones, are shown.

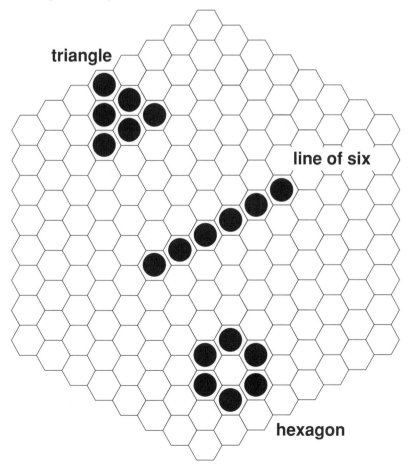

triangle

line of six

hexagon

Diagram 7.37

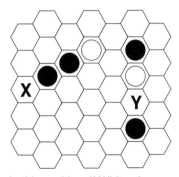

In this position, if White plays at X, the two adjacent Black stones will be captured. But a White play at Y does not result in the capture of two White stones.

The capturing rule is like that of Pente: If a placement causes a pair of adjacent opposing stones to be "sandwiched" on opposite sides, that pair of stones is removed from play. And, as in Pente, a stone may safely be placed into a sandwiched position (see Diagram 7.37).

The object is to form any one of three possible winning formations: six stones in an unbroken row, a compact triangle of six stones, or a small hexagon of six stones (see Diagram 7.36). It makes no difference what other stones are next to these formations; forming an "overline" of seven or more stones in a row still wins.

In Pente, a player can win by capturing a certain number of stones. This is not so in Hexade, where capturing is simply a means to an end.

Havannah

This game was marketed in Europe by Ravensburger about 10 years ago and won critical acclaim. It is a connection game in the same broad category as Hex, but it has a subtler strategy and much more varied tactics.

Rules are simple. Each player in turn places a stone of his color on any empty board space. Once placed, a stone is never moved or captured.

A player wins by forming any one of the following three shapes with his stones (see Diagram 7.38):

1. A "fork," which is an unbroken path connecting any three of the board's six edges (corner points do not count as belonging to any edge);

2. A "bridge," which is an unbroken path connecting any two of the board's six corner points; or

3. A "ring," which is a closed loop of any size and shape that surrounds at least one point that is either vacant or enemy-occupied.

In practice, it's virtually impossible to form a ring, but threats to form one can be used to gain time and complete a fork or bridge faster than the opponent. Draws are theoretically possible in Havannah, but are extremely rare.

A pie rule may be invoked for the opening move of the game, although the first player's advantage is only slight. Early in the game, a move played three, four, or five spaces in from one of the board corners is good, as it threatens to connect to two different edges.

Once players get used to playing Havannah on the 169-cell grid shown in Diagram 7.38, they may find it interesting to play on a 271-cell board, which has ten hexes on an edge instead of eight. Experienced players in Holland have come to prefer this larger board.

Lotus

In the early 1980s, a game called Kensington was invented in England by Brian Taylor and Peter Forbes. It was marketed with some success both there and in the United States.

The board uses an interesting grid made up of a combination of regular hexagons, squares, and triangles (see Diagram 7.39). This pattern can also be found in some books on polygons as an example of how a mix of different regular shapes can completely tile, or fill in, a plane.

The play of Kensington is reminiscent of the old three-in-a-

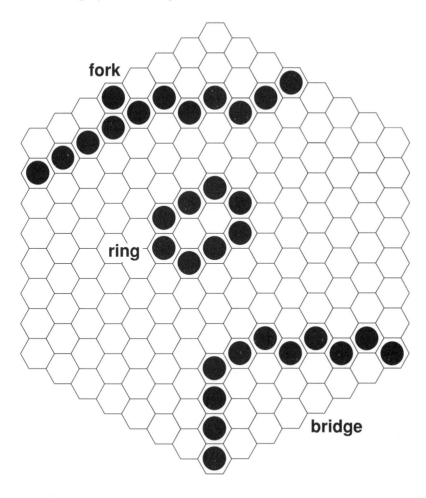

Diagram 7.38

The commercial version of Havannah produced by Ravensburger used a board the same size as that of Hexade, although experienced players now regularly use a board with an extra ring of hexagons. Examples of the three kinds of winning formations are shown.

row game Nine Men's Morris (also known as Mill). Each player has a differently colored set of 15 pieces. With the board initially empty, players take turns placing one of their pieces on any empty intersection on the board. Once a player has placed all his pieces on the board, his turns consist of moving one of his pieces along a line to an adjacent point.

During both the placement and movement phases of the game, players try to form triangles, squares, and hexagons with their pieces. Completing a triangle allows a player to reposition any one opposing piece by moving it to any empty point on the board. Completing a square allows a player to reposition two opposing pieces. Completing a hexagon wins the game, unless it's one of the two hexagons of the opponent's color, in which case nothing special happens and the game continues.

Diagram 7.39

Except for the absence of a color scheme, the Lotus board resembles the board used in Kensington. Play is on the intersections, which are highlighted by small circles. A track with a marker is used to record endgame points and to neutralize the advantage of going first.

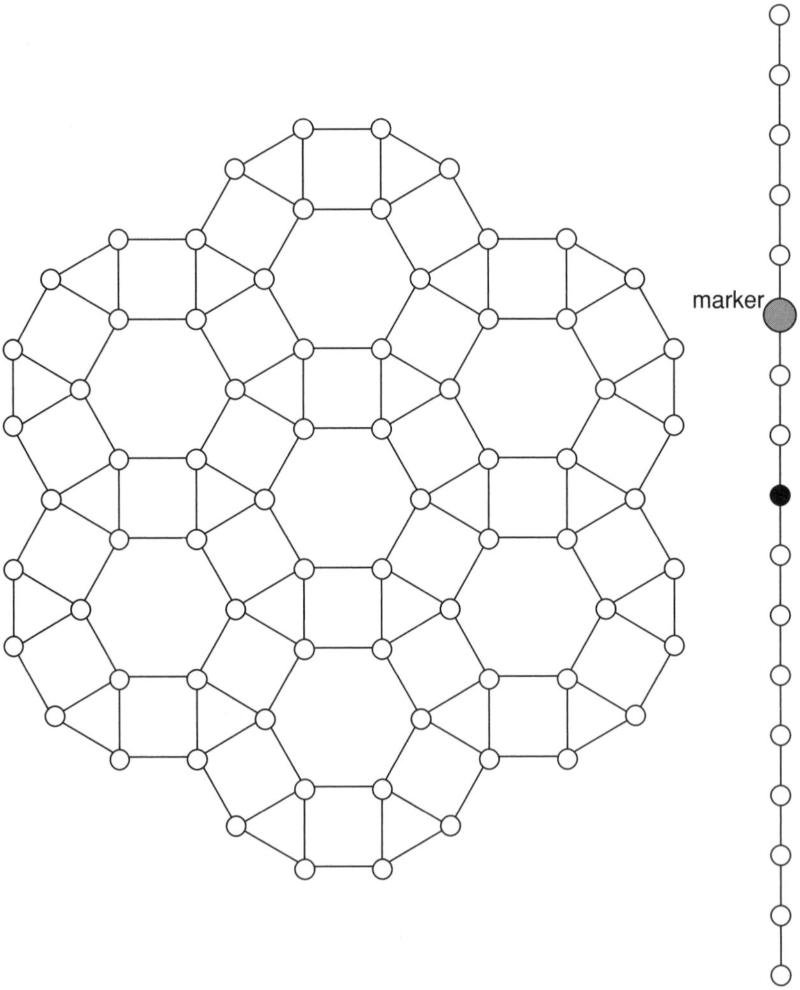

marker

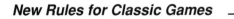

Kensington is an interesting game, but it can be long and drawn out. I think that Christiaan Freeling's game of Lotus puts the same board design to better use.

To play Lotus, it's most convenient to use pieces from a small Reversi or Othello set. That's because captured pieces are not removed, but instead change color. Lotus is officially played with 72 pieces, black on one side and white on the other. If you don't have enough Reversi pieces (only 64 come in a set), you can use go pieces or small checkers instead. You'll just need to substitute pieces of one color for the other when captures take place.

Play starts with the board empty. Off the board, players draw a 19-point track on a piece of paper and place a marker on it. The marker begins three points closer to the player who will go second; this is the game's komi.

In turn, each player either places a piece, usually referred to as a "stone," on any empty space on the board, or passes. A player who passes moves the marker one space closer to himself. Once

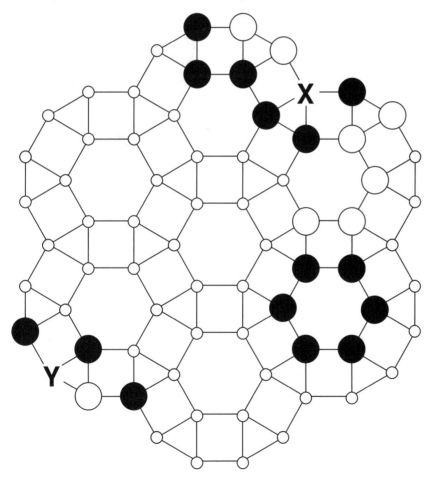

Diagram 7.40

In this position, a Black play at X captures two White stones, which are then transformed into Black stones. If instead White plays at X, the group of three White stones (including X) has no liberties, but is safe because the Black stone to the right of X is captured, thereby linking the White stones to the five White stones that do have liberties.

In the bottom left, a White play at Y would be a suicide move, causing both the placed stone and the adjacent White stone to turn Black.

Black's stones in the lower right occupy one of the board's seven hexagons, which are known as "lotuses." As a result, these six stones, as well as any Black stones connected to them, are permanently safe from capture.

placed, a stone is never moved or removed—but its color may change

As in go, a stone or a solidly connected group of stones of the same color is captured if it loses its last liberty—that is, if it no longer is adjacent to at least one vacant point. But in Lotus, capture results in the reversal of color of the captured stones rather than their removal. A move may result in the capture of more than one enemy group at the same time.

If a player places a stone on a point where it is itself surrounded or is part of a group that is then surrounded, there are two possibilities:

1. If the placement causes the capture of an enemy group, that capture is immediately made. Now there are two possibilities:

   a. The reversal causes the capturing side to be linked up to at least one liberty. In this case, the capturing side's stones are safe. An example is a White play at X in Diagram 7.40.

Diagram 7.41

Compare this position to the top of the previous diagram. If Black plays at X now, the two White stones are captured, and so turn Black. But the resulting Black group now has no liberties either, so a second reversal occurs, making all the stones White.

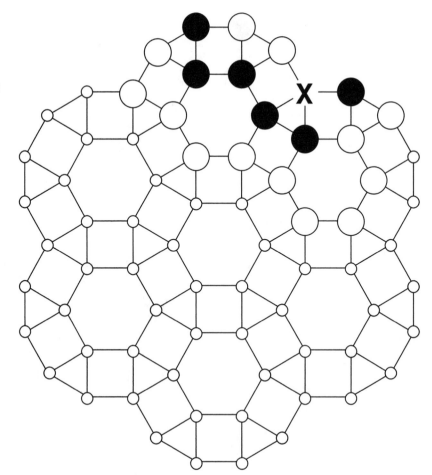

New Rules for Classic Games

b. After the reversal, the capturing side's stones are left with no liberties. In this case, a second reversal takes place, as in Diagram 7.41. This means that the capturing move was really a "suicide" play.

2. If the placement does not cause the capture of an enemy group, the placement is a suicide move (such as a White play at Y in Diagram 7.40). The placed stone, along with any stones of the same color connected to it, is reversed to the opponent's color.

There is, however, an important exception to all of the above capturing rules, and it is based on an idea from the go variant Rosette (see Chapter 5). A group that contains a "lotus"—the six points around one of the board's seven hexagons—can never be captured. If a group can make a solid connection to a group containing a lotus, of course, it, too, becomes permanently safe.

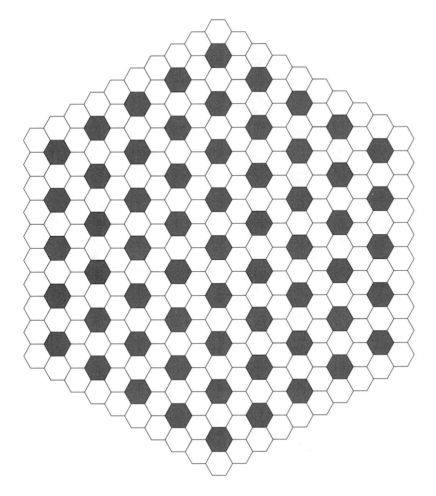

Diagram 7.42

Medusa, a sophisticated strategy game, is played on the white cells of the board shown. It is closely related to Lotus, except that in Medusa stones have the ability to move.

If you are playing on a Kensington board, by the way, note that the colors of the hexagons play no role in Lotus.

If both players in turn move the marker (i.e., pass instead of placing a stone on the board), the game ends. "Dead groups"—those that will inevitably be captured, since they do not include a lotus and cannot connect to a safe group—are reversed.

The winner is the player who has the most points. A player gets one point for each stone of his color and one for each empty point surrounded by his stones. Also, the player who ends up with the marker on his half of the track gets one point for each space the marker is from the center of the track.

Diagram 7.43

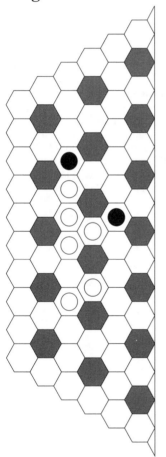
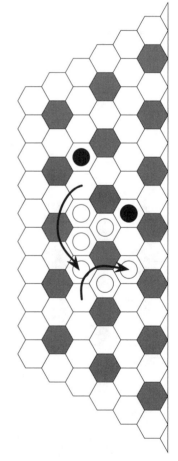

Left: White's two-stone group has two ways to move, while the four-stone group has four different options—as well as the option not to move.

Center: This is one way that White can move from the position in the previous diagram.

Right: Here is another option, in which one stone is jumped over two cells. In order to make both of these moves, White would have to move the two-stone group first. Otherwise, it would lose its power of movement for that turn when the other group came in contact with it.

As in go, a seki can occur that prevents one or more vacant points from becoming part of either player's territory. Such points, of course, do not score for either player.

Medusa

Like Lotus, this game involves both a go-like object (getting the most territory) and Othello-like captures. But it also has an element not found in either go or Lotus: Pieces can move. In a single turn, a player can both place a new stone and move any or all of his groups of two or more stones.

The board is a hexagonal grid of hexagons in which certain cells are out of play (see Diagram 7.42). Players will need about 210 stones. Most suitable are Othello or Reversi pieces, but a set of go stones is adequate, as it is not much trouble to replace one color stone with the other when a capture is made. As in Lotus, there is also a track of spaces with a marker on the middle space at the beginning of the game. The official number of spaces on the track is 19, although it is unusual for the marker to move more than three or four spaces toward either player.

The board is empty when the game begins. Black has the first turn, after which play alternates. Each turn, a player has two options:

1. He may place a stone of his color on any vacant space. (If Reversi pieces are used, the player places a piece with his own color face up.)

2. He may move one or more of his groups.

A player may use both these options; and if he does, he must do them in order (placement must precede movement). But a player may also choose to exercise only one of the options or to pass.

For movement purposes, a "group" is defined as two or more connected stones of one color. Moving a group means taking *one* of its stones and moving it in a straight line (in one of the six main directions defined by the lines of hexagons) over any number of friendly stones to land on the first vacant space beyond. A player may move each of his groups once in a turn, but no group may move more than once in a turn.

By moving, groups may split or join. If a group makes a move that joins it with a group that has not yet moved that turn, the other group loses its right of movement for that turn. Diagram 7.43 shows some examples of movement.

A stone or group that loses its last liberty (the meaning is the same as in Lotus or go) is captured, which means that its color is immediately reversed—either by flipping over Othello-type pieces,

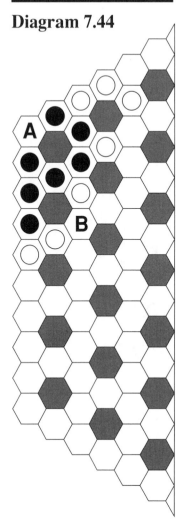

Diagram 7.44

White can capture Black's group by playing at A. As in go, when both players lose their last liberties at the same time, the player who made the move captures the other player's stones.

if they are being used, or by substituting pieces of the opponent's color for them.

Capture may result from a placement, a movement, or both. If a capture occurs because of placement, the stones are *immediately* reversed in color, *before* the movement phase takes place.

Stones captured by placement gain the right to move in the

Diagram 7.45

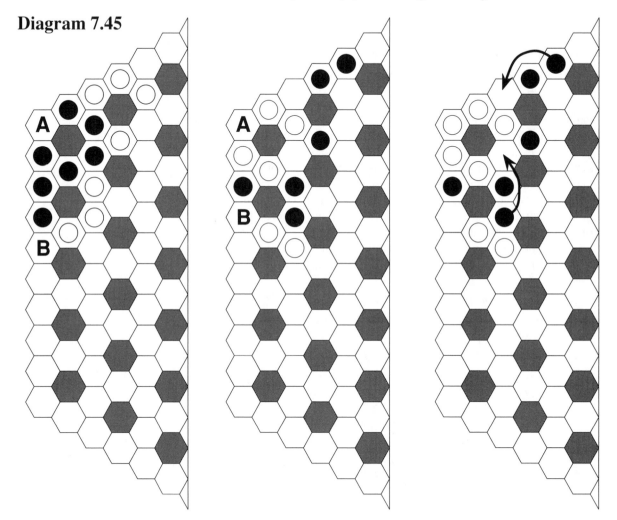

Left: Here Black is safe. Since placement must always precede movement, White cannot occupy both A and B. As soon as White puts a stone at A, it is reversed to Black before White has a chance to move to B. White's suicide move at A gives Black a hexagonal ring—a rosette—that makes his group permanently safe from capture.

Center: In Medusa, suicide can sometimes lead to

immediate resurrection. Here, White is threatening to play at B, capturing a Black stone and saving his corner stones. But if it is Black's turn, he can play a stone at A himself, a suicide play that is only temporary, as shown in the next diagram.

Right: Now Black makes the moves shown, surrounding and capturing five White stones. In the process, Black also gets a rosette.

same turn. But stones captured by movement cannot move in the same turn, since they are now part of a group containing at least one stone that has already moved.

As in Lotus, there is an exception to the rule that a surrounded group is captured: A group that contains a rosette (a hexagonal ring of six stones) is safe from capture. In Medusa, though, the safety isn't necessarily permanent, since a player might choose to break up his rosette by moving one of its pieces.

The play of a stone where it has no liberties is a "suicide move," which causes the stone to be turned over to the opponent's color. This happens immediately, before movement. But just as in go or Lotus, if a stone is placed in such a way that both it and an opposing stone or group have no liberties, the opposing stone or group is captured, and the stone just placed is not.

In Diagram 7.44, White can capture the Black group by putting a stone on A. There's no suicide, since the Black stones are surrounded and immediately reversed. If it were Black's turn, he could save the group by playing at A himself to make a rosette.

In the first position in Diagram 7.45, Black is safe. A White placement at A would be suicide, immediately giving Black a rosette; and White cannot occupy B by moving stone C until *after* the placement phase.

The middle position in Diagram 7.45 shows how, in Medusa, suicide can lead to immediate resurrection. White is threatening to save his corner group by capturing at B, which will also connect the White stones. But Black, on move, can turn the situation around with a temporary sacrifice. Black begins by playing on the corner (point A), a suicide stone that immediately turns white. Then Black moves both two-stone groups as shown in the last position in Diagram 7.45, surrounding the five White stones and turning them all Black.

If a player does not make a placement in a turn—that is, if all he does is to move groups or to pass—he gets to move the marker on the track one space closer to himself.

The object of Medusa is to get more territory than the opponent. Points are determined exactly as in Lotus: points occupied plus surrounded vacant points plus points, if any, earned by moving the marker along the track. The marker can also be used to handicap the player who goes first (though no standard komi has been established yet) or to equalize games between unequal players. Sekis can occur, as in go and Lotus.

CHAPTER 8

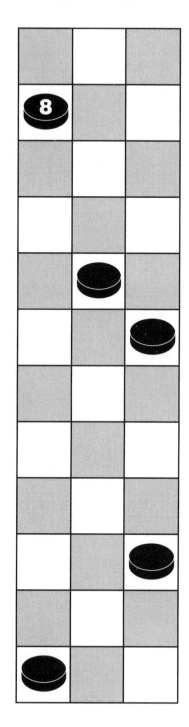

PAPER & PENCIL AND NO-EQUIPMENT GAMES

As the other chapters in this book demonstrate, a small game library is all you need to have a wealth of game-playing possibilities. But even if you own no games at all, you can find unlimited play possibilities with nothing more than paper and pencil.

CROSSWORD SQUARES

This elegantly simple, underrated word game dates back at least several decades and has appeared in both books and boxed editions under several different names. It is a highly strategic game that is usually played by two players, but it can be played—with some lessening of the game's strategic possibilities—by a larger number.

To begin, each player draws a 5x5 grid on a sheet of paper. Players keep their grids hidden from one another throughout the game.

Each player, in turn, calls out any letter of the alphabet and writes it in any empty square in his grid. At the same time, each of the other players also writes the same letter into an empty square of his grid. The turn to call the next letter passes to the next player.

After 25 letters have been called out, all the grids will be filled. Players then determine their scores, which are based on how many three-letter, four-letter, and five-letter words they have managed to form in their grids. To count, a word must read across or down in crossword fashion, in an *uninterrupte*d line of squares in any row or column. Thus, a row reading PARWN from left to right contains the three-letter word PAR but not the four-letter word PAWN.

Scoring systems vary. It is a good idea to give four-letter words a value twice that of a three-letter word, but half that of a five-letter word. For instance:

Word Length	Score per Word
3 letters	10
4 letters	20
5 letters	40

Overlapping words score separately. But if a word is wholly contained within another word, such as CAT within CATS, only the longer word counts. Note that a line such as SCATS scores the same whether it is counted as one five-letter word or as two overlapping four-letter words (SCAT and CATS); that's one of the reasons it's a good idea to double the value of a word for each additional letter. Some players also use the rule that if a word appears more than once in a player's grid, it scores full value only the first time; after that, it is worth only half (which is why it is convenient to use a scoring system in which the value of three-letter words is a multiple of 2). Diagram 8.1 shows a game in progress.

Some strategies will be apparent just from thinking about the game, but others will be discovered only with experience. The players' style will have a great deal to do with how high the final score is. Some players may prefer to choose lots of easy-to-use letters such as A, S, E, R, and T, while others may be fond of the kinds of low-scoring struggles that can result from choosing letters such as J, Q, X, and Z. It's not hard to arrange some long words by calling the letters yourself; the real key to winning is making maximum use of the letters your opponent calls.

For a more complicated variation, players can also score words that are formed diagonally in any direction.

GHOST AND SUPER GHOST

Ghost is a popular word game for situations in which players have no equipment, such as on a long car trip. It's normally played by two or three players, although more can participate.

Each player, in turn, names a letter of the alphabet aloud. When the sequence of letters completes a word that is at least four letters long, the player who named the final letter is given a "G." A new round starts and play continues the same way, except that if a player who already has a "G" again completes the spelling of a word, he gets an "H." In later rounds, upon completing words, the player will pick up an "O," "S," and "T," spelling "GHOST," which eliminates the player from the game.

The object, then, is to *avoid* completing the spelling of a word. There's a big catch, though: If you name a letter that doesn't finish the spelling of a word, but the opponent thinks that there is no word beginning with the sequence you have just made, the opponent can challenge. Upon being challenged, you must state a word that begins with the sequence given so far, or you must take a "G" (or whatever other letter in "GHOST" you are up to). If you are able to come up with a legitimate word, however, the challenger gets the letter.

One way to vary Ghost is to increase the minimum word length to five, so that sequences may start with any four-letter words, which ordinarily would cause the round to end.

Diagram 8.1

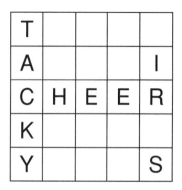

In this game in progress, each player is making a very different crossword from the same set of letters.

Another variation, which many Ghost players quickly come to prefer, is Super Ghost. Play is the same as in Ghost, except that a player may add a letter at either the end *or the beginning* of the sequence.

Thus, if a sequence begins PERSO, instead of being forced to complete the word PERSON, a player can complicate things by adding a letter before the sequence. The player could add an M to make MPERSO (thinking of IMPERSONAL or IMPERSONATE), or a U to make UPERSO (thinking of SUPERSONIC).

Trying to calculate all the possibilities in this game is mind-boggling. But it's a lot of fun.

CRASH

This two-player game is similar to Double Jotto (see Chapter 1) and is ideal for postal play. Each player thinks of a five-letter "target word" that the opponent will try to discover. Players must agree on a dictionary of record, and it is usual to exclude words that are contractions, proper names, abbreviations, plurals, or other inflections of main dictionary entries. Words containing repeated letters are allowed, however, which is not the case in Jotto.

Each player then simultaneously makes a series of "salvos." Each salvo consists of one or more five-letter words, which are restricted in the same way as the target words. The players must agree on the number of words in each salvo, and the same numbers are used by each player during the game. A good way to play is to have four words in the first salvo, three in the second salvo, two in the third, and one word per salvo thereafter. In multiword salvos, the words should be numbered 1, 2, etc.

Each player replies to a salvo by scoring it, which means indicating the number of "crashes" between the target word and each salvo word. A "crash" occurs when the same letter of the alphabet appears in the same position in both the salvo word and the target word. For example, HEART and SPADE would score 1 crash (for the As), while TRICK and TREAT would score 2 crashes (for the initial TRs).

Choosing an illegal target word automatically loses the game, as does giving an incorrect score to a salvo word. Otherwise, the winner is the player who scores a 5 (thus identifying the word) in the fewest salvos. If both words are identified in the same salvo, the winner is the player who scored a 5 with the lower numbered word within the salvo.

NIM AND MISÈRE NIM

Mathematician Charles Bouton invented the game of Nim in 1902. Although it is relatively easy to learn to play the game perfectly, it has variations that are quite interesting.

Nim is played with three or more piles of objects—coins, toothpicks, or cards, it makes no difference. In turn, each player removes any number of objects from any one of the piles. The player who takes the last object in the last remaining pile wins.

To figure out the best move in any Nim position, express the number of objects in each pile as a binary (base two) number, then add together the three numbers using the special Nim-addition rule that $1 + 1 = 0$. And so, with piles of three, five, and nine objects, you would calculate the Nim-addition as $11 + 101 + 1001 = 1111$.

This Nim-sum is the key to winning. When the Nim-sum is 0, whoever is about to move will lose, provided both players make the best moves for the rest of the game. When the Nim-sum is not 0, the winning strategy is always to remove enough objects to make the Nim-sum equal to 0. As it happens, it is possible to accomplish this if and only if the Nim-sum is not already 0. In the above example, removing three objects from the pile of nine will work, since the resulting Nim-addition will be $11 + 101 + 110 = 0$.

Misère Nim is a variation in which the play is the same but the object is the opposite: The player who takes the last object *loses*. Surprisingly, the winning strategy turns out to be much the same as in regular Nim. The exceptions are: (1) don't allow your opponent to reduce the position to an even number of piles, each of which contains a single object; and, of course, (2) if there is only one pile left, take all *but one* of the objects in it.

Nim can be played with paper and pencil by drawing groups of circles to represent the objects and having players cross out the circles that are "taken."

Two-Dimensional Nim

Nim gets a lot harder when extended to a second dimension. In the rectangular array of objects shown in Diagram 8.2, a player may remove any number of objects that lie in any row or column; optionally, players may also allow objects to be removed along diagonals. In the triangular array shown, a string of objects may be removed along any line parallel to any edge of the triangle.

The player who takes the last object wins, although it makes just as good a game to play a Misère version in which the last

Diagram 8.2

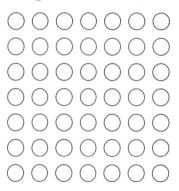

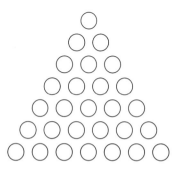

Extended to two or more dimensions, Nim becomes much more challenging. Both rectangular and triangular arrays work well.

Diagram 8.3

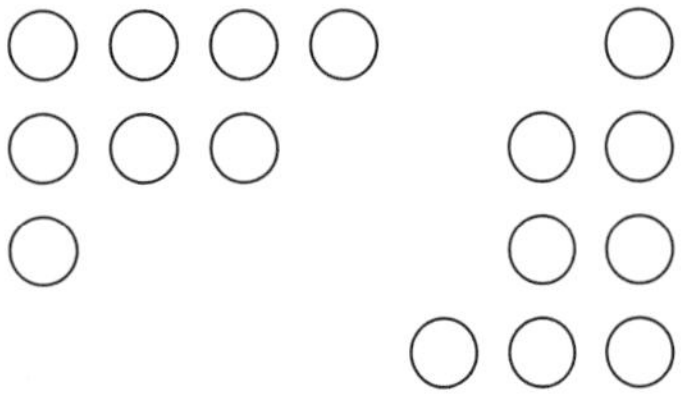

In a Nim variation in which players may not remove objects separated by a gap, a player who can divide the position into two separate but equal parts has an easy win. In the position above, whoever moves next will lose, since the opponent can keep imitating his moves in the other half of the "board."

player loses. A variation is to prohibit players from taking pieces that are separated by a gap caused by the earlier removal of other pieces. If you play this way, be sure that the first player cannot immediately divide the opening position into two equal sections. Once two identical sections are left, as in Diagram 8.3, the first player to move will lose. All the second player has to do is to watch what the first player does in one section and then imitate it in the other section to be sure of an easy win.

Nim can be thought of as a special case of the much more complex taking-away game of Hackenbush, which is described and analyzed in *Winning Ways* (see page 112).

TSIANSHIDSI

There are many other Nim-like games. One example is Tsianshidsi, invented in 1907 by W. A. Wythoff. Two piles of objects are used, and each player, in turn, may either (1) remove any number of objects from one pile, or (2) remove an equal number of objects from each pile. This game, too, has a known winning strategy, which involves trying to make a move that leaves a "safe" pattern of objects in the two piles. Safe patterns are 1 object in one pile and 2 in the other; 3 objects in one, 5 in the other; 4 and 7; 6 and 10; 8 and 13; 9 and 15; and so on (the difference between the two numbers keeps increasing, and no number is repeated). When you make a safe pattern, then no matter what your opponent does, you will be able to make a move that reduces the position to another safe pattern, until you eventually win by taking the last object.

Like Nim, though, Tsianshidsi can be complicated by adding additional piles, by creating a two-dimensional array of piles in which equal pieces may be removed from all piles lying in the same line, and/or by playing a Misère version.

MAP-COLORING GAMES

By drawing an irregular grid on a blank piece of paper, players can create their own "board" for a group of related, Nim-like games. The grid should consist of a number of regions that touch each other in various ways, much like an outline map showing the state borders of the United States. We'll call the irregular grid a "map," even though it does not have to be a real map of anything.

In the simplest game, players take turns coloring in any uncolored region on the map, with one restriction: If two regions touch along a border, only one of them may be colored in. It's all right to color in two regions if they touch only at a corner point, as Colorado and Arizona do, for example. The first player unable to color in a region loses.

To complicate the game, players can use two or three pencils or crayons of different colors. Again, players take turns coloring in a region, and they each may use any color they wish each turn. In this game, regions that touch along a border may both be colored, provided they are given different colors. The first player unable to make a legal move loses.

The game gets still harder if each player is given a different color to use throughout the game—say, one may only use red and the other green. This game, by inventor Colin Vout, is extensively analyzed in *Winning Ways* under the name Col. And it's harder still if each player gets two different colors to use. This can be played in two interesting ways: Players can have two completely different pairs of colors (e.g., one player uses red and yellow, the other uses green and blue), or players can have one common color (e.g., one player has red and yellow, the other has green and yellow).
Misère versions of all these games are possible, too.

CHOMP

This game, another two-dimensional Nim-like game, was invented by David Gale in 1973. Any rectangular grid of squares can be used for this paper-and-pencil game, as long as it is larger than 6x6 in size and is not perfectly square. For beginners, 7x10 and 10x13 boards work well; for more experienced players, an 11x17 board is recommended.

Each player in turn draws an X in any square in the grid, then completely crosses out all rows above the X and all columns to the right of the X. Players may not place an X in a row or column that has been crossed out. The player who is forced to choose the square in the lower left corner loses.

SPROUTS

This paper-and-pencil game, invented in 1960 by John H. Conway and M.S. Paterson, is much harder to analyze than Nim. In fact,

Diagram 8.4

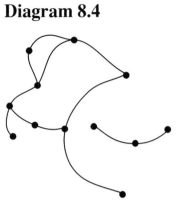

Sprouts and its Misère variation are excellent games to play in a home tournament, since they are easy to explain and quick to play, and require no equipment other than paper and pencil. In this game in progress, four of the dots have three lines extending from them and thus can no longer be used.

except for some of the simplest forms of the game, it is unknown whether the first or second player should win.

Players begin with a sheet of paper on which several dots have been drawn. Each player, in turn, draws a line connecting a pair of dots and then draws a new dot somewhere near the midpoint of the line he just drew. Lines do not have to be straight. Diagram 8.4 shows a game in progress.

Player's choices are restricted in two ways:

1. No line may cross another line.

2. No more than three lines may extend out of one dot. Thus, when a new dot is added to the middle of a line, it already has lines extending from it in two directions, and only one more line may be connected to it.

In regular Sprouts, the last player to be able to make a move wins. An equally good game is Misère Sprouts, in which the last player able to make a move loses.

DOTS-AND-BOXES

Children often play this game, in which players take turns connecting adjacent dot pairs with horizontal or vertical lines. When a player completes a square, he puts his initial in it and goes again. The object is to get your initials in the most squares.

This game, too, resembles Nim, because there comes a time when players run out of safe moves. But there is no easy way to analyze dots-and-boxes; it's a hard game to play well.

To vary dots-and-boxes, players can compete to complete triangles instead of squares, using a dot pattern like one of those shown in Diagram 8.5.

ARITHMETIC CROQUET

This two-player game was invented in 1872 by Lewis Carroll, author of *Alice in Wonderland* and *Through the Looking Glass*. The first time you play, you will probably feel like you have no idea what you are doing—but that will change with experience.

The object of the game is to go through the "hoops," which are the numbers 10, 20, 30, ..., 90, and then to be the first to name the number 100. Here's how it works.

Players take turns naming a whole number out loud. The first number each player names must not be higher than 8, and the player who goes second must choose a number that is different from the first player's. Each turn, a player must name a new number. The new number may not be more than 8 higher than the number the player named on his previous turn.

The amount by which a player increases his number from one turn to the next is known as a "step." A player may not take a step that is equal to the most recent step his opponent took, nor may a player take a step that is equal to the difference between his opponent's last step and 9. Thus, if a player takes a step of 6—by going, say, from 7 to 13—his opponent may not take a step of either 6 or 3 on the next turn.

Each number ending in 0 is a "hoop" that must be "played through" in one of two ways:

1. By going from a number below a hoop to a number that is the same distance above the hoop (for example, getting through the 30 hoop by going from 28 to 32); or

2. By going into a hoop on one turn (as by going from 28 to 30) and then going above it on the next turn by taking the same size step as was used to play into it. (In this case, the player in the 30 hoop would have to move to 32.) When a player moves into a hoop in this manner, he loses the power, for that turn only, to bar his opponent from taking a step of the same size or a step of 9 minus the same size.

A player may miss a hoop by deliberately playing beyond it without following the above rule; but then he must move backward on his next turn to go to any number below the hoop. Missing the same hoop twice loses the game.

A player can get temporarily stuck in a hoop if his opponent takes a step of a size that bars the player from using the number he needs to get out of the hoop. If this happens, the player loses his turn and must wait for the opponent to take a step of a size that will allow him to move. If a step of a certain size will keep the opponent stuck in a hoop, a player may not take such a step more than once in a row—but he may alternately take steps equal to that size and the difference between that size and 9 in order to cause the opponent to lose more than one turn.

A player moving from any number between 90 and 100 has no power to bar the opponent from taking steps of certain sizes, unless the opponent is also on a number between 90 and 100, in which case the usual barring rule applies.

The winner is the first player to name 100. The 100 "winning peg" may, like each hoop, be missed once; but missing it twice loses the game.

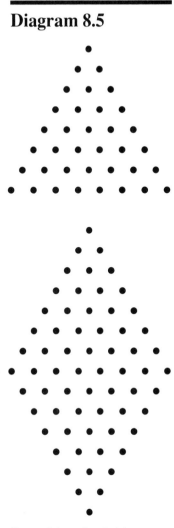

Diagram 8.5

For an interesting twist on Dots-and-Boxes, try Dots-and-Triangles on a grid such as one of these.

FINGER BASEBALL

All you need for this old two-player game are the fingers of one hand and, if you like, a paper and pencil to keep score.

One player is chosen randomly to "bat" first, which makes the other player the "pitcher." Both players put one hand behind their backs, then bring those hands forward simultaneously to reveal either 1, 2, 3, 4, or 5 outstretched fingers. Each combination of "batter" fingers and "pitcher" fingers leads to a particular outcome, as follows:

- If the number of fingers on the two players' hands don't match, the batter is out.

- If the number of fingers on the two players' hands do match, then the batter gets one of the following results:

If Each Player Shows:	Batter Gets:
1 finger	single
2 fingers	double
3 fingers	triple
4 fingers	home run
5 fingers	walk

Runners, if any, advance the same number of bases as the batter.

There is, of course, no pure strategy that will assure success in this game. If you always choose the same number of fingers, your opponent will catch on and will always be able to make a successful countermove.

According to game theory, the best strategy is a mixed one in which you make choices that are random, but that are weighted in such a way as to take into account the relative benefits and disadvantages of each possible pair of outcomes.

For an introduction to game theory and details on how to determine what percentage of time you should use each strategy, see *The Compleat Strategyst* by J.D. Williams (McGraw-Hill, 1966). This is hard to do in the context of a nine-inning baseball game, however, because strategies can be influenced by the number of men on base, the score, and the number of innings left in the game.

In addition, the importance of psychology is not to be underestimated. It is very hard not to become predictable in a way that will allow an observant opponent to take advantage of your pattern of plays.

ONE-CAPTURE GO: PAPER BOARDS

Complete rules to playing this game on a board were given in Chapter 5. But since pieces, once placed, are never moved or removed in this game—until a capture is made, which ends the game—it can be played as a paper-and-pencil game. This has the advantage of giving players much more freedom over the kinds of grids on which the game is played.

Players choose a grid to play on. It can be a regular square or hexagonal grid, or a semiregular or irregular grid. Four possibilities are shown in Diagram 8.6.

Each player takes a pencil of a different color. Each player, in turn, colors in one region in the grid. Any region at all may be chosen, as long as it has not already been colored in. Experienced players should adopt a pie rule to balance the game.

The winner is the first player to completely surround a region, or a connected group of regions, that the opponent has colored in. Surrounding a region or group of regions means coloring in the last uncolored space *touching* that region. "Touching" means sharing an edge; regions that share only a corner point are not considered to be

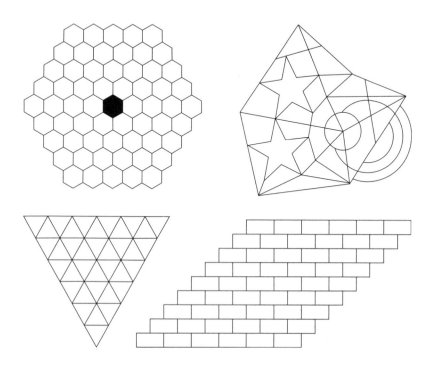

Diagram 8.6

One-Capture Go can be played with two pencils of contrasting color on any kind of grid that players wish to draw on paper. For variety, it's even possible to play on a board containing holes, such as the blackened hexagon in the upper left grid.

touching. If a move causes both players to have regions or groups that are surrounded, the player who made the move wins.

A player may not pass when it is his turn. If, by coloring in a region, a player is forced to cause one of his own regions to be surrounded, he loses the game.

CONNECTION GAMES

Hex and Havannah

Any abstract board game in which pieces are placed on a space but never removed can be played with paper and pencil. Two games described earlier in this book, Hex (Chapter 2) and Havannah (Chapter 7), are excellent examples. As in the paper and pencil version of One-Capture Go, each player uses a pencil or pen of a different color, and a "move" consists of coloring in an uncolored region on the paper board.

Octagons

Because of the uniform way in which they cover a plane without meeting at corners the way squares do, hexagons are the shape of choice for most connection games. An exception is my own game Octagons, which is played on a grid with an octagon-square pattern in which the octagons have been cut in half to make irregular pentagons.

The board is shown in Diagram 8.7. The top and bottom board edges are colored red, and the left and right edges are colored blue. One player is Red, who uses a red pencil, and the other is Blue, who uses a blue pencil.

Each turn, a player colors in either *one* half-octagon or *two* squares. The pie rule is in effect: One player, chosen randomly, moves first by making a move for Red, after which the other player has the choice of playing Red or Blue. Once the choice is made, players take turns normally for the rest of the game.

As in Hex, the winner is the first player to complete a path of his color between the two edges of his color (i.e., Red tries to connect the top and bottom edges with red-colored spaces, and Blue tries to connect the left and right edges with blue spaces).

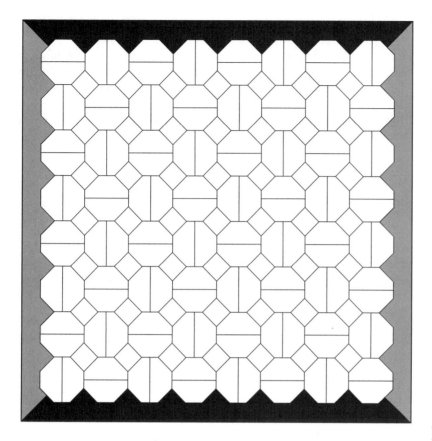

Diagram 8.7

In Octagons, players alternately fill in either one half-octagon or two squares per turn, trying to connect the two edges of their color with a path of their color.

Diagram 8.8

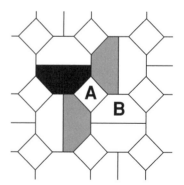

The Gray regions have a loose connection that cannot normally be broken by Black, since if Black fills in A, Gray can answer at B, and vice versa. But if Black can play at A and make a similar threat elsewhere in the same turn, Gray will be in trouble.

Octagons offers players an unusual tactic. Since half-octagons generally border seven spaces, they are much more important to occupy than squares, which border only four. The fact that two squares can be filled in at once does not fully compensate for this, and so it is better, early in the game, to fill in a half-octagon than to fill in two squares. But as the board fills in, positions come about in which filling in a square will threaten an important connection, as shown in Diagram 8.8. If a player can bring about positions of this kind in two different parts of the board, he can fill in both key squares in one turn, making it impossible for the opponent to defend both threats.

Otherwise, the strategy of Octagons is much like that of other connection games. Craige Schensted and Charles Titus, inventors of several outstanding connection games, summarized strategy succinctly in their remarkable book *Mudcrack Y and Poly Y* (Neo Press, 1975) by stating, "The best offense is a good defense." For some reason, it's easier to see how to block the opponent's connection than to see how to solidify your own connections. But if you can do the former, you don't need to worry about the latter, since it is impossible for a game of Octagons to end in a draw.

It's also important to spread out your moves, even though it may look as though the opponent can keep you from connecting them into a solid path. If you color in spaces that are too close together, some of them may end up doing the same job; and if you find that one of your moves has become unnecessary, it's as if you have given your opponent an extra turn.

CHAPTER

9

PARTY GAMES

If you want to give a party and you're looking for a theme, why not make it a game party? You can set up a few different games around your house or apartment, run minitournaments, and award prizes to the winners of certain events. And the games in this chapter may be just what you need to make the party truly memorable.

HAGGLE

This invention of Sid Sackson's is one of the most successful party games I've ever participated in. It requires some advance preparation by the host, some work scoring the game later, and, ideally, a prize to give players an incentive to do their best. But it's well worth the effort.

In the original version of Haggle, which is detailed in the inventor's book *A Gamut of Games*, pieces of paper of different colors were used as the "cards" to be traded by the players. I have adapted the game for use with ordinary playing cards; otherwise, the play is unchanged.

At the party, each player will receive an envelope containing 12 playing cards and 2 pieces of paper known as "secret information sheets." The information sheets give some of the information about how much different cards are worth, either alone (their "basic value") or in combination with other cards.

During the course of the party, or during a time period set aside just to play the game, players trade cards and information with one another, making any deals they wish. They can trade however they see fit: cards for cards, information for information, or cards for information.

At a predetermined time, each player places all of his cards, or whichever of his cards he wishes, into his envelope and hands the envelope (with the player's name on it) to the host. The host then determines each player's score according to the cards in the envelopes and the scoring rules as set forth in the full set of information sheets. The player with the highest score wins.

To play Haggle, you'll need at least eight players. And the more, the better. The number of players determines how many cards you'll need. For 8 to 13 players, use three decks of cards; for 14 to 26 players, use six decks; for 27 to 39 players, nine decks; and so on.

You will also need to prepare two identical sets of information sheets, with each set containing as many sheets as there are players. Finally, you'll need one envelope for each player.

Preparation

1. Sort the decks into suits. For eight players, use the A, 2, 3, 4, 5, 6, 7, and 8 of each suit, and leave the 9 through king out of the game. For nine players, use the ace through 9; for 10 players, the ace through 10; for 11 players, the ace through jack; and so on. For 14 players, use six decks, but use only the ace through 7 of each suit. For 15 players, include the 8s; for 16 players, include the 8s and 9s; and so on. The idea is to have an equal number of cards in each suit and to have a total of 12 cards in the game for every player.

   Note: You can simplify this procedure by ignoring the card values and just picking the right number of cards from each suit. By keeping the card ranks uniform, however, you will be better able to create information sheets that make use of card ranks as well as suits, as some of the examples below illustrate.

2. Create two identical sets of information sheets, such as the one in the example below.

3. Mix the cards thoroughly, and randomly put 12 cards into each envelope. Mix the information sheets up, and put two of each of those into each envelope as well, taking care not to give any player two information sheets that match. (Remember, there are two of each kind of sheet.)

4. Give the envelopes to participants at the same time and explain the game. Set a time limit for turning in the envelopes to you for scoring.

Secret Information Sheets

Here's an example of how you might prepare information sheets for a game with 12 players. A good way to approach the task is to start by assigning a basic value to each suit, so that any card of that suit will have particular point value. Suppose you decide that hearts will be worth 4 points each, clubs 3, spades 2, and diamonds 1. You put this information into four information sheets, preferably in such a way that players can learn more by piecing together two or more sheets than by reading each sheet independently. For example:

1. Clubs have a basic point value of 3 points each, which is as much as a diamond and spade together are worth.

2. Hearts have the highest basic point value and are each worth as much as a diamond and club together.

3. In terms of basic value, a spade is worth half as much as a heart and twice as much as a diamond.

4. A diamond is worth 1 point less than a spade.

Next, add rules that complicate the scoring. It is a good idea to place limitations on the highest-valued cards and to create bonuses favoring the lower-ranking cards. This has two desirable effects:

a. Players who happen to be dealt a lot of one particular suit—or one or two particular pieces of information—will not have an overly great advantage or disadvantage.

b. Trading will be lively, because it will not be easy for players to figure out which suits to concentrate on collecting.

Here are some examples:

5. If a player's hand has four or more hearts in it, all the hearts in the hand count zero.

6. The player with the most diamonds gets a bonus equal to the square of the number of diamonds in his hand. In case of a tie, no one gets the bonus.

7. For each pair of diamonds a player has, one spade in his hand scores triple its usual point value.

8. A hand only scores for as many clubs as it has spades.

It's a good idea, too, to place some general limitation on the number of cards a player may turn in with his hand.

9. Players may turn in as many or as few cards as they like; but if a player turns in more than 15 cards, the excess over 15 will be removed at random before the hand is scored.

Finally, add a few whimsical rules to make things really tricky to figure out. But remember, you as host will be responsible for scoring the hands later and determining the winner!

10. The player with the most aces gets a bonus equal to twice the number of aces in the hand. In case of a tie, each tying player gets the bonus.

11. A hand that contains only black cards or only red cards gets a bonus equal to twice the number of cards in the hand.

12. A hand containing exactly one card of one suit, two cards of another suit, three cards of a third suit, and four cards of a fourth suit scores double.

Whimsical rules such as these can be dropped or added at the last minute if the number of participants in the game turns out to be different from what you anticipated when doing your advance preparation. If you had prepared the above information sheets and unexpectedly found that a thirteenth player had shown up, you could add another whimsical information sheet, such as, "13. If a hand contains at least three hearts, rule 8 is ignored when the hand is scored." Such cross-referential rules can be interesting; but when creating them, be sure you have not inadvertently contradicted any other rules.

Here's how some sample hands would be scored under rules 1 through 12 above:

Hand 1:	Suit	Number of Cards
	♥	3
	♣	none
	♠	none
	♦	7

This hand scores as follows:

> 3 hearts x 4 points each = 12 points
>
> 7 diamonds x 1 point each = 7 points
>
> all-red bonus = 2 points per card x 10 cards = 20 points

That makes a total of 39 points. If no other player has as many as seven diamonds, the player also earns a bonus of 7 x 7 = 49 (rule 6). This would make the hand worth a total of 88 points.

The player who turned in Hand 1 also had a club and a fourth heart, but discarded them just before putting the hand in the envelope. The player thereby avoided the loss of points for having more than three hearts (rule 5), and gained the bonus for a one-color hand (rule 11).

Hand 2:	Suit	Number of Cards
	♥	1
	♣	4
	♠	3
	♦	2

The hand scores as follows:

> *hearts:* 1 x 4 = 4
>
> *clubs:* 3 x 3 = 9 (under rule 8, only three of the four clubs score, since the hand has only three spades)
>
> *spades:* 1 x 6 (under rule 7, one spade has triple its usual value, since the hand contains one pair of diamonds) + 2 x 2 = 10
>
> *diamonds:* 2 x 1 = 2

The total is 25 points. But because of the bonus for 4-3-2-1 distribution (rule 12), the hand doubles in value to 50 points.

Hand 3:	Suit	Number of Cards
	♥	3
	♣	3
	♠	3
	♦	5

Assume that among this hand's 14 cards are five aces and that no other player turns in a hand that has more aces. The hand then scores as follows:

hearts: 3 x 4 = 12

clubs: 3 x 3 = 9

spades: 6 x 2 (there are two pairs of diamonds, so two of the spades are tripled) + 2 x 1 = 14

diamonds: 5 x 1 = 5

aces: 2 x 5 = 10 for the aces (rule 10)

This makes a total of 50 points.

SUPER BABEL

A great party game for a large number of players, Super Babel is the creation of Robert Abbott. Like Haggle, it uses cards as objects to be traded.

The game can be played with as few as 6 players, but is really best for 15 or more. In addition, one person needs to act as a non-playing scorekeeper and reshuffler.

The number of decks needed is approximately one-third the number of players. To begin, shuffle together all the decks and deal them into piles of ten cards each. It's a good idea to do this in advance. The scorekeeper should also prepare a scoresheet in advance, divided into columns. Each player's name should appear at the top of one of the columns.

The rules of the game are explained to all the players, and a time limit is set, such as 20 minutes, after which the game will end. The scorekeeper then gives each player one packet of ten cards.

Players then attempt, by trading cards with one another, to form ten-card hands that will let them "go out." Such hands must either be a combination of two poker hands that are straights or better, or they must be one of three special ten-card hands, as described in the following chart. Each player should be given a copy of this chart to refer to during the game.

Five-Card Hands (Two of These Are Needed To Go Out)

Hand	Point Value	Description
straight	5	any five cards in numerical sequence
flush	7	any five cards of the same suit
full house	10	three cards of one rank plus two cards of another rank
four of a kind	15	four cards of the same rank (plus one of any other card)
straight flush	20	five cards of the same suit in numerical sequence
royal flush	21	the ace, king, queen, jack, 10 of one suit

Ten-Card Hands (One of These Is Needed To Go Out)

Hand	Point Value	Description
double straight	20	any ten cards in numerical sequence
double flush	40	ten cards of the same suit
double straight flush	80	ten cards of the same suit in sequence

According to the rules of the game that appeared in *Abbott's New Card Games* (Funk & Wagnall's, 1963), players are not allowed to turn in duplicate cards—such as two queens of clubs—as part of the same combination. Thus, Q-Q-9-3-2 of clubs was not a valid flush. This is a good rule to follow, but the inventor has found that some players may not like the added complexity of having to check for matching numbers in, say, a ten-card hand of all hearts. If players prefer a slightly simpler form of the game, they can play without this restriction.

When a player goes out, the game does not end. He turns in his cards to the scorekeeper, who records their point value by writing it in the player's column on the scoresheet. The scorekeeper then gives a new packet of ten cards to the player, who immediately rejoins the trading action and tries to get a new set of cards to turn in. A player may turn in any number of sets of cards during the game, as long as time allows.

There are no restrictions on the kinds of trades players may make, except that trades should always be between equal numbers of cards (one for one, three for three, etc.) to ensure that players will always be able to turn in ten cards. Players may call out what they have and wait for the best offer or keep their hands secret; they may bargain in the open or move into another room for closed-door discussions; they may form alliances or work alone.

As players turn in more and more sets of cards, the scorekeeper should start to reshuffle them together after the scores have been recorded in order to avoid running out of new ten-card packets to give players. Depending on the number of players and the pace of the action, it may be a good idea for the scorekeeper to have an assistant to help with the reshuffling and redealing.

When time is up, the scorekeeper adds up the scores of all the players to determine the winner.

The inventor has recently come up with an alternative scoring system for Super Babel, which allows players to make trades of unequal numbers of cards. Point values are based on the difficulty of getting each kind of hand, as measured by the average number of cards a player needs to be randomly dealt in order to get such a holding.

Hand	Point Value
4 cards of the same rank	15
6 cards of the same rank	50
5 cards of the same suit	5
9 cards of the same suit	40
5 cards in numerical sequence	7
8 cards in numerical sequence	30
5 cards of the same suit in numerical sequence	20

In this version, a card used in one combination cannot be used in another. A player may turn in a hand of any size, provided it contains a minimum of 20 points.

CHARADES

Tabloids and Fortune Cookies

The old parlor favorite can be varied by altering the subject matter, introducing bidding, and adding handicaps. Ordinarily, players act out a familiar phrase—a name, title, saying, etc.—in an attempt to get their teammates to guess the phrase as quickly as possible. But for variety, it can be fun to act out stranger phrases, such as tabloid newspaper headlines ("Two-Headed Man Gives Birth to Twins") or fortune cookie sayings ("You are wiser than your years"). It's best to use only authentic headlines and fortunes. Players should be told what kind of phrase it is they are trying to guess, since that will help them figure out what otherwise might be an unlikely string of words.

Beating the Clock

If players have an accurate timer or stopwatch available, they can make charades more competitive by introducing bidding. One player from each team (there can be any number of teams) is shown the next name, phrase, etc., that is to be acted out. These players then take turns bidding for the right to become the actor.

Bids are made in units of time. If one player starts the bidding at two minutes, he expects to be able to get a teammate to name the phrase in two minutes or less. If the other player thinks he can succeed more quickly, he might bid 1 minute 45 seconds. The first player might counter with 1 minute 15 seconds. Each bid should be required to be less than the previous bid by a certain minimum amount, such as 10 or 15 seconds.

When no one wants to bid anymore, the player with the low bid gets to be the actor. If a teammate figures out the answer within the time limit, the team earns a point; if not, the team loses a point as a penalty.

For Experts Only

As a real test of their abilities, experienced charades players may wish to try a version in which they are handicapped in various ways. They may be required to act out something with one or both hands behind their back, with their back turned toward their teammates, with their hands inside mittens (so that they can't hold up specific numbers of fingers), or with their eyes closed.

Make a list of all the handicaps you think would be fun to try, then write each one on an index card and shuffle the cards. Each time something is about to be acted out, turn over the top index card to determine what handicap rule the actor will have to obey.

It's possible to combine this version with bidding by letting a player from each team see both the phrase to be acted out and the handicap, and then having them bid on how quickly they think they can convey the message.

BOARDLESS PICTIONARY

The charades bidding method can also be applied to certain other party games, such as Pictionary. The board is not used; instead, play and scoring follow the method outlined for charades (in "Beating the Clock," above). One player from each team gets to peek at the subject to be drawn before bidding on it.

RUNNING A TOURNAMENT

If you're hosting a party with a game theme, your guests may find it interesting to compete for a prize in a minitournament that allows any number to participate. Tournaments can be run in various ways, such as a round robin, single or double elimination, or Swiss system (in which players with like records are paired against each other each round). The best format depends on the number of players, the amount of equipment you have (that is, the number of games that can be going on simultaneously), and the number of rounds people have time to play.

Don't hesitate to improvise a format just because it's not one of the standard ones. For example, suppose you have one croquet set, which comes with equipment allowing six players to play at once. You want to run a croquet tournament for 18 people, but you are not sure there will be time for more than four games. In this situation, you would probably do best to divide the players into groups of six and have each group play a game. Players who finish first or second in each group's game qualify for a final round, a six-player game in which the first-place finisher will win the tournament.

It's also interesting to have a kind of "decathlon" of game events, with players earning points according to their finish in each event.

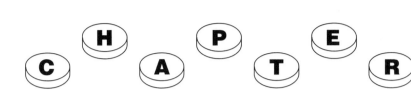

OUTDOOR GAMES

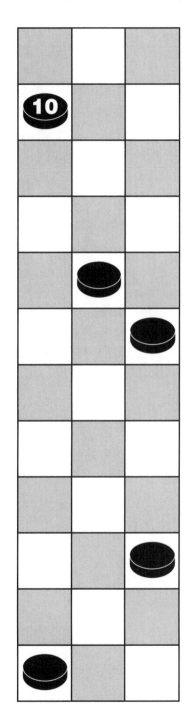

As baseball fans will attest, equipment as simple as a stick and a ball can lead to hours of enjoyment. Almost anyone who played a lot of stickball, touch football, and one-on-one basketball while growing up has already improvised a variety of ground rules for these sports. In this chapter are rules for some backyard games that are not so well known.

KICKBALL GOLF

When I was in high school, I spent a lot of time one summer designing and playing a nine-hole pitch-and-putt golf course on my family's front lawn. I dug nine holes in various locations, sank flowerpots into them, used sticks as "pins" to mark the holes, and mowed low-cut "greens" around them. I even added a small sand trap at the edge of the woods near the ninth green.

I experimented with different tee locations and orders in which to play the holes, and finally created a scorecard including yardage for each hole and a schematic diagram of the course. Then I played the course over and over, usually by myself—in which case I played against an imaginary "Mr. Par," who always shot a 3 on every hole.

I never got tired of the game. I was constantly challenged to beat my own best score and to set other personal records such as most consecutive birdies. Of course, there was also the satisfaction of improving my skill at something—and I did find that it carried over to real golf, in that short approach shots and chip shots became by far the strongest part of my game. Eventually, I expanded the course to 18-holes, not by adding more holes but by figuring out a way to play them from new tee locations and in a different order. I even had a par-4 eighteenth hole, a dogleg around a patch of woods.

Years later, I became a homeowner with a smaller lawn. Setting up a golf course like the one I had as a teenager seemed like a bad idea, not only because of the shorter distances (which would put my windows at risk) but because of safety considerations. Children, both mine and neighbors', were often running around the property or hiding behind bushes. Still, I wanted to find a substitute for my old pitch-and-putt golf game that would allow me to get a little exercise, relax, and have the same kind of fun.

One of my children had a pre-inflated ball of the kind you can find at supermarkets in the springtime—the kind of ball that can't be reinflated. This one was about 10 or 11 inches in diameter and happened to have a picture of the old TV character ALF on it, but they come in a wide variety of colors and patterns, as well as slightly different sizes and weights. Size is not too important for this game, but heavy ones work better than light ones.

One day, I tried kicking the ball toward a small tree at the end of the back yard and got it pretty close. Then I wondered how easy it would be to "putt" such a ball with my foot, and took two more short shots before hitting the tree's trunk. Sure that I could improve on the three shots it had taken me to hit the tree, I played again and again, until I finally did it in two kicks.

It wasn't long before I went looking for new targets around the lawn. Soon I set up a "course" of five "holes"—all tree trunks— that took me on a complete circle around the house, ending up back near the first "tee."

I began playing several rounds of the game every weekend. Each round only took a few minutes, so I could play as a break from other outside chores. Soon I was taking the game more seriously: I made adjustments on tee locations, created a dogleg around one corner of the house, established "par" results for each hole, and kept mental records of my best scores. I also refined the rules to specify that, to count as being "in the hole," the ball had to hit the target tree trunk either at ground level or no more than a yard above ground level.

If you don't have trees in your lawn, or if you don't have a lawn but want to try the game in an open field, you can always substitute other targets, such as large coffee cans.

The final course, shown in Diagram 10.1, had the dimensions given in the following table.

Hole	Distance (yards)	Tree Diam. (inches)	Par
1	40	3	3
2	24	9	2
3	30	5–13*	3
4	33	21	2
5	28	9	2
Total	155	—	12

*The tree has a double trunk, so the width depends on the direction from which it is approached.

The values of par were modified over time as I got better at the game. With the final values, it's quite a challenge to break or even equal par. I have birdied each hole, even the par 2s, more than once, but the best score I have ever achieved on a single round has been a 2-under-par score of 10.

I find it nearly impossible to kick the particular ball I use more than 30 yards without a good wind at my back. An exception is the fourth hole, where a good kick will land on the driveway and take a sizable bounce toward the hole, which is also slightly downhill from the tee. In addition to distance and obstacles, hole difficulty is a function of the diameter of the target tree. Small trees, such as the three-inch diameter first hole, can be hard to hit consistently even from six feet away, except where the lawn is smooth and flat, whereas large trees should require only a single putt from 15 feet away.

I also developed different techniques for kicking the ball. I found fairly quickly that the game is best played in bare feet. With shoes on, unless you're good at kicking soccer-style, it's too easy to have the ball angle off one side or the other from the tip of your sneaker.

With bare feet, I found it best to hit the ball in one of two ways. For long shots, I would bring my right foot back and slightly to the left, with my foot stretched out pointing backward and its toes curled down. I would then bring the foot forward quickly, but

Diagram 10.1

This schematic drawing of the author's Kickball Golf course is accurate, but does not indicate such hazards as overhanging branches. The outer boundary shows the property line. Note that one tree is used as both the second and fifth holes.

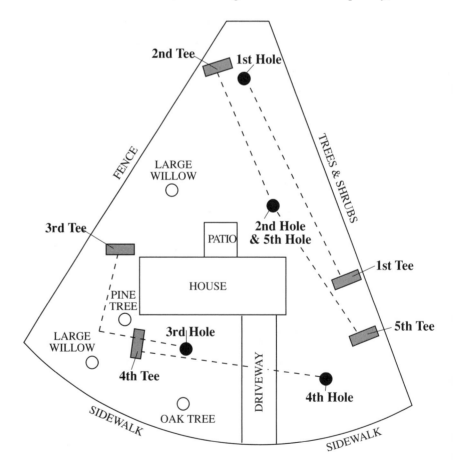

as smoothly as possible, striking the ball with the flat area on top of my foot in a slightly left-to-right direction. When done correctly, this shot makes the ball take off at the same kind of low trajectory as a good golf tee shot, and the ball tends to hook slightly from right to left. A running start can be used for greater distance.

For short shots—say, those under 25 feet—I devised a special "putting" technique. I would curl my toes *up* this time, bring my leg straight back, then strike the ball gently—in almost a pushing motion—with the ball of my foot or with the area between the ball of my foot and my toes. This technique allows very accurate putting, but works poorly for long distances.

Eventually, I played "ALF-Ball Golf," as I took to calling it, with my wife and others, with each player using his or her own ball, and it worked well as a competitive game, too. The only additional rule for competitive play involves what to do when one player's ball gets in the way of another's. As in modern golf, we allowed a player to mark an obstructing ball's location with a leaf or twig, then temporarily remove it to allow other players to take their turns without being "stymied."

We tried for the lowest total score, but the game would also work well using the objective of winning the most holes. Either way, ties are broken by sudden-death playoffs beginning at the first hole.

Will my Kickball Golf game replace croquet and badminton as America's favorite lawn sports? Probably not. But it doesn't require much equipment, and it has the advantage of being a good game to play solitaire.

Kickball Ricochet

If you've played a lot of pool, you know that the position you leave the cue ball in is just as important as making your shot. In Kickball Golf, an interesting variation is to play the course not as a series of holes but as one continuous route that must be covered in as few shots as possible.

None of the tees are used except the first. The holes are played in order, as usual; but after hitting each tree, you head for the next tree from wherever your ball has ended up. If you're close enough to a hole to take a risk, you can kick the ball hard at the target, trying to ricochet it so that it will bounce a good distance toward the next hole.

If you wind up so that the tree you've just hit lies directly between you and the next hole, too bad—going around obstacles is part of the game. The winner is the player who needs the fewest shots to complete the course by hitting the final hole.

OTHER "GOLFS": CROQUET AND FLYING DISC

A course similar to that for Kickball Golf, but using wickets as targets, can be set up with a croquet set. Of course, you'll probably want to use much smaller distances than for Kickball Golf. Try to make use of any natural obstacles you have, such as trees or slopes, to make the course more interesting.

With a croquet set, it seems more natural to play a version that is analogous to the Kickball Ricochet variation. Rather than designating tees for each wicket, let each ball begin from wherever it was when it passed through the previous wicket. The winner is the player who takes the fewest total shots to pass through all the wickets on the course.

Flying discs such as the Frisbee work very well in target games. In fact, Disc Golf is an organized game with many officially recognized courses around the country. Some holes emphasize distance, others accuracy. Setting up a Disc Golf course takes a lot of room, but you may be able to find enough space to create a kind of pitch-and-putt version. An old tire or inner tube hanging from a tree branch or propped against a wall makes a good target; players try to throw the disc through the center hole.

BACKYARD BASEBALL

The kinds of baseball games people play while growing up mainly depend on the size and nature of the field and the number of players available. I often played with just two or three people on a team, in a small area that was part lawn, part dead-end street. The rules we came up with might work in many backyard games in which both space and the number of players are limited.

We used a large Wiffle Ball, baseball gloves, and wooden bats. There were only three bases: first, third, and home, which were set up just where those bases normally go, except that the distance from home to each of the other two bases was only about 45 feet.

Most rules of baseball applied. The key exceptions were:

1. No stealing was allowed, and a player on base could not take a lead until the ball was pitched.

2. A team could only have one player on base at a time. This

meant that a man on first could be forced out at home when a ground ball was hit; all the fielder had to do was to step on home holding the ball.

Typically, a run would be built as follows. The first player would single, which was not too hard with only the pitcher and one or two other fielders on defense. Then the second player would hit the ball far enough so that the runner on first could not be forced at third. The defensive team would have to throw home to force the runner out, giving the batter time to reach third. From third, with just one out, it was usually easy for the runner to score.

TIEBREAKER TENNIS

Looking at tennis from the point of view of a game inventor, I really cannot understand the logic of its scoring. In a three-set match, a player can quite easily win the majority of points without winning a set. A player can also win the majority of games without winning a match.

What would be wrong with playing a match to, say, 50 points, with serves alternating every two points? I suppose this would eliminate the moments of special tension that audiences like, when a key game is at deuce or when a player must fight back from love–40 to hold his serve. But the outcome might be a lot fairer.

One thing I do like about tennis scoring is the tiebreaker rule. I like it so much, in fact, that I would like to suggest a tennis variation that consists of nothing but a series of tiebreakers. Each tiebreaker is played in the usual way: The first player to get seven points wins, provided he is at least two points ahead. Serves change after the first point, and every two points thereafter.

To win a match in this variation, a player must win seven tiebreakers. If players have a lot of stamina, they can even require the winner to be two tiebreakers ahead for the match to end.

CROQUET VARIATIONS

Croquet is a rare example of a multiplayer game in which the best player can win even if everyone else tries to gang up on him. It requires complex decision-making as much as dexterity and ranks among my favorite games.

Multiball variations for two or three players were discussed in Chapter 4. Here are two other suggestions to vary the play.

Rough Terrain

When setting up a croquet set, many people try to place it on the flattest, most wide open area they can find in their lawn. But the play can be very amusing if, instead, some wickets are set up on steep, smoothly mowed hills, while others are placed close to trees, the edge of the woods, or other obstacles. Remember, everyone will be playing under the same harsh conditions.

Poison

This popular variation is played the same way as normal American croquet, except that the game does not end when a player completes the course. Going through the last wicket makes a player's ball "poison." A player whose ball is poison must avoid hitting the stake, on penalty of being eliminated from the game.

When a poisoned ball hits any other ball—even one that is also poisoned—the other ball is eliminated from the game. The last player with a ball left in the game is the winner.

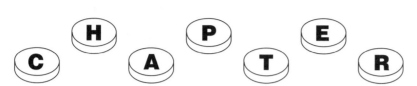

BEYOND

BACKGAMMON

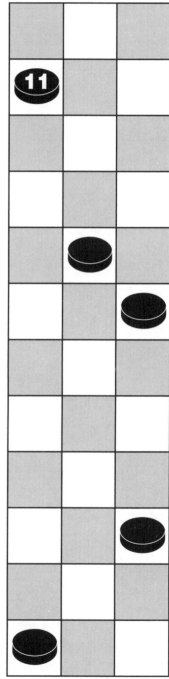

The oldest board games known to archaeologists, such as the ancient Egyptian game of Senet (dating to the Old Kingdom) and the 5,000-year-old game found in an excavation of the Sumerian city of Ur (now in Iraq), were race games in which players moved pieces along a track according to dice throws. Gradually, these games evolved into backgammon and some of the medieval and modern variants found in this chapter.

THE DOUBLING CUBE

The doubling cube is the twentieth century's contribution to the evolution of backgammon. The cube has made the game much more interesting by greatly increasing the importance of skillful decision-making in determining the winner of a series of games.

The doubling cube can have the same effect when used for many other games of mixed chance and skill. Other race games, such as Parcheesi or Sorry!, are particularly suitable for using the cube.

For readers unfamiliar with the way the doubling cube is used in backgammon, here's an explanation. The cube itself is the size of a die, the faces of which bear the numbers 2, 4, 8, 16, 32, and 64. At the start of play, the cube's "64" face is turned up, and the cube is placed between the two players to show that neither player "owns" the cube.

At any point during the game, but always just before rolling the dice, a player may take the cube, turn it so that the "2" face is up, and offer it to the opponent. This is an offer to double the stakes of the game from one to two points (or to double the size of the wager if the game is being played for money). The opponent may either accept the offer, in which case he takes possession of the cube and continues to play the game at doubled stakes, or he may decline, in which case he loses the game, but the stakes are not doubled.

If a player who accepts the cube finds that his chances to win improve, he has the right to offer the cube back to the other player by turning the "4" face up. If the opponent accepts, the game becomes worth four points; if he declines, he loses the two-point value that was showing on the cube prior to the offer. Redoubling may occur any number of times during a game.

Playing with the doubling cube requires that players exercise very fine judgment about their chances of winning a game. Note that a player who estimates his winning chances at 25 percent has a close decision in whether or not to accept a double. It's a matter of odds: If he were to accept and play out the game four times, he would be likely to lose three times and win once, for a net loss of 6 − 2 = 4 points. But declining to accept each time would also result in a four-point loss (one point per game), so the choice would seem to be a tossup.

But in fact, a player is often right to accept a cube when he has less than a 25 percent of winning. One reason is the value of owning the cube. If his position improves, he may be able to redouble, forcing his opponent to give up some games that the opponent might have won had he suddenly gotten very lucky. The earlier the stage the game is in, generally, the more time a player has for his luck to change, and the more valuable is possession of the cube.

Estimating winning chances with any precision is by no means easy. And there are still more complications to consider, such as the possibility of a gammon, which will double the value of whatever number is showing on the cube when the winner bears off all his men before the opponent has borne off any men at all. There is even the possibility of a backgammon to consider, which is a gammon in which the losing player still has at least one man left in his opponent's home board when the game ends.

Note: A backgammon scores as a triple game in the United States, but only as a gammon elsewhere.

Also significant in tournament play may be the score of a match. If players are playing a match to ten points, for example, a player who is down eight to one may need to accept almost any double, since conceding another point will make it very hard to win the match. In such a case, a player needs to take into account how his chances of winning the match will be affected by declining the double.

It's equally complicated, of course, for players to try to figure out when to offer a double. Generally, a player needs to have significantly more than a 50 percent chance of winning the game, since doubling means giving the opponent control of the cube. But again, the score of the match, the stage of the game, and the possibility of a gammon must be taken into account, complicating the decision. Occasionally, a player will even be right to double when his opponent is the favorite to win the game.

Some players like an "automatic doubling" variation in which to turn the cube to "2" at the start of the game if, in rolling to see who goes first, the players throw matching numbers. The cube remains in the center, unowned by either player. If any additional rethrows also result in ties, however, no further automatic doubling occurs.

CHOUETTES

A popular form of backgammon is the chouette, which allows three or more players to take part in a single game. By high die roll, one player is chosen to be the person "in the box" who plays against a team consisting of all the other players. The team has a captain, also determined by die roll, and the other players are ranked according to the order in which it will be their turn to become captain.

Team members may consult about their moves, but the captain actually moves the men and has the power to make the final decision when teammates disagree about the best move. If the team doubles, it does so as a whole; but if the player in the box doubles, team members may decide as individuals whether to play on or drop out.

If the player in the box wins, the team rotates so that the second person in line becomes captain, while the previous captain becomes last in line. If the team wins, the captain becomes the player in the box, the team rotates as usual, and the losing player becomes last in line to be captain of the team.

There is no reason the chouette formula cannot be adapted to other games besides backgammon, although it makes the most

Diagram 11.1

In Tabula, the Ancient Roman forerunner of backgammon, all pieces begin off the board and move in the same direction.

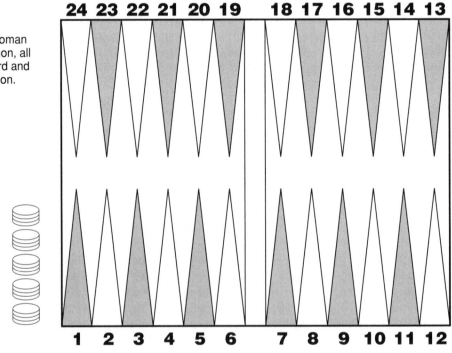

sense to use it in conjunction with a doubling cube in two-player games that depend on a combination of luck and skill.

TABULA: THE WAY IT WAS

Tabula, the forerunner of backgammon played by the ancient Romans, is not the oldest race game, but it was the first that clearly reminds us of the modern game. The game can be played with a standard backgammon set, using the following rules:

1. Each player starts with 15 pieces, all of which begin off the board.

2. Players throw three dice each turn. At the start, pieces are entered into play according to dice rolls, just as pieces reenter from the bar in backgammon, in the lower left quadrant of the board. Thus, on a roll of 1-2-5, a player could enter pieces on the points numbered 1, 2, and 5 in Diagram 11.1.

3. Both players move their pieces in the same direction, counter-clockwise from the 1 point to the 24 point. Otherwise, rules of movement are as in backgammon, except that no extra moves are made as the result of throwing doubles (or triples).

4. A player can use all or some of the numbers to move pieces already on the board even when he still has pieces to enter. In *Board and Table Games from Many Civilisations* (Oxford University Press, 1960), R. C. Bell suggests that the game is improved by adding a rule prohibiting each player from moving a piece beyond the 12 point until all of his pieces are on the board.

5. As in backgammon, men cannot be moved onto a point occupied by two or more enemy men, but a "blot" (a man alone on a point) can be landed on, in which case it is removed from the board. Such a piece must be reentered in the same way as pieces are entered at the start, and players are required to reenter a blot that has been hit before moving any other pieces.

6. The first player to bear off all his pieces wins.

FAYLES

Fayles (or Fallas) was a form of backgammon played in Europe in the Middle Ages. Although it died out around the seventeenth century, it is a good game with an exciting "sudden death" element to it. Rules are as follows:

1. The starting position is as shown in Diagram 11.2. Black moves clockwise from 24 to 1, and White moves in the opposite direction.

2. Three dice are thrown each turn. Alternatively, players use two dice and treat the lower of the two numbers thrown as having come up an additional time (e.g., a throw of 4-1 is played as 4-1-1, while 3-3 is played as 3-3-3).

3. Pieces move as in backgammon, except that no extra moves are made as the result of throwing doubles (or triples).

4. As in backgammon, men may not be moved onto a point occupied by two or more enemy men, but blots may be landed on, in which case they are returned *to their starting point*. To keep track of which pieces should be returned to which points, players should mark the checkers starting at positions 24 and 1 prior to the start of the game.

5. If a player cannot use all three numbers in his throw, he *fails* ("fayles") and loses the game at once.

6. If no one fails, the winner is the first player to bear off all his men. Bearing-off rules are as in backgammon.

Diagram 11.2

The opening setup is shown for the medieval game of Fayles. A unique rule adds a lot of tension: A player who is unable to use all three dice thrown in a turn immediately loses the game.

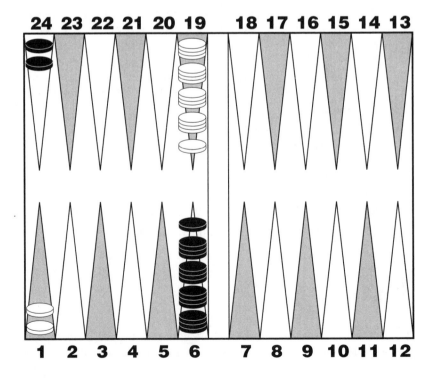

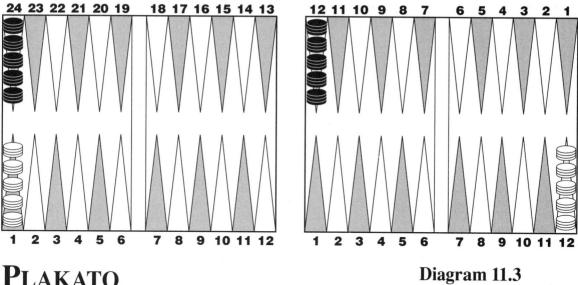

PLAKATO

This Greek version of backgammon uses the opening setup shown in the first position in Diagram 11.3. Play is as in regular backgammon, except that when a blot is hit by an opposing piece, the blot is not removed from the board. Instead, the blot stays where it is and becomes "pinned." A pinned piece may not move until the piece that landed on it (and any allied pieces that may have joined it there) move off the point. To indicate that a piece is pinned, a player who hits a blot should place his piece on top of the blot and leave it there until it moves away.

MOULTEZIM

In this Turkish version, players set up and bear off on opposite ends of the board. Rules are as in backgammon, except as follows:

1. From the opening position shown in Diagram 11.4, both players move clockwise.

2. A player must move a piece into his own outer or inner table (i.e., at least as far as the point where the opponent's pieces begin) before moving any other piece.

3. A piece may not land on an opponent's piece, *even when it is the only piece on the point.*

4. A player is not allowed to occupy more than four points in his outer table.

Diagram 11.3

In Plakato, players set up the board as shown above left. Black moves clockwise and White moves counterclockwise. Blots that are hit are "pinned" rather than sent to the bar. Gioul also uses this opening position.

In Moultezim, which is set up as shown on the right, Black and White both move clockwise but bear off at opposite ends of the board. Thus Black's inner table is the lower left quarter of the board and his outer table is the lower right, while White's inner and outer tables are the upper right and upper left, respectively.

GIOUL

This Middle Eastern variant uses the same opening setup as Plakato and the same prohibition against hitting blots as in Moultezim. The intriguing rule that distinguishes this variant is what happens when a player throws doubles: The player gets to move the two numbers in the pair, *plus every higher pair of doubles up through 6-6.*

On throwing 4-4, for example, a player would get to move 4-4, then 5-5, and finally 6-6; while on 6-6, he would only get to move 6-6.

It sounds as though throwing doubles gives a player an overwhelming advantage, but there's a catch that makes such a throw double-edged: The player must begin by moving the double thrown, then must move up to the next higher double and try to play those moves, and so forth. Thus, on a throw of 4-4, the player tries to use one 4, then another 4, then a 5, then another 5, and then two 6s. If at some point, however, the player is unable to use a number, *the opponent may use that number, as well as all higher numbers not yet used by the player.* The opponent, too, must try to use the numbers in ascending order. If the opponent is unable to use a number, the turn is over for both players.

Diagram 11.4

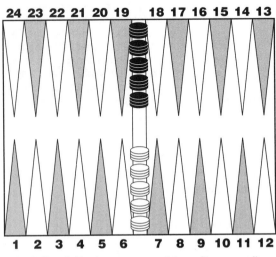

In both Dutch Backgammon and Acey Deucey, all pieces begin on the bar as shown above.

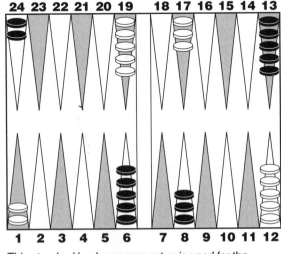

This standard backgammon setup is used for the 1,000-point variation, with no doubling cube.

Dutch Backgammon

Rules are the same as in backgammon except as follows:

1. All pieces begin off the board. Traditionally, they are stacked on the bar (see Diagram 11.4).

2. Pieces are entered by dice throws, as in Tabula, but move in opposite directions as in regular backgammon. In Diagram 11.4, Black enters pieces in the upper left and moves clockwise, while White enters pieces in the lower left and moves counterclockwise.

3. A player may not move a piece that is on the board until all his pieces have been entered.

4. A player may not hit a blot until at least one of his pieces has reached his inner table (the last six points a piece must pass before bearing off).

Acey Deucey

Rules are as in Dutch Backgammon, except that on a throw of 1-2, two things happen:

1. A player gets to follow his move of 1 and 2 by playing any double he chooses; and

2. The stakes of the game double.

It is also common for wagers to be based on the number of pieces left on the board when the game ends.

1,000-Point Backgammon

This variation was created by Robert A. Schmittberger, who was looking for a more varied way to score the game. The setup and rules of play are as usual (see Diagram 11.6), but there is no doubling cube—all games are played to conclusion. The winner then receives points in three categories:

1. 100 points for a regular win, 200 points for a gammon, or

1,000 for a backgammon. (The latter number is so high because backgammons are so rare.)

2. 1 point for each opposing piece left on the board. (An interesting variation is to award 10 points per piece.)

3. 1 point for each point that the opponent's pieces would still have to move to be borne off.

A match is won by the first player to reach 1,000 points.

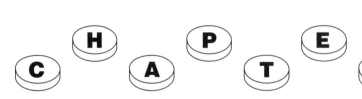

BEYOND CHECKERS

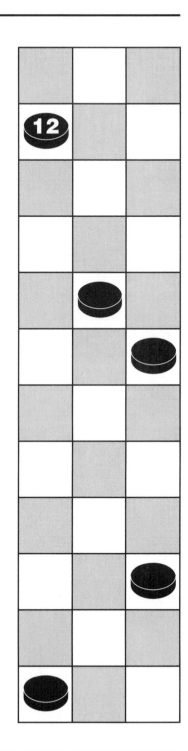

Most households have at least one old checkers set lying in a closet. Often, it gets little or no use because few people are aware of the rich variety of games that can be played with it.

As shown in Chapter 7, a wide variety of uncheckerlike games can be played with checkers equipment. But there are also many interesting games that do resemble checkers, including both regional variations and unorthodox games that put players on little-known ground. Many of these games offer richer tactics than the ordinary game.

ANGLO-AMERICAN CHECKERS

In Europe, the rules of checkers vary a great deal from country to country. The version most Americans know is also the one played in England. Men move one square diagonally forward; they capture only in a forward direction, by jumping over an adjacent piece and landing on the square immediately beyond. On reaching the last rank, they promote to kings that move and capture as men do, but in either a forward or backward direction. Captures are compulsory, but a player need not choose the move that results in the greatest possible number of captures, as long as the piece that is moved does not end its move on a square from which a further capture can be made.

Unfortunately, this game is one of the least interesting varieties of checkers. It's not so much that Anglo-American Checkers isn't a good game—it is, despite its "drawishness" (that is, its tendency to end in a tie). It's just that the other major forms of the game are better.

Here, then, are some little-known ways to make your checkers set into a treasure chest of games.

INTERNATIONAL CHECKERS

One of the more complex forms of checkers is International Checkers, also known as Polish Checkers or Continental Checkers. Invented in France in 1723, the game is played on a 10x10 board with 20 checkers on each side (see Diagram 12.1). It is very popular in France, Belgium, the Netherlands, Switzerland, Russia, and several other countries.

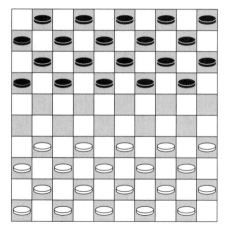

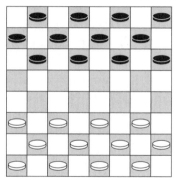

Diagram 12.1

International Checkers is played on a 10x10 board with 20 checkers per side. But in many countries, an 8x8 version of the game is popular. The opening setups for both versions are shown.

The rules of International Checkers can also be applied to an 8x8 checker set with 12 pieces on each side. This "Little International Checkers" is also known as German or German-Polish Checkers, since it is popular in many parts of Germany and Poland. There is also an extra-large version of the game, Canadian Checkers, played on a 12x12 board with 30 pieces on each side.

Here are the basic rules of the 8x8 form of International Checkers. Apart from the opening setup, the same rules apply to the 10x10 and 12x12 games.

1. The setup is the same as in Anglo-American Checkers (the smaller board in Diagram 12.1). White moves first.

2. The object is to capture or blockade all opposing pieces.

3. Men (unpromoted pieces) may only move one square at a time, diagonally forward, when not making a capture.

4. As in Anglo-American Checkers, a man may capture a diagonally adjacent opposing man by jumping over it and landing on the square beyond (which must be vacant). But a man may capture *diagonally backward as well as diagonally forward*. A man may make multiple jumps, capturing more than one piece in a turn, in any combination of forward and backward directions (see Diagram 12.2).

5. A man *ending* its move on the last rank becomes a king. If a man jumping to the last rank can make another capture that takes him off the back rank, he must make that capture and does not become a king that turn.

Note: More accurate than "king" is the term "queen," since promoted men are called *dames* ("ladies") in French, and the game itself is called *les dames*. (And in France, the "men" are known as *pions*, or pawns. The French terms "pion" and

Diagram 12.2

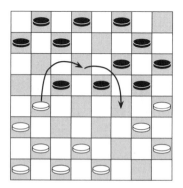

Men may only move forward, but they can jump in any direction. Here, White can—and must—make the double jump shown.

Diagram 12.3

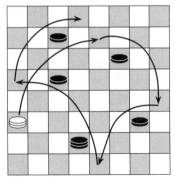

White's king can make a quintuple jump, ending the game in a single turn.

"dame" are also used in chess to mean "pawn" and "queen," and "dame" is also the queen in a deck of cards.) But in English-speaking countries, "king" is the term generally used and better understood, and so it will be used in this book.

6. Kings move like bishops in chess: any distance along an open diagonal.

7. A king may capture an opposing piece lying on the same diagonal by jumping over it—and the king may travel over any number of empty squares on either side of the jump. A king may not, however, jump over two adjacent enemy pieces, nor over one of its own pieces.

8. Kings may make multiple jumps, changing directions and lengths of jumps in any manner (see Diagram 12.3). When a king makes a multiple jump, all jumped pieces are left on the board until the end of the turn and only then are removed. During a multiple jump, a king may not jump over the same piece twice.

9. Capturing, for both men and kings, is always compulsory. If a player can make more than one jump, he must always choose the one that will capture the most pieces, without regard to whether the pieces are men or kings. If two or more jumps will result in the same maximum number of captures, the player may choose any one of them.

RUSSIAN CHECKERS

Also known as Shaski, Russian Checkers is played the same way as 8x8 International Checkers, with two differences:

1. A man reaching the last rank always becomes a king, even in the middle of series of jumps. Such a man can continue his turn by jumping as a king.

2. A player must make a capture when able to, but may choose any capture—not necessarily the one that takes the most pieces.

Note: This does *not* mean that a player may complete only part of a capture. Whatever capturing move is chosen, the moving piece may not stop on a square from which it can make another jump.

POOL CHECKERS

This game is played the same way as Russian Checkers, except that:

1. A man moving onto and off the last rank during a series of jumps does not promote that turn. (In other words, the International Checkers rule applies.)

2. The usual convention is that Black moves first.

SPANISH CHECKERS

Sources often conflict about which set of checkers rules go with which game—one reason being that players themselves use the terms in an inconsistent way.

Pool Checkers is sometimes referred to as Spanish Pool Checkers, or just Spanish Checkers. But another kind of Spanish Checkers is played with a set of rules that have the following differences from Pool Checkers:

1. The board setup is a mirror image; that is, players have empty squares on their lower left instead of their lower right (see Diagram 12.4). White usually moves first.

2. Men (nonkings) can only move and capture forward, as in Anglo-American Checkers. Kings move and capture as in Pool Checkers

3. As in International Checkers, a player must choose the move that captures the most pieces possible, without regard to whether the captured pieces are men or kings.

ITALIAN CHECKERS

In this game, men and kings move and capture as they do in Anglo-American Checkers. There are some interesting differences, however.

1. The board setup is the same as in Spanish Checkers.

2. A man may not capture a king.

Diagram 12.4

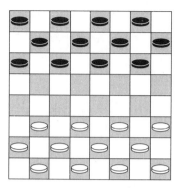

In Spanish Checkers and Italian Checkers, the board is set up as shown, which is a mirror image of the opening position in Anglo-American or Russian Checkers.

Diagram 12.5

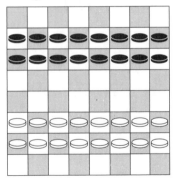

Turkish Checkers requires 16 pieces per player.

Diagram 12.6

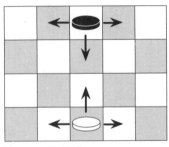

Unpromoted pieces may move one square forward or sideways.

Diagram 12.7

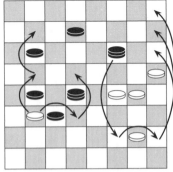

White has a choice of two double jumps. If it is Black's turn, he must take the triple jump shown but has a choice of three final landing squares.

3. A player who has more than one capture available must choose according to the following priorities:

    a. He must take the most pieces possible.

    b. In case of tie, he must make a capture with a king rather than with a man.

    c. If more than one capture by a king is possible, he must make the capture that takes the most kings.

4. A game is considered a double loss if a player loses without ever having promoted a man to a king.

TURKISH CHECKERS

This form of checkers can be found not only in Turkey but in many former parts of the Turkish Empire, ranging from Egypt to the Balkans. It can be thought of as an orthogonal version of Russian Checkers.

1. The board is set up as shown in Diagram 12.5 (although traditionally, board squares are all one color). White moves first.

2. Men may move one square straight ahead or sideways—not backward or diagonally (see Diagram 12.6).

3. Men capture by jumping in the same directions they move, that is, forward or sideways (see Diagram 12.7).

4. Kings move any number of spaces along an empty rank or file, like rooks in chess.

5. Kings capture horizontally or vertically at any distance, in a manner analogous to king captures along diagonals in International Checkers (see Diagram 12.7).

6. A man reaching the last rank by means of a jump immediately becomes a king and continues to jump as a king *as part of the same turn* if able.

7. Captured pieces are removed just as they are jumped and so do not block further jumps as they do in International Checkers.

8. A player must capture when able and must always choose the move that captures the most pieces, without regard to whether the pieces are men or kings.

9. A player wins by capturing or blockading all opposing pieces

or by reaching a position in which he has a king against an opponent's man. (If not for the latter rule, a man could avoid capture by the king indefinitely.)

OTHER REGIONAL VARIANTS

Here are several other notable European 8x8 checker variations:

Armenian Checkers. This game is set up and played the same way as Turkish Checkers, except that men may also move diagonally forward, giving them five possible directions of movement (as shown in Diagram 12.8) and kings may move in any horizontal or diagonal direction, like a queen in chess. Capturing moves for both men and kings, however, are restricted to the horizontal and vertical jumps of Turkish Checkers.

Central-South German Checkers. This version is played like Spanish Checkers, except that a king must stop on the first square beyond the last jumped piece when making a series of captures and also when making a single capture.

Gothic Checkers. Reportedly the oldest form of checkers to have been played in Germany, this game has the starting position shown in Diagram 12.9. Men move one square diagonally forward, but may capture in any of the five nonretreating directions (vertically, diagonally forward, or sideways). Kings move one square diagonally in any direction, but may capture along any horizontal, vertical, or diagonal line (eight possible directions). Kings may not move or capture at a distance, however; they may only capture adjacent pieces and must land immediately beyond them.

Scandinavian Checkers. This variant is played like Spanish Checkers, except that men may capture at a distance the same way kings do, but only in a forward direction.

Frisian Checkers. Played on and near the Frisian Islands (in the North Sea, off the coasts of the Netherlands, Germany, and Denmark), this 10x10 version can be adapted to an 8x8 board. Rules are as in International Checkers, except that both men and kings may capture orthogonally as well as diagonally—provided that pieces always remain on squares of the same color, as in Diagram 12.10. Noncapturing moves, however, are confined to diagonals as usual.

Diagram 12.8

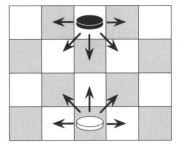

In Armenian Checkers, men have five possible directions of movement, but captures may not be made diagonally.

Diagram 12.9

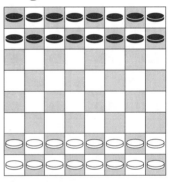

Gothic Checkers may be the oldest German variant.

Diagram 12.10

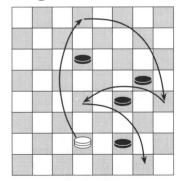

In Frisian Checkers, a king can jump diagonally or orthogonally provided it stays on squares of a single color.

OFFBEAT VARIANTS

Giveaway Checkers

In this well-known variant, the winner is the first player to lose all his pieces, or who cannot make a move because his only piece or pieces are blockaded. For variety, the game can be played with any of the movement and capture rules of any of the preceding variants. As usual, capture is compulsory; whether a player must take the most captures possible depends on the rules of the particular variant.

Lasca

This challenging and original game was invented by former world chess champion Emanuel Lasker. It is played on a 7x7 board, which can be improvised by covering up one edge row and column of an 8x8 checkerboard.

Each player starts with 11 pieces, known as "soldiers." All the pieces are marked on one side, such as by affixing a small sticker in the center. In the initial setup shown in Diagram 12.11, the marked sides are face down.

Pieces move and capture as in Anglo-American Checkers with this difference: When a piece is jumped, instead of being removed from the board, it is placed directly under the jumping piece (see Diagram 12.12). It continues to stay with the jumping piece wherever that piece moves and can no longer be moved by its owner. This column of pieces is controlled by the owner of the piece on top (see Diagram 12.13). If the column makes further captures, it places each jumped piece at the bottom of the column.

When a piece or column jumps over a column, only the topmost piece of the column is captured. Sometimes this will free a friendly piece that was trapped underneath.

As usual, promotion occurs on the last rank. It is indicated by

Diagram 12.11

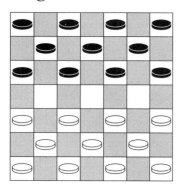

Lasca, played on a 7x7 board with 11 pieces per side, was invented by former world chess champion Emanuel Lasker.

Diagram 12.12

Each time a piece is jumped, it is placed under the piece that jumped it. If a stack is jumped, only the top piece of the stack is placed under the jumping piece.

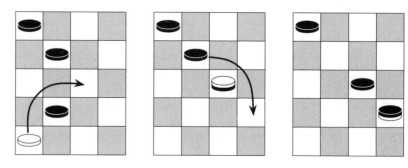

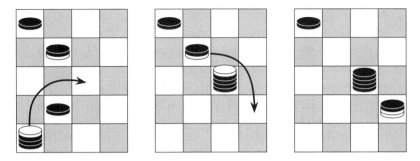

Diagram 12.13

A stack moves and jumps as a unit and is controlled by whichever player owns the man on top of it. In this sequence, White captures a Black piece, but Black immediately liberates his stack of four men.

flipping over the promoted piece, known as an "officer," so that its marked side is up. Officers move and jump forward or backward, just like kings in Anglo-American Checkers. Like soldiers, officers collect the pieces they jump by placing them in a column underneath as they go. Captures are compulsory, but a player is free to choose among more than one capturing move.

There is one other rule, which is designed to prevent an officer from jumping back and forth over a column of enemy pieces: A piece may not jump over the same column twice consecutively in a turn.

The object is to immobilize the opponent's army by trapping it entirely under one's own pieces or by completely blockading any pieces left uncovered.

Emergo

I find Lasca more interesting than most forms of checkers. But as if to prove that nearly any game can be made better, Christiaan Freeling took the key idea in Lasca, did away with the checkers-like rules of initial position, forward movement, and promotion, and came up with one of the best little strategy games ever devised. And I use the term "little" here to refer to the small board size—just 37 hexes—not the game's complexity. Indeed, in terms of complexity, Emergo's tactics rival those of any game I can think of.

Two sets of 12 checkers each are used. Officially, the colors are red and yellow. The board, shown in Diagram 12.14, is initially empty, and Yellow moves first. (See Appendix B for tips on how to improvise such a grid.) After that, moves alternate.

A "move" consists of one of three kinds of actions: *entering, moving,* or *capturing.* A capturing move must be made whenever possible; when no capture is available, entering takes precedence over moving.

Throughout these rules, the term "piece" refers to either an entire stack of pieces or a single piece. A single piece can be thought of as a "stack" consisting of one checker. As in Lasca, the color of the topmost piece in a stack determines ownership of that stack.

Entering. "Entering" means placing one checker in a vacant cell, subject to two restrictions:

1. A player may not enter a checker on the central cell of the board.

2. A player may not, in entering, put himself under attack (that is, on a cell where the checker can be captured) *unless he is already under attack*. (What this means will become clear under "Capturing," below.)

Diagram 12.14

Emergo begins with the checkers off the board. With minor exceptions, a player may place a piece on any vacant cell during the entering phase.

Diagram 12.15

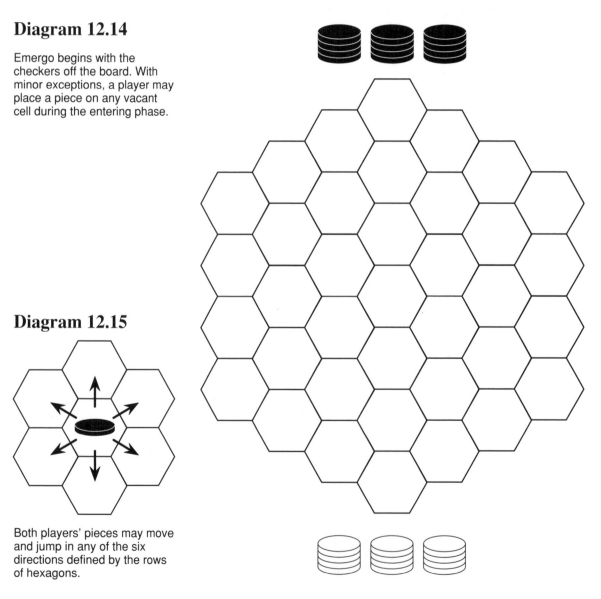

Both players' pieces may move and jump in any of the six directions defined by the rows of hexagons.

A player with checkers left to enter must use his turn to enter one, unless he can make a capture, in which case he must make the capture instead of an entering move.

If one player has entered his last checker, the other player *must* enter his last checker or checkers (there may be several, since one player may have been busy capturing while the other was entering) as a single piece (that is, all stacked together), subject to the same restrictions. This last piece is called a "shadowpiece," and it plays an important role in entering strategy.

Moving. "Moving" means moving a piece of one's own color to an adjacent cell, as in Diagram 12.15.

Capturing. "Capturing" is accomplished as follows: A piece captures by jumping over an adjacent, enemy-controlled piece and landing on the cell beyond, which must be vacant for the jump to be made. The effect of a capture is that, as the jump is made, the topmost checker of the jumped piece (or the only checker, if there is but one) is placed under the jumping piece, as in Lasca.

After a jump, further possible captures must also be made in the same turn, in any direction except the direction immediately opposite that of the preceding jump. Thus, jumping back and forth over the same piece by making a 180° turn is not allowed. But it is permissible to jump the same piece more than once in a turn, as long as at least one other jump intervenes. This can happen, for example, when jumping a set of three pieces arranged in a triangle, as in Diagram 12.16.

When a player is faced with a choice of captures, he must take the one that leads to the maximum number of captures. If there is more than one way to make the maximum number of captures, the player may choose any of these ways.

A player wins when he controls (i.e., has one of his checkers on top of) every piece on the board. Draws are possible if neither player has sufficient force to win; or, very rarely, by repetition of a sequence of moves; or by "stalemate," which is defined as a situation in which a player whose turn it is has at least one piece left but cannot make a legal move.

Strategy and tactics are subtle, as players must walk a fine balance. Being first to get all your checkers on the board is good because it lets you take the initiative with your first nonentering move; but a tall shadowpiece may give your opponent more than enough compensation. Losing a lot of checkers to a single enemy piece can be good, because when you recapture the opposing checker on top of your checkers, you will be left with a "strong" stack of several of your checkers, which the opponent will have to jump many times to whittle down (see Diagram 12.17).

Diagram 12.16

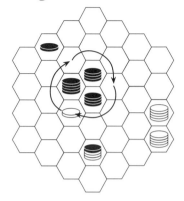

A stack may be jumped more than once in the same turn, provided at least one other jump intervenes. Here the White piece will capture ten Black pieces by making a clockwise series of jumps. The White piece may not jump counterclockwise, since that would capture only nine pieces.

Diagram 12.17

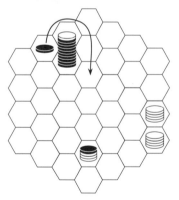

But Black comes out better from this exchange, as he is immediately able to liberate his powerful stack.

Diagram 12.18

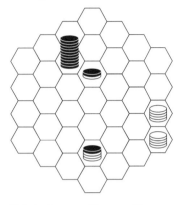

This is the resulting position (see previous diagram). Inevitably, the average height of the towers grows as the game progresses.

Diagram 12.19

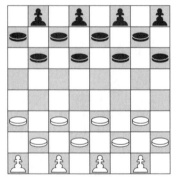

The Good-for-Nothings can be played on either an 8x8 board (above) or a 10x10 board (see Diagram 12.20). The same setup can also be used for the game Dragon.

Note that the game inevitably progresses toward a state in which the number of pieces is smaller, but the average height of each piece is greater (see Diagram 12.18).

The Good-for-Nothings

This whimsical but challenging game is a creation of V. R. Parton's. It can be played on an 8x8 or 10x10 board, set up as in Diagram 12.19 or as in the first position in Diagram 12.20.

On the back rows, checkers are replaced by chess pawns. If you don't have a chess set handy, simply mark each back-row checker in some way, as by attaching a label or sticker.

The basic rules of movement and capture are the same as in Pool Checkers (see above). The back-row pieces are known as "good-for-nothings" (or "ne'er-do-wells"—the game seems only to have been described in French, under the name *Les Vauriens*, which has the same meaning). These pieces move and capture the same way as ordinary men.

What makes this game different from regular Pool Checkers is its object. There are three different ways to win:

1. By *capturing* all the opponent's *regular* checkers;

2. By *losing* all your own *good-for-nothings*;

3. By forcing the opponent to *promote a good-for-nothing* (such as by forcing him to jump onto the last row with a good-for-nothing).

Conversely, a player loses if he captures all the opponent's good-for-nothings, if he only has good-for-nothings left himself, or if one of his own good-for-nothings reaches the last rank.

This is a very quick game of subtle strategies and sharp tactics. The 10x10 version is even more challenging.

Dragon

This is another of Parton's games, and it is extremely fast-moving. Although he devised it for a 10x10 board, it can be adapted to an 8x8 board. In either case, the setup is the same as for The Good-for-Nothings, and rules are as follows.

1. Each player starts with two kinds of pieces: men (checkers) and dragons (chess pawns, or checkers marked in some way in order to make them distinct).

2. Men move and capture as in Anglo-American Checkers.

3. Dragons may move and capture like a king in International Checkers, *but only in a forward direction.*

4. Both men and dragons promote to kings. Kings move like kings in International Checkers, with one exception: Unless there is no alternative, a king making a capture may not end its move (i.e., after making its final jump of the turn) on the edge of the board. The purpose of this rule is to make it harder for the weaker side to salvage a draw in multiple-king endings.

5. Captures are compulsory, but a player need not choose the move that makes the most captures possible.

6. A player who captures or blockades all opposing pieces wins a complete or "Dragon" victory. A player who cannot achieve this can still win a demi-victory if he has more pieces left than his opponent when the game ends.

7. Draws occur only when both players have the same number of pieces left (one, two, or three), and it is clear that neither side can capture any more pieces.

Diagram 12.20

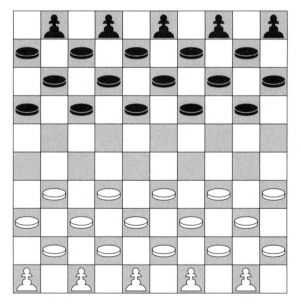

Both Grand Kinger and the 10x10 version of The Good-for-Nothings use the above setup.

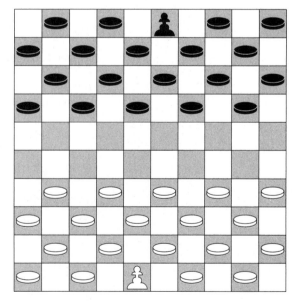

This single-pawn setup is used for both Simple Kinger and Royal Checkers.

Kinger

This is yet another of Parton's games designed for a 10x10 board. Depending on the form of the game being played, each player has at least one special piece known as a "kinger," plus an army consisting of a mix of men and kings. (The inventor also suggested a variation in which dragons, as in the game Dragon above, are substituted for the kings.) The opening setup for Simple Kinger is the second position shown in Diagram 12.20. Grand Kinger's opening setup is the same as the setup for The Good-for-Nothings.

Rules are as follows:

1. Men move and capture as in Anglo-American Checkers.

2. Kings move and capture as in International Checkers.

3. A kinger moves and captures like a king in International Checkers, except that, unless there is no alternative, a kinger making a capture may not end its move (i.e., after making its final jump of the turn) on the edge of the board. This makes the kingers much more vulnerable to being captured.

4. A kinger cannot be captured by a man or king—only by an opposing kinger. This makes the kingers less vulnerable to being captured.

5. Captures are compulsory. A player need not choose the move that captures the most pieces.

6. The object of the game is to eliminate the opposing kinger (Simple Kinger) or all the opposing kingers (Grand Kinger).

Royal Checkers

Frenchman Joseph Boyer, who wrote one book on checkers variants and two books on chess variants in the 1950s, came up with a pair of interesting games by applying the object of chess to a checkers setting. His versions use a 10x10 board and follow International Checkers rules of movement and capture, but can easily be adapted for other checkers variations and board sizes.

One of each player's checkers is designated as a "royal" piece and is specially marked (or replaced by a chess pawn). The royal piece is placed on the first rank, exactly as in the setup for Simple Kinger (Diagram 12.20).

The object of the game is to capture the opponent's royal piece. In one version of the game, known as *le pion royale* ("royal pawn"), the special checker moves, captures, and promotes like any other man. In the other version, *la dame royale* ("royal queen"), the royal piece moves like a king in International Checkers throughout the game.

Hexdame

In most forms of checkers, pieces have at most four possible directions of movement. When a checkers-type game is played on a hexagonal grid, however, the number of lines increases to six, as in Emergo. This greatly complicates the tactics without sacrificing the charming simplicity of checkers rules.

The best translation of International Checkers rules to a hexagonal board is this game of Christiaan Freeling's. One advantage of Hexdame over International Checkers is that draws are less common, since in Hexdame, three kings can always defeat one king in an endgame. In International Checkers, a player usually needs four kings to hunt down a lone enemy king.

The opening setup is shown in Diagram 12.21. Rules are as follows:

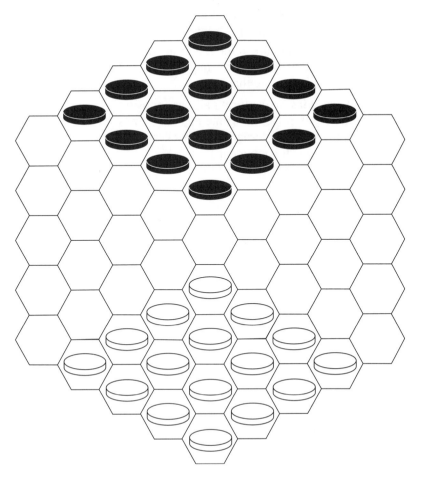

Diagram 12.21

Hexdame, a translation of International Checkers to a hexagonal grid, is more complex than the 10x10 orthogonal game.

1. White moves first. A man moves one space at a time in any of the three forward directions (the nonretreating directions shown in Diagram 12.15).

2. A man captures an adjacent piece by jumping over it in in any of the six directions defined by the rows of hexagons, as in Emergo. Multiple jumps can be made in any direction or combination of directions. Captures are compulsory, and a player must always choose the move that captures the most pieces possible, without regard to whether the captured pieces are men or kings. If there are two or more jumps that capture the most pieces, the player is free to choose any of them.

3. When a man *ends* its move on any of the nine spaces on the opponent's edge of the board, it promotes to a king. A man that jumps onto and off the last row during a capturing sequence does not promote.

4. A king may move any number of spaces along an open row, and may jump a piece that lies any distance away, in a manner analogous to king jumps in International Checkers.

5. Captured pieces are removed from the board only after the entire move has been performed. A man or king may not jump the same piece more than once.

6. A player wins by capturing all the opposing pieces. If a player has no legal move, the game ends in a draw. (This is different from the rule in International Checkers, where a player wins if he blockades the opponent.)

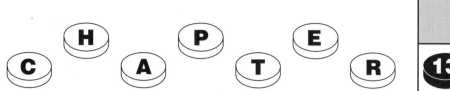

CHAPTER

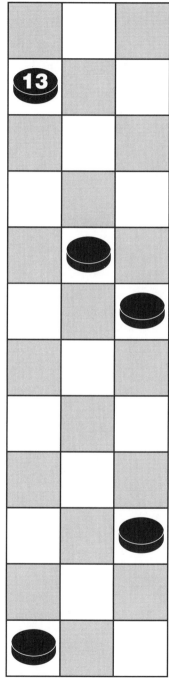

BEYOND CHESS

In Chapters 7 and 12, we saw how such simple equipment as a checkers set could be used to create many unusual and very different games. If we substitute chess pieces for the checkers, the possibilities for new play grow astronomically.

One of my hobbies over the years has been to invent chess variants, such as the game Extinction Chess found in Chapter 1. Relatively few people share my enthusiasm for such games, but I find them endlessly fascinating. More than that, I find that the process of coming up with new chess variants often gives me ideas for new kinds of play in nonchess games.

The form of chess most people know—which is sometimes referred to as Western chess, orthodox chess, or orthochess—is itself just one of many that have been played throughout history. Even today, it's just one of the three major chess games played in the world, the others being xiang qi (Chinese chess) and shogi, the latter being by far the most complex form of chess that has ever achieved widespread popularity.

Rules for hundreds of chess variants have been published, and no doubt thousands of others have been created and played but never published. They come in all sizes and shapes. Some use extra pieces, some use larger boards, and some are played in three or more dimensions.

In this book, I'll confine myself—with a few exceptions—to some of the better games you can play using an ordinary chess set, or an ordinary chess set supplemented by some checkers or a second board. Many of these games can be enjoyed by chess novices and experts alike.

As you try these games, or just as you read through their rules, think about how some of the ideas in these games could be tried in other games you have. The principle of Refusal Chess, for example, can be applied to almost any abstract two-player strategy game, from checkers to Reversi, with intriguing results.

PRE-CHESS

One of the simplest ways to vary chess is by altering the opening setup. This makes memorization of openings almost worthless, while expanding the number of different kinds of positions that players will have to learn to cope with. Many variants have been tried that use this idea, but only Pre-Chess has reached a status that has seen grandmaster-level games published in the U.S. Chess Federation's official publication, *Chess Life*.

Rules are as in orthodox chess, except:

1. Pawns are placed on the board as usual, but each player's first rank is initially empty.

2. Beginning with White, each player in turn chooses any one of his eight pieces and places it on any square of his first rank. The only restriction is that each player must place his bishops on squares of different colors. (In practice, this is an unnecessary restriction, since players will want their bishops on opposite colors anyway. In a Pre-Chess tournament in which I played in New York City, players decided at the outset to drop this rule and also to completely disallow castling.)

3. After all the pieces are placed, play begins as usual, with White moving first.

4. Castling is not permitted unless a king and rook are placed on their normal squares (e1 or e8 for the king, a corner square for the rook).

In playing this game, my preference is to place knights near the center, at least one bishop in a corner, and the king (and often the queen) on b1 or g1. Rooks are effective almost anywhere, though not in a corner in which they would be hemmed in by the king.

SHATRANJ

Played for about 1,000 years in Islamic countries, Shatranj produced a considerable literature of opening analyses, games, and problems. It evolved into Medieval Chess, which in turn changed into the modern game of orthodox chess.

But does evolution always go in the right direction? Shatranj has less powerful pieces than modern chess, but it also has great subtlety, depth, and charm, as well as elements of positional play that are absent in modern chess. It will remind chess players of the most challenging endgame they have ever encountered, and I recommend it highly.

The game can be played using a standard chess set, with the pieces set up in the usual way at the start. In some manuscripts, the starting positions of the king and general are reversed, but the standard chess setup was the most common.

Pieces have different names (given below in parentheses) and, in some cases, different moves:

1. Rooks (chariots) move as in orthodox chess.

2. Knights (horses) move as in orthodox chess.

3. Bishops (elephants) jump two squares diagonally; e.g., an elephant at e3 can move to c1, c5, g1, or g5 and would not be blocked by pieces of either color at d2, d4, f2, or f4.

4. Kings (shahs) move as in orthodox chess, except that there is no castling move.

5. Queens (generals) move one square diagonally; e.g., a general at e2 can move to d1, d3, f1, or f3.

6. Pawns (foot soldiers) move and capture as in orthodox chess, except that they may not move two squares on their first move.

The object is to checkmate *or stalemate* the opposing king, *or to capture all opposing pawns and pieces other than the king*. The latter way of winning is known as the "bare king" rule. However, if one king is "bared" but can bare the other king on the very next turn, the game is a draw. Perpetual check and repetition of moves are also draws.

Abu-Bakr Muhammad Ben Yahya as-Suli (c. 880-946), who played at the court of the caliph in Baghdad in the early 900s, wrote the first book on the game and is considered to have been one of its greatest players. Another good player was Aladdin—actually Ala'addin at-Tabrrizi—who, besides being famous in children's stories, was a real-life Persian lawyer and historian of the late fourteenth century.

In as-Suli's book, the following piece values are given, and no doubt are based on decades, if not centuries, of experience: rook 5, knight $3\frac{1}{3}$, general $1\frac{2}{3}$, elephant $1\frac{1}{4}$, center pawn $1\frac{1}{4}$, knight's or elephant's pawn between $\frac{5}{6}$ and 1, and rook's pawn $\frac{5}{8}$. But the kingside elephant was regarded as more valuable than the general-side elephant, because it could support and be supported by the general.

An opening commonly regarded as one of the strongest, known as the "mujannah" or "flank opening," involved advancing the c and f pawns two squares each, moving the knights up behind them, advancing the b, d, e, and g pawns one square each, and moving both rooks to the knights' original squares. A typical follow-up would be to advance the kingside rook's pawn, then the knight's pawn next to it, and to transfer the general-side rook via b2 to either f2 or g2. (See Diagram 13.1.)

One thing players need to be aware of is that certain squares are strong for one player but weak for the other. For example, White (actually Red, traditionally) can eventually attack f5 with both his general and his king-side elephant, while Black can do the same to f4. For a great deal of detailed information on shatranj, including many opening analyses and composed problems to solve, see H. J. R. Murray's *A History of Chess* (Oxford University Press, 1913; since reprinted by Benjamin Press).

Diagram 13.1

In this shatranj position, White has played the mujannah opening and is ready to transfer his rook from b2 to either f2 or g2.

New Rules for Classic Games

DICE CHESS

Strong tournament chess players, and even grandmasters, have been known to play this variation for light relaxation between serious games. Rules are as in orthodox chess, except that movement is determined by dice rolls. Each player in turn throws a die, and the result of the throw determines which piece(s) the player may move. A typical assignment of numbers is as follows:

If Player Throws	Player May Move
1 or 2	king or pawn
3	queen
4	bishop
5	knight
6	rook

A player throws again if the piece thrown is missing or cannot legally move. Some players allow a player to pass his turn without moving if he has a legal move but does not wish to make it. Castling is permitted on either a king or rook move. The object is to capture, not simply to checkmate, the opposing king.

Two variations that are sometimes seen are as follows:

1. Either player throws a die. White moves on even throws, Black on odd. (Warning: With inexpensive dice not weighted as accurately as casino dice are, a 6 may be significantly more likely to come up than a 1.)

2. Each player in turn throws a die and then makes as many moves as the number thrown. No piece or pawn, however, may be moved more than once.

For a more elaborate game that uses a similar principle, see Modern Chaturanga in Chapter 7.

CHECKLESS CHESS

This old variant is also known as Prohibition Chess. *The Oxford Companion to Chess*, by David Hooper and Kenneth Whyld (Oxford University Press, 1984), gives a sample game of it won by German master Max Lange in 1856.

The rules are as in orthodox chess, with one big difference: A player may not check the opponent's king unless the resulting position is checkmate. It takes a moment to fully appreciate the effect of this rule. If you move your king out into the center of the board, the opponent's pieces must avoid squares that would check the king and can become cramped. Thus, the king in this game becomes a formidable offensive weapon.

Screen Chess

Also known as Battle Chess, this is a game for players who like to skip openings and move right into middle-game combat. Rules are as in orthodox chess, except for the opening setup. Before the game, a screen is placed across the board between the fourth and fifth ranks. Each player then sets up all his pieces and pawns anywhere he likes on his half of the board, without the opponent's seeing. Alternatively, players may simultaneously write down their setups on separate pieces of paper, then set up the position on the board.

The following placement restrictions apply:

1. Only one pawn may be placed per file, and pawns may not be placed on the first rank.

2. A player's two bishops must be placed on squares of different colors.

Giveaway Chess

Several variations of this game have been published. Here's a fairly standard one, followed by NOST:

1. Capturing is compulsory. A player with a choice of captures may choose whichever one he wishes.

2. No check or checkmate rules apply; kings are captured like any other piece, and the game continues.

3. When a pawn reaches the last rank, the player owning it must promote it, but has the choice of promoting it to a queen, rook, bishop, knight, or king.

4. The winner is the first player to lose all his pieces (including pawns and king) or to have no legal move (such as when he is left with only blockaded pawns).

DOUBLE MOVE CHESS

Rules of this game, invented by Fred Galvin, are as in orthodox chess, except as follows:

1. White makes one move on his first turn; thereafter, each player makes two moves per turn. The moves may be made with the same piece or with different pieces.

2. The object of the game is to *capture* the opposing king. The concepts of check and checkmate are abolished. Thus, a player is free to move into check on his first move and then parry the check with his second move; and a player may check the opponent's king on his first move and then capture the king on his second move.

3. Each move must change the position. A player may not move a piece off and back onto the same square in one turn, except to make a capture.

Although the king is a very strong piece in this game—being able, for example, to capture a protected piece on an adjacent square and then move away—the power of the other pieces more than makes up for it. This extremely dynamic, complex game tends to end quickly, making it ideal for postal play.

REFUSAL CHESS

This game and the one that follows are closely related. Both were invented by Fred Galvin.

Rules are as in orthodox chess, except: On each turn, a player can refuse to accept the opponent's move. If this happens, the opponent must retract the move and play a different move, which the player must accept. Different promotions of the same pawn count as two different moves; and if there is just one legal move, it must be accepted.

The game is challenging not only tactically but psychologically. Compare it to Compromise Chess, below.

COMPROMISE CHESS

Rules are as in orthodox chess, except: Each turn a player chooses two moves, and the opponent tells him which of the two to make. Different promotions of the same pawn count as two different moves; and if there is just one legal move, it must be played. Compare this game to Refusal Chess, above, by the same inventor.

POCKET KNIGHT CHESS

This game was popular in Europe around the turn of the century, but is still seen occasionally. Rules are as in orthodox chess, except that each player starts with his queen's knight off the board (b1 and b8 are left vacant). During the game, a player can use a turn to drop this knight onto any empty square, even to deliver checkmate.

KINGLET

This game of V. R. Parton's was part of my inspiration for Extinction Chess (see Chapter 1). Rules are as in orthodox chess, except that the object is to capture all eight opposing pawns rather than the opposing king. All rules regarding check and checkmate are suspended: Kings may be moved into check freely and may be captured like any other piece. Pawns promote as usual, but if a player is forced to promote his last pawn, he loses.

SPUTNIK CHESS

This game was invented by J. Berthoumeau and R. Loiseau. Rules are as in orthodox chess, except:

1. On crossing the center line of the board (between the fourth and fifth ranks), a rook, bishop, or knight becomes a "sputnik"

piece. On crossing back to its own side of the board, it becomes a normal piece again.

2. Each turn, a player *must* move one normal piece; in addition, he *may* move *any or all* of his sputnik pieces (once each), and in any order.

GRASSHOPPER CHESS

In the early twentieth century, "fairy chess" problems using unorthodox pieces and/or rules were at the peak of their popularity. In 1912, probably the greatest fairy chess problem composer, T. R. Dawson, invented a piece known as a grasshopper, traditionally represented in diagrams by an upside-down queen symbol. The piece proved very popular to problemists and was used in thousands of problems by Dawson and others.

A grasshopper moves in the same directions as a chess queen, and, like a queen, may move any distance; but it cannot move at all without jumping over another piece. The piece jumped over may belong to either side.

After jumping over a piece, a grasshopper must stop on the very next square in the line of movement. If that square is occupied by an enemy piece, that piece is captured. If the square is occupied by a friendly piece, the move cannot be made; a grasshopper may not jump over more than one piece in a turn.

The piece jumped over by a grasshopper is never captured,

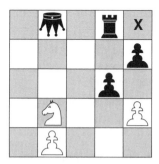

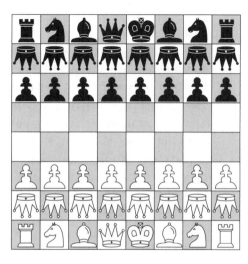

Diagram 13.2

Left: The grasshopper, conventionally depicted with an upside-down queen symbol, may jump to X, or it may land on and capture either White pawn.

Right: This is the opening setup for Grasshopper Chess. Checkers may be used for the grasshoppers.

even if it belongs to the opponent (see Diagram 13.2.)

Grasshoppers were relegated to the esoteric world of fairy chess problems until Joseph Boyer came up with this game to put them to a new use. Rules are as in orthodox chess, but each player has an entire row of grasshoppers, as well as the usual pieces and pawns. Grasshoppers start on the second rank and pawns on the third (see Diagram 13.2).

Because of the starting position, pawns may not move two squares on their initial moves. A pawn reaching the eighth rank may be promoted to a grasshopper, as well as to any of the usual choices.

One of the interesting problems players face is deciding what is a fair exchange for a grasshopper. Early in the game, when the board is crowded with pieces to jump over, a grasshopper may be worth almost as much as a knight, but its value decreases steadily as exchanges are made, until it is worth less than a pawn.

AVALANCHE CHESS

This game of prolific chess variant inventor Ralph Betza has proved very popular in postal competition.

Rules are as in orthodox chess, except: Each turn, after making a normal chess move, a player must (if he can) advance one enemy pawn one square forward. That's the only special rule, but the following clarifications are helpful for certain situations:

1. The first, or normal, part of a move must be legal according to the normal laws of chess. A player may not, for example, move into check in anticipation of getting out of it by pushing a pawn.

2. The second, or "avalanche," part of a move must be a simple one-square pawn advance and may not be a capture or a two-step pawn advance by a pawn on the second rank.

3. The second part of the move must be made if possible. If a player must make a push that puts his own king in check, he loses the game.

4. A pawn that is avalanched to the eighth rank promotes immediately to whatever type of piece its *owner* (not the player who pushed it) wishes. If the promoted pawn gives check, it wins the game.

5. No *en passant* capture can involve a pawn that was just avalanched.

The avalanche rule lets players expose the opposing king rather easily, but what makes the game even more exciting is the speed with which passed pawns march toward promotion.

EMPEROR KING CHESS

In medieval Japan, a 25x25-square chess game with 354 pieces was invented. Known as Tai Shogi (where "tai" means "great," as in "taipan" or "typhoon"), it is quite playable and interesting. More than that, it contains many unusual pieces, such as the hook mover described in 3D Hook-Move Chess in Chapter 7, and ideas that can be applied experimentally to other games.

> *Note:* Rules and sets for Tai Shogi and several other fascinating historical shogi variants are available from G.F. Hodges, P.O. Box 77, Bromley, Kent, United Kingdom. Rules for one of these games, Chu Shogi, appear at the end of this chapter.

The object of the game, in part, is to capture the opposing emperor. You also have to get the king—literally a "jade" or "jeweled" general—as well as the crown prince, if the opponent has obtained one by promoting his drunk elephant (no, I'm not kidding).

The emperor has a uniquely powerful move: It can jump directly to *any square on the board, occupied or not!* If it lands on an opposing piece, that piece is captured. There is only one restriction on an emperor's move: It may not land on the opposing emperor *unless the opposing emperor is undefended.* An emperor is defended if at least one of its side's pieces attacks the square that it is on.

At first you might wonder how you are supposed to capture a piece that can move anywhere—until you realize that you can do it with your own emperor, once you knock out the other emperor's defenders. Indeed, the powers of the two emperors tend to offset each other to a large degree, so that, for example, an emperor cannot simply pick off an opposing piece that seems undefended, because no matter where that piece is, it's actually defended by the other emperor.

Rather than play 1,000 moves to reach a Tai Shogi endgame, I decided to try to get the feel of how emperor endgames work by giving the emperor's power to kings in ordinary chess, while leaving all other rules the same as in orthodox chess. It so happened that the resulting game was fun to play, with some interesting differences from orthodox chess.

For example, in an opening such as 1.e4 e5 2.Bf4 Bf5? 3.Bf7+, the Black emperor-king cannot now take the bishop, since the bishop is defended by its own emperor and no other black piece guards f7. (It's not checkmate, though; the Black king can fly to a defended square such as b6.) In the middle game, a player cannot sacrifice very much to achieve a breakthrough near the enemy emperor, since the emperor can simply fly to the other wing. Endgame tactics tend to focus on attacking the emperor's last defender.

KNIGHT RELAY CHESS

Invented around 1970 by Mannis Charosh, this variant differs from orthodox chess in the following ways:

1. Knights can neither make captures nor be captured.

2. Any of a player's pawns and pieces—other than kings and knights—that are a knight's move away from one of the player's own knights may move or capture like a knight, in addition to retaining their own powers. Once no longer a knight's move away from a knight, a piece loses this power, but the power may be regained and lost any number of times.

3. Pawns may not use a knight's power to jump to the first or eighth rank. A pawn may jump back to the second rank, whereupon it regains its two-step move option.

4. Pawns may be promoted to any of the usual choices, including knights, which function in the same special way as the other knights in the game.

Diagram 13.3

The game of Rettah is set up as shown, with kings representing the powerful yet vulnerable rettahs.

RETTAH

This game of V. R. Parton's is based on the premise that kings, because of their singular importance, also ought to be the most powerful pieces in the game. The opening setup is shown in Diagram 13.3.

Kings are known as "rettahs" (from "hatter" spelled backward, referring to the Mad Hatter in *Alice in Wonderland*), and have the combined powers of queen and knight (i.e., a rettah can move as either).

When a player's rettah is checked, the player *must* capture the checking piece. This is true even if the only way to do so is to capture with the rettah, and even if such a recapture by the rettah exposes it to immediate capture. The winner is the player who captures the opposing rettah.

ALICE CHESS

Lewis Carroll's novel *Through the Looking Glass* inspired V. R. Parton to invent this imaginative chess variant. In a sense, it is a three-dimensional game, since the board can be thought of as measuring 8x8x2 (in squares). To play, a chessboard is set up as usual, and an empty second board is placed next to it.

Rules are as in orthodox chess, except as follows:

1. On each board, pieces move as in orthodox chess.

2. On completing a move on either board, a piece is immediately transferred to the corresponding square on the other board. For example, if White opens 1.e3 on the fully set up board, the moved pawn ends up on the e3 square of the board that began empty (see Diagram 13.4).

3. In transferring to the other board, a piece may not land on a square occupied by another piece, regardless of which player owns the piece. This means that a piece may not move to a square if the corresponding square on the other board is occupied.

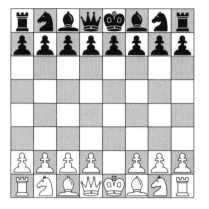 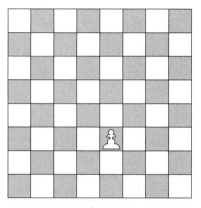

Diagram 13.4

In the Alice Chess position shown, White has played 1.e3 on the board on the left, after which the moved pawn is immediately transferred to e3 on the other board.

4. A move must be legal on the board on which it is played, before the moving piece transfers to the other board. Thus, a king may not move into a position that would temporarily be check, even though the king's transfer to the other board would put him on a safe square.

Note: When in check on one board, a player *may* legally move a piece on the other board if the piece will then transfer to a square where it interposes against the check. Even though the king might seem to have been left in check temporarily, the move played was legal on the board on which it was played, and the final position is also legal, since the check was blocked.

To be faithful to the mirror world that inspired the game, players may wish to rotate the empty chessboard 90° at the start, so that a black square is in the lower right, and then transfer pieces to the mirror image of the square they were on. But most players find it hard enough to figure things out with both boards oriented the same way. Another variation is for the two players to set up their armies on different boards at the start.

DOUBLE KING CHESS

Diagram 13.5

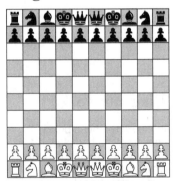

In Double King Chess, a player wins by capturing *either* opposing king. Each side, therefore, has two main targets to attack and two to defend.

This is another game by V. R. Parton, who also called it Chess Tweedle or Twin Orthodox Chess. The setup is as shown in Diagram 13.5.

All pieces move as in orthodox chess, except that:

1. Pawns have the option of advancing up to three squares on their initial move. *En passant* captures may be made against either a two- or three-square advance. (As an alternative, players may find it interesting to use the pawn rules of Wildebeest Chess, given later in this chapter.)

2. A kings may only castle with the nearer rook. A player may make two castling moves during a game, one with each king.

The object of the game is to capture *either* opposing king. Thus, it is possible to win not only by checkmating one king but by forking or skewering both kings with a piece that cannot immediately be captured.

With two queens to attack with, two targets to aim at, and two kings to defend, players will find this game extremely challenging both strategically and tactically.

DOUBLE BUGHOUSE

Also known as Double Speed Chess or Double Drop-In, this shogi-like, four-player chess variation can sometimes be seen between rounds at chess tournaments.

Two boards are set up side by side, and a chess clock is placed by each board, as shown in Diagram 13.6. Both clocks are set at five minutes per player.

Two games of Speed Chess are played simultaneously. Players form two teams, with each team consisting of the White player on one board and the Black player on the other board.

When a player captures a piece, he hands it to his partner. His partner may use a turn to drop this piece onto any empty square on his board, after which it becomes part of his army. The only restriction is that a pawn may not be dropped onto the eighth rank.

A player does not have to drop a newly acquired piece right away. It's perfectly legal to accumulate as many pieces as you can off the board, waiting for an opportunity to drop one effectively. However, only one piece may be dropped per turn.

A team wins if either of the opposing players runs out of time or is checkmated. Sometimes you will find yourself just a move

Diagram 13.6

PLAYER C **PLAYER D**

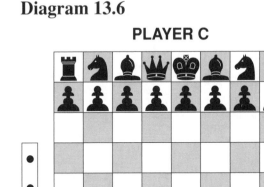 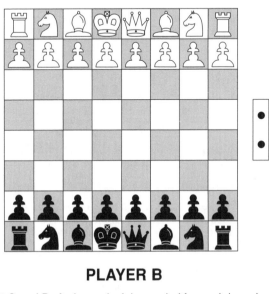

PLAYER A **PLAYER B**

In this Double Bughouse setup, A and B are teamed against C and D. A chess clock is needed for each board.

away from being checkmated; in this case, your only hope is not to move. You have let your clock run, hoping that your partner will win on the other board before your time is up. This tactic won't work, though, if your partner's opponent has more time left on his clock than you do on your clock, since he can also stop moving and wait for your flag to fall.

During the game, players are allowed to make such comments as, "Partner, I can really use a knight—trade a queen for one if you have to," or "Don't trade queens right now whatever you do, or I'll be mated." It gets noisy, frantic, and very exciting.

MISSILE CHESS

This and the next two variants in this chapter are my own inventions. The setup for Missile Chess is as in orthodox chess, except that a checker—representing a missile—is placed under every piece and pawn (see Diagram 13.7).

Diagram 13.7

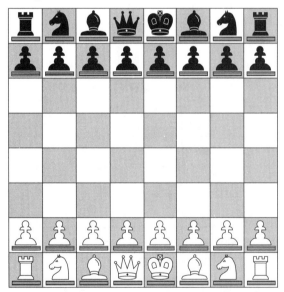
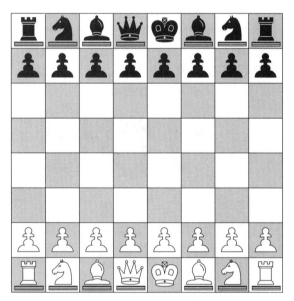

Left: Missile Chess is set up with a checker under each piece. Each checker represents a missile that can only be fired once. When a piece fires its missile, the checker under it is removed.

Right: Teleportation Chess has as similar setup, but kings and pawns do not have special powers and so are not placed on checkers. A piece on top of a checker may jump to any empty square on the board, but then loses its checker.

Both Missile Chess and Teleportation Chess are forms of Exotic Chess. In some kinds of Exotic Chess, there may be more than one checker per piece, and checkers of different colors may be used to represent different powers.

Play is as in orthodox chess, except that a player has the option of using his turn to "fire a missile" instead of making a move. A piece can only fire its missile at a square to which the piece could legally move.

The effect of firing a missile is to capture an opposing piece on the target square, without the attacking piece itself having to move there. After a piece fires its missile, the checker underneath is removed to show that it cannot fire again.

Pieces may also move and capture normally, whether or not they have used their missiles. Unused missiles (checkers) accompany their pieces wherever they move.

Many variations are possible. Players may choose to:

1. Give different numbers of missiles to different types of pieces.

2. Give each player an equal number of missiles, and let him allocate them among his pieces as he sees fit.

3. Give pieces both missiles (white checkers) and "shields" (black checkers) in varying numbers. A shield defends a piece against one missile attack, but is wiped out in the process.

TELEPORTATION CHESS

Rules are as in orthodox chess, except that once during the game, each piece other than the kings and pawns may make a special "teleportation" move to any vacant square on the board. Since the destination square must be vacant, no captures may be made by teleporting—but checkmate can be delivered that way.

As in Missile Chess, checkers are used to represent the special power and are removed when the power is used. At the start, a checker is placed under every piece other than the kings and pawns (see Diagram 13.7).

In the sample game record that follows, an asterisk at the beginning of a move denotes the use of the teleportation power and signifies that the checker should be removed from under the piece.

Sample Game

White: Paddy Smith
Black: R. Wayne Schmittberger

1.e4 e6 2.d4 d5 3.Bf4 Bb4+ 4.c3 *Bb4-c4 5.Bc7 Qc7 6.Bc4 dc (If 6. … Qc4?? 7. *Ng1-d6+) **7.*Ng1-b5 *Ng8-d3+ 8.Qd3** (If 8. Kf1 Qf4! leaves Black with the better of the ensuing complications.) ***Qc1+ 9.Qd1 *Nc2+ 10.Ke2 *Bd3+ 11.Kf3 *Ra8-f4+ 12.Kg3 Qd1 13.*Ra1-b8+ Ke7 14.Rb7+ Kf6 15.e5+ Kg6 16.*Nb1-e7+?**

(White should have kept this power in reserve and played Rd1 immediately.) **Kh6 17.Rd1 *Rh8-g4+ 18.Kh3 Rh4+ 19.Kg3 Be2** (threatening mate, as well as to take the rook) **20.Nf5+ ef 21.*Rd1-d6+** (Now, with the last exotic power having been used, it becomes a chess game with normal rules but an abnormal position.) **Kg5 22.h3 Re4 23.Rf7 f4+ 24.Kh2 g6 25.e6 Ne3 26.fe fe 27.e7 Bd3 28.Rd8 e2 29.e8=Q Re8 30.Re8 Re4 31.Resigns.**

EXOTIC CHESS

The use of checkers to represent special powers with limited numbers of uses suggests a new class of chess variants, infinite in number. Taken as a whole, I call these games Exotic Chess.

The general rules are as follows. The setup is as in orthodox chess, except that checkers are placed under the pieces and pawns. Each checker represents a special power, usable once in the game; thus, once the power is used, the checker is removed.

Depending on the variation chosen, different pieces can have different powers (which may be represented by checkers of different colors), similar powers (as in Teleportation Chess and Missile Chess, both of which may be considered forms of Exotic Chess), or different numbers of powers (represented by placing more than one checker under a piece).

Here's an example of a game in which each kind of piece is given a specific power, making it possible to represent all the different powers with checkers of a single color. The powers, each of which can only be used once in this game, are as follows:

1. Queens may, without moving, destroy one enemy piece that is either one or two squares away. The destroyed piece may lie either a queen- or knight-move away from the queen, and the power is not affected by any other pieces that may intervene.

2. Rooks may make a king-move in any direction, but only onto an adjacent square that is occupied by either a friendly or enemy piece. In so doing, the rook pushes the displaced piece one square farther in the same direction, and may set off a chain reaction of pushes if additional pieces lie in the same line. A piece pushed off the board is captured; a player may capture one of his own pieces in this manner.

3. Bishops may switch places with any friendly pawn anywhere on the board. If a switch brings a pawn to the eighth rank, it is immediately promoted.

4. Knights may, without moving, rearrange in any desired fashion all pieces that are on the eight squares adjacent to them. These pieces are put back on these same eight squares; both friendly and enemy pieces may be rearranged; and pieces may be moved to squares previously vacant or occupied, or may be left where they were, without restriction. Pieces may not be "rearranged" off the edge of the board.

5. Kings may switch places with any friendly piece anywhere on the board.

6. Pawns may, without capturing, move one square diagonally forward.

A checker, of course, accompanies its piecs wherever the piece moves until the piece uses its exotic power. Pawns promote as usual on the eighth rank. If a pawn has not yet used its exotic power, then promotion also has the effect of transforming the pawn's power into the power assigned to the kind of piece to which the pawn is promoted. If the pawn has already used its exotic power, it will not have any exotic power after promotion.

In the game record, the long form of algebraic notation is used for the sake of clarity. An asterisk at the beginning of a move denotes the use of an exotic power. If multiple moves are made by one player in a single turn, the moves are separated by "/". A capture made by a queen without moving is shown by "x!"

Sample Game

White: Paddy Smith
Black: R. Wayne Schmittberger

1.d2-d4 d7-d5 2.Qd1-d3 c7-c6 3.Bc1-f4 *e7-d6 (Early in the game, the knight's exotic power may be better than the bishop's; hence Black blocks the possible capture.) **4.Ng1-f3 Bc8-g4 5.*Nf3/e2-e4/Bf4-e3/g2-f4/Bg4-g3 *Ra8-b7/Nf3-g2/e4-f3/ d5-e4/c6-d5/b7-c6 6.f3xe4 d5xe4 7.Qd3xe4+ Rb7-e7 8.*f4-e5 *Bg3-h7/h7-g3 9.Qe4-f4 g3xf2+ 10.Be3xf2 *Ng8/Rh8-f7/f7-h8/ Bh7-g7/Bf8-h7/g7-f8 11.Qf4-d2 Qd8-b6 12.*a2-b3 d6xe5 13.*d4-c5 Qb6-c7 14.Qd2-g5 Rf7xf2 15.Ke1xf2 Bh7xc2 16.*Qg5x!e7 Bg7-h6 17.Qg5-h5+?** (Better was 17.Qg5xg8, with an unclear position.) **f8-f7 18.Qh5-g4?! *Bc2-f7/ f7-c2 19.Bf1-c4** (Using the exotic power of the knight at b1 won't stop the pawn on c2 from promoting, since it can advance diagonally as well as straight ahead.) **c2-c1=Q 20.Rh1xc1 Bh6xc1 21.Bc4xf7+ Ke8xf7 22.*Kf2-a1/Ra1-f2+ Ng8-f6 23.h2-h4?!** (This was played with the idea of *h4-g5, but perhaps some queenside defensive move might have held the position.) **Qc7-a5+ 24.*Nb1/Ka1-c1/Bc1-a2/b2-c2** (If the bishop is put on a1, Black plays Qa5-a2+, threatening to use its exotic power, and then chases the king across the board.) **Ba2xb1 25.Rf2xf6+ Kf7xf6 26.Qg4-g5+ *Kf6-a7/a7=f6 27.Qg5-d2** (Black was threatening Qa5-c3, which is mates on account of the queen's unused exotic power.) **Qa5-a3+ 28.Kc1-d1 Qa3-b2+ 29.Resigns.** (On 29. Kd1-e1 *Qb2x!d2.)

Diagram 13.8

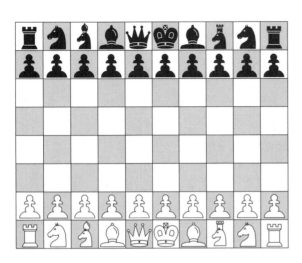

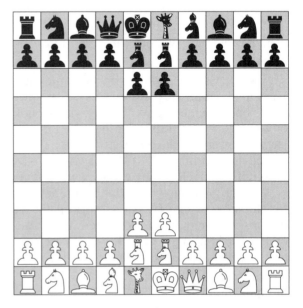

Capablanca's Chess, also known as Lasker-Capablanca Chess because it was played extensively by both José Capablanca and Edward Lasker, is set up as shown above. In addition to the usual pieces, each player has an archbishop (also called a cardinal), which is placed on the queenside, and a chancellor (or minister) on the kingside. The archbishop can move as knight or bishop, and the marshall as knight or rook.

When castling, a king moves three squares left or right instead of the usual two. A pawn may promote to an archbishop, a chancellor, or any of the usual alternatives. Otherwise, the rules are the same as those of orthodox chess.

Similar games were tried as early as 1617, when Pietro Carrera, a priest, chess player and author from Militello, Sicily, suggested adding a centaur (combined knight and bishop) between the queenside rook and knight, and a champion (combined knight and rook) between the kingside rook and knight.

Rules to Turkish Great Chess (above) were published around 1797 in a central Indian book, *Sardarnama*, by Shir Muhammad-Khan. With the exceptions of shogi and its variants, I rate this as the best of all the "historical" chess variants described in H. J. R. Murray's *A History of Chess*.

The giraffe moves as either a knight or queen; the war machines (the pieces starting on the second rank) move as either a knight or rook; and the vizir (starting between the giraffe and the bishop) combines the powers of knight and bishop.

The other pieces move as in orthodox chess, except that pawns have no special two-move option when they start out, and there is no castling move. Pawns may only promote to queens.

Note: The name used for the queen actually translates as "general," and the bishop is actually an "elephant." The pieces that move as rooks, knights, and pawns translate as "chariots," "horses," and "foot soldiers," respectively, as expected.

GRAND CHESS

In orthodox chess, the queen combines the powers of the rook and bishop. But why not combine the powers of knight and bishop, or the powers of rook and knight?

In fact, many game inventors have tried doing just that. One version of an eighteenth-century game, known as Turkish Great Chess, used two such "rook-knights," one "bishop-knight," and even one "queen-knight," for each player, in addition to a normal set of chess pieces. Each player also had two extra pawns, since the game was played on a 10x10 board (see Diagram 13.8).

Early in this century, world chess champion José Raoul Capablanca and U.S. master Edward Lasker experimented with a similar game, as others had done before. They tried it on both 10x8 and 10x10 boards but came to prefer the former (see Diagram 13.8). Both players liked the game better than orthodox chess; games were faster, more exciting, and less likely to end in a draw.

Christiaan Freeling's Grand Chess uses the same set of pieces as Capablanca's Chess, but Freeling's opening setup (shown in

Diagram 13.9

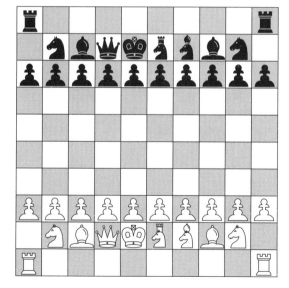

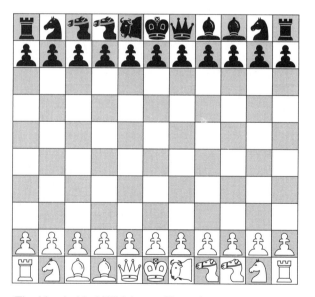

Grand Chess, set up as shown above, adds two new pieces. The marshall (f2 and f9) combines the powers of rook and knight, while the cardinal (g2 and g9) has the powers of bishop and knight. These form a natural complement to the queen, which is a combined rook and bishop.

The idea behind Wildebeest Chess (set up as shown above) is to equalize the number of "riders"—pieces moving along straight lines—and the number of "leapers"—pieces that jump directly to their destination square. Camels start on h1, i1, c10, and d10, and wildebeests on g1 and e10.

Diagram 13.9), I believe, yields the better game. The "rook-knights" and "bishop-knights," shown in the diagram by combining the usual piece symbols, are known as "marshalls" and "cardinals," respectively. A marshall may move as either a rook or knight, and a cardinal as either a bishop or a knight, just as a queen moves as either a rook or a bishop. A marshall is as powerful as a queen; a cardinal is worth about a pawn less.

Rules are as in orthodox chess, except as follows:

1. There is no castling move. (Nor is there a need for one, since rooks are already connected and easy to develop at the start of the game.)

2. As in chess, pawns may move one or two squares forward on their initial move only, and one square forward thereafter. *En passant* capture may occur as in chess.

3. A pawn may only promote to a piece that has been lost by its side.

4. A pawn may promote on the eighth, ninth, or tenth rank, at the option of the player owning it. A pawn moving to the tenth rank *must* promote; if no pieces have been lost by its side, it may not move to the tenth rank, although it still attacks (gives check to) an enemy king on that rank.

WILDEBEEST CHESS

This game is my attempt to balance the number of "riders"—pieces that move along open lines—with the number of "leapers"—pieces that jump directly to a square a certain distance away, regardless of what intervenes.

The opening setup is shown in Diagram 13.9. The extra pieces starting on c10, d10, h1, and i1 are camels, which move like elongated knights. A camel jumps from one corner to the other of a 2x4 rectangle (instead of a knight's 2x3 rectangle), regardless of what intervenes. Thus, in the starting position, White's camel on h1 may jump to g4 or i4, and could go to e2 or k2 if those squares were vacant.

The pieces starting on e10 and g1 are wildebeests, which combine the powers of knights and camels in the same way that queens combine the powers of rooks and bishops.

Other pieces move as in orthodox chess, with the following exceptions:

1. Castling is subject to the same restrictions as in chess: There

must be an open line between king and rook, neither may have moved, the king must not be in check, and the king may not pass over an attacked square. But, subject to these restrictions, a player has the freedom to castle by moving his king *any number of squares* (one, two, three, or four) toward either rook, then jumping his rook over the king to land on the square next to the king.

2. A pawn on the second rank may move one, two, or three squares. A pawn on the third rank may move one or two squares. A pawn on the fourth rank or beyond moves just one square per turn. Pawns capture exactly as in chess, except that *en passant* captures are available against both two-square and three-square advances. If a pawn bypasses a square on which it could have been captured by an enemy pawn, the enemy pawn may capture it *en passant*, provided it does so at once.

3. A pawn may promote only to a queen or wildebeest.

A player wins by checkmating *or stalemating* the opposing king. That's because I find the stalemate rule in chess to be illogical. I much prefer the rule of shatranj and xiang qi, where a stalemated player loses.

Camels, by the way, are not as valuable as knights. Both knights and camels can attack a maximum of eight squares, but there are fewer squares for which this is true of camels. Paradoxically, they are hindered by their greater range. Wildebeests are better than rooks, the difference being the greatest in the opening and middle game stages of play.

CHU SHOGI

The modern game of shogi (see page 69) dates back 400 or 500 years. But several other forms of shogi have also been played in Japan, some predating modern shogi by centuries.

Most of these games are more like Western chess than modern shogi, in that captured pieces remain off the board. But they are much larger than chess, using boards ranging up to 25x25 (Tai Shogi). There is even a recorded mention of a 36x36 game, but rules have never been found.

The most popular of these games was Chu Shogi. Also known as Middle Shogi, the game is mentioned in diaries as early as the twelfth century, and it still had a fair number of followers in Japan, particularly around Kyoto, until World War II. I am presenting its rules here, despite the game's complexity, for two reasons: It is my favorite chess variant, and its unusual pieces may give readers ideas for creating many other chess variants. For example, you might play chess with a regular set, but replace the powers of the rooks and bishops with those of Chu Shogi's whales and white horses.

Note: Players should be careful *not* to follow rules for Chu presented in H. J. R. Murray's *A History of Chess,* where Chu is referred to as "Intermediate Japanese Chess." These rules and others that used them as a source, such as the rules found in John Gollon's *Chess Variations: Ancient, Regional, and Modern* (Charles E. Tuttle Company, 1968), contain many major errors. The correct rules were carefully researched in Japan and brought to the West by George F. Hodges and John Fairbairn in the 1970s.

Chu Shogi sets are still available commercially in Japan, and they may also be obtained from G. F. Hodges (see page 195). Or,

Diagram 13.10

Chu Shogi uses a total of 92 pieces, set up as shown. The diagram uses abbreviations of the full piece names, which are given in the table beginning on page 210.

Black, who plays first, sits at the bottom, and White sits at the top. Black's pieces may promote upon reaching any of the ranks a through d, while White's promotion zone consists of ranks i through l.

A standard board measures approximately 16½"x18".

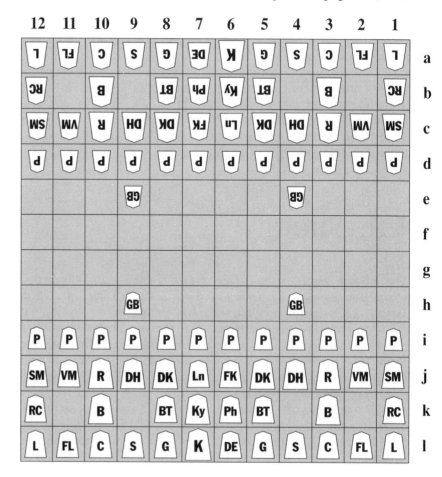

players may improvise their own pieces from cardboard or from standard shogi sets. In writing the promoted values, as explained below, on the backs of the pieces, it is a good idea to use a different color or type style in order to distinguish promoted and unpromoted pieces that have the same name.

Rules of Play

Chu is played on a 12x12 board. Each player has 12 pawns and 34 other pieces, set up as shown in Diagram 13.10. Although the diagram shows only the abbreviations of the names of the pieces, standard sets show the full names of the pieces, written in Japanese. The full English equivalents of the piece names are given below under "Powers of movement."

As in shogi, pieces are wedge-shaped (see Diagram 6.1) and are all the same color. Ownership is indicated by the direction the pieces face: They always point toward the opponent.

Despite the lack of a color difference, the first player is known as Black and the second player as White. Moves are recorded with an algebraic system in which ranks are lettered a through l from the top of the board (where White sits) down, and files are numbered from 1 through 12 from right to left (from Black's point of view). This is an extension of the recording system used for regular shogi.

Promotion

Just as in chess, players take turns moving one of their pieces per turn, trying to capture the opposing king. In this game, unlike chess, not only pawns but nearly all of the other pieces can achieve promotion. There's even a piece that promotes to an extra king, giving its owner a spare in case he gets checkmated!

Promotion occurs when a piece reaches any of the four farthest ranks on the board, which together are known as the "promotion zone." On moving a piece into the promotion zone, a player may promote the piece by turning it over to reveal its new, more powerful identity. Promotion is optional; but if a piece does not promote upon entering the zone, it may not promote on that player's next turn unless it makes a capture. Thereafter, the piece may promote on making any move wholly or partially within the zone, including a move that ends outside of the zone.

A special rule applies to pawns. If a player forgets to promote a pawn when it reaches the ninth rank (that is, when it enters the promotion zone), the pawn must remain unpromoted until it reaches the last rank, at which time it must promote.

Powers of Movement

The following table gives, for each piece, the English and Japanese names, the English abbreviation as used in Diagram 13.10, a description of how it moves, and its promoted value. Movement powers of the promoted pieces are given at the end of the table.

Most of the pieces' moves are described by reference to the moves of orthodox chess pieces. Thus, "like a bishop" means any number of squares along an open diagonal. "Forward" means in a direction toward the opponent, "backward" means in a direction toward the player who owns the piece, and "sideways" means orthogonally (not diagonally) left and right.

None of the pieces may jump over other pieces, with the exceptions of the lion, phoenix, kylin, and, in certain directions, the horned falcon and soaring eagle. Diagrams 13.11 through 13.15 illustrate all the moves.

Piece (Abbreviation)	Japanese Name	Movement Power	Promoted Value
bishop (B)	kakugyo	like a chess bishop	dragon horse
blind tiger (BT)	moko	like a king, but not orthogonally forward	flying stag
copper general (C)	dosho	like a king, but not sideways and not diagonally backward	side mover
dragon horse (DH)	ryume	like a bishop, or one square orthogonally	horned falcon
dragon king (DK)	ryuo	like a rook, or one square diagonally	soaring eagle
drunk elephant (DE)	suizo	like a king, but not orthogonally backward	crown prince
ferocious leopard (FL)	mohyo	like a king, but not sideways	bishop
free king (FK)	hon'o	like a queen	does not promote
go-between (GB)	chunin	one space orthogonally forward or backward	drunk elephant
gold general (G)	kinsho	like a king, but not diagonally backward	rook

Piece (Abbreviation)	Japanese Name	Movement Power	Promoted Value
king (K)	osho	like a chess king	does not promote
kylin (Ky)	kirin	one square diagonally or two squares orthogonally, jumping if necessary	lion
lance (L)	kyosha	like a rook, but not sideways or backward	white horse
lion (Ln)	shishi	see "The Lion" below	does not promote
pawn (P)	fuhyo	one space orthogonally forward*	gold general (or *tokin*)
phoenix (Ph)	hoo	one square orthogonally or two squares diagonally, jumping if necessary	free king
reverse chariot (RC)	hensha	like a rook, but not sideways	whale
rook (R)	hisha	like a chess rook	dragon king
side mover (SM)	ogyo	horizontally like a rook, or one square vertically forward or backward	free boar
silver general (S)	ginsho	like a king, but not orthogonally backward or sideways	vertical mover
vertical mover (VM)	shigyo	vertically forward or backward like a rook, or one square horizontally	flying ox

*Pawns, like other pieces, capture the same way they move, which is a major difference from Western chess.

Some pieces occur only as the result of promotion. Their moves are as follows:

Promoted Piece (Abbreviation)	Japanese Name	Movement Power
crown prince (CP)	taishi	like a king
flying stag (FS)	hiroku	like a king, or forward or backward like a rook
flying ox (FO)	higyu	like a bishop, or forward or backward like a rook
free boar (FB)	honcho	like a bishop, or sideways like a rook
horned falcon (HF)	kakuo	orthogonally forward like a lion; like a queen in all other directions
soaring eagle (SE)	hiju	diagonally forward like a lion; like a queen in all other directions
whale (W)	keigei	forward like a rook; backward like a queen
white horse (WH)	hakku	forward like a queen; backward like a rook

Diagram 13.11

The pieces shown in the diagram are all "step-movers." Each can only move one square at a time, and (except for the king) only in certain directions, as indicated by the dotted squares adjacent to each piece.

The emphasis is on forward movement for some pieces, as illustrated by the movement patterns of the opposing copper generals at the top left and top center of the board.

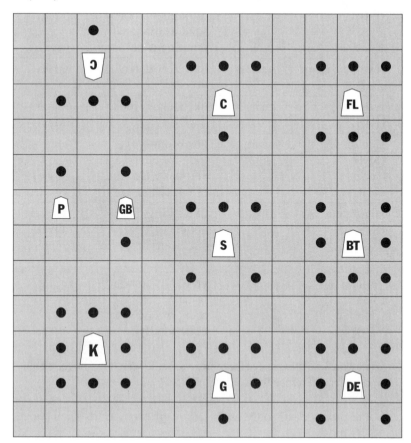

The Lion

The lion has a very unusual move, as well as some special rules associated with its own capture. If the eight squares around a lion are called A squares and the squares two away from a lion are called B squares, as shown in Diagram 13.12, then a lion may do any one of the following things in a single turn:

1. Move directly to any A or B square, jumping if necessary and capturing a piece if it lands on one.

2. Capture a piece on an A square and continue moving one more square in any direction from the point of capture, making a second capture if the second square landed on is also enemy-occupied.

3. Without moving, capture a piece on any A square (this is known as "igui," and counts as a turn).

4. Move to a vacant adjacent square and return to its starting square, effectively passing the turn. (As a practical matter, this power will never be used.)

Diagram 13.12

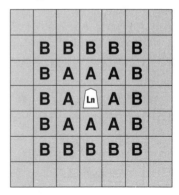

The lion's complex move makes it more valuable than two free kings early in the game.

Diagram 13.13

The "ranging" pieces shown in the diagram can travel any distance along an open path in any of the directions indicated with arrows, but they may only move a single square in the directions in which there are dots on adjacent squares.

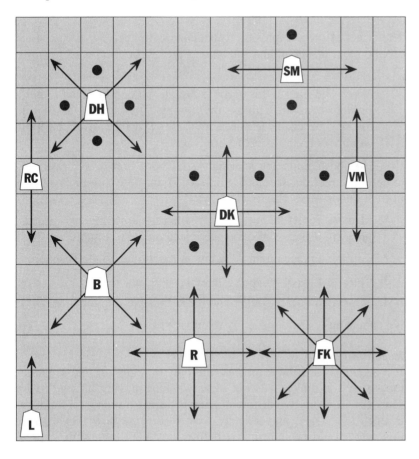

Diagram 13.14

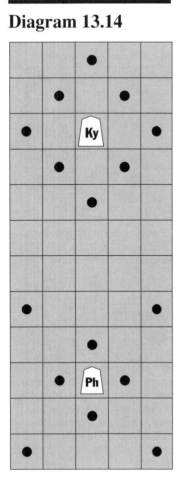

The kylin and phoenix move either one or two spaces in the directions shown. Unlike most other pieces in the game, they may jump over occupied squares to reach their destination.

Though initially weaker than most of the ranging pieces, these pieces promote more powerfully than any others, with the kylin becoming a lion and the phoenix becoming a free king.

The following special rules pertain to capturing lions:

1. A lion may capture an opposing lion on a B square only if the opposing lion is unprotected. A lion is considered "protected" for the purpose of this rule by a pinned piece, as well as by a piece that is blocked from the defense of the lion only by the attacking lion (e.g., a free king on 1a defends a lion on 1h from capture by a lion on 1f, assuming no other pieces intervene).

   Exception: A player may always use a lion to make a double capture of a piece on an A square and a lion on a B square, whether the lion is defended or not, provided that the first piece captured is neither a pawn nor a go-between.

2. If one player captures a lion with a nonlion piece, the opponent may not capture a lion, except with another lion, on his next turn.

3. A lion may always capture an opposing lion on an A square, either normally, by igui, or by capturing and moving on (to either an A or B square).

The effect of these capturing restrictions is to keep the lions, which are the most powerful and interesting pieces, on the board for most of the game.

   Note: The lion in this game is not an African lion, but rather a lionlike beast of Chinese mythology. The phoenix and kylin, too, are based on Chinese mythology; a picture of the kylin can be seen on labels of Kirin beer.

Horned falcons and soaring eagles have lion power restricted to certain directions (see Diagram 13.15). In these directions only, a horned falcon or soaring eagle may:

1. Move directly to an A or B square, capturing or not, and jumping if necessary over any piece on the A square;

2. Capture a piece on an A square and continue to the B square;

3. Capture a piece on an A square by igui; or

4. Move to a vacant square and back, thus passing the turn.

No capturing restrictions apply to either of these pieces.

Repetition of Moves

If a sequence of moves repeats, the player beginning the sequence must vary the move. It is not clear whether moving a piece to the same square from two different squares during a sequence counts as a repetition. Thus, players may wish to discuss how they believe this rule should be interpreted before they play (although in practice, repetitions do not seem to come up very often). I recommend a ko-type rule in which repetition of a position, rather than repetition of a sequence, is prohibited.

Winning

Generally, a player wins either by capturing the opponent's king or by capturing all opposing pieces except the king (this is the same as the bare king rule in Shatranj). It can be assumed that a bare king earns a draw if it can also bare the opposing king on the first turn after it was bared.

There is a complication, however. If a player has promoted his drunk elephant to a crown prince, the crown prince acts as a second king. If a player has both a crown prince and a king, the opponent must capture *both* of these pieces to win.

Relative Values of the Pieces

In Chu, the concept of relative piece values is less useful than it is in Western chess. The size of the board and the slow movement rate

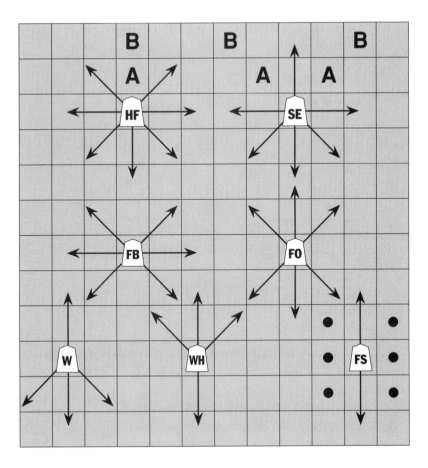

Diagram 13.15

The diagram shows movement powers of the pieces that are encountered only upon promotion. Omitted from the diagram is the crown prince, which has the same move as the king.

The horned falcon and soaring eagle have lion power limited to the directions in which nearby squares are marked "A" and "B." These squares function in the same way as the A and B squares in Diagram 13.12.

of many of the pieces means that a player with a small material advantage may not have time to exploit it before being mated in a sector of the board where the opponent has local superiority. Another complication is that values change when pieces promote.

Still, players should find the following table, which is based on my own experience in playing the game, a useful guide. Instead of assigning point values to pieces as in chess, I have ranked pieces in order of their average value during a game, from most valuable (the lion) to least valuable (pawn). Pieces grouped together have approximately the same value, with the pieces listed first within each group being slightly better.

In the table, names of pieces not in parentheses refer to unpromoted types only. That is, "rook" means a rook that still can promote to a dragon king, and not a promoted gold general, which is referred to as "+ gold." There is one exception: "lion" and "free king" also refer to a promoted kylin and phoenix, respectively.

1. lion
2. free king
   (soaring eagle)
   (horned falcon)
   dragon king
   dragon horse
3. (flying ox)
   (free boar)
4. (+ rook)
   rook
   phoenix*
5. (+ bishop)
   bishop
   vertical mover
   (+ gold)
6. kylin*
   side mover
7. (white horse)
   (whale)
   (crown prince)**

8. reverse chariot
   lance
9. (flying stag)
10. gold
    drunk elephant*
11. (+ ferocious leopard)
12. (+ silver)
    (+ copper)
13. ferocious leopard
    blind tiger
    silver
14. (+ go-between)
    (+ pawn)
    copper
15. go-between
    pawn

* Value varies greatly according to how close the piece is to promotion.
** But if the player has lost his king, the crown prince is priceless.

Players should also be aware of the following:

1. Early in the game, do not give up your lion unless you can get something more than two free-king-type pieces (pieces listed

under 2 above) in return. As the game progresses, the relative values of the lion and free king get close together, and by the time you reach an endgame a free king is stronger than a lion unless the lion is near the enemy king.

2. It is often good to exchange a strong piece (other than a lion) for two or three weaker pieces. But be careful, because the player with more rook-type pieces in the endgame will enjoy a kind of "air superiority" that makes it easier to advance and promote remaining pieces.

3. Sacrificing a piece in order to promote a second piece is generally to be avoided unless both pieces are weak or unless the piece to be promoted is a kylin, phoenix, side mover, or vertical mover.

The following is one of six sample games of Chu published in a Japanese book in 1778. Although Chu is known to have been played for centuries, and some books of problems are known, the six games in this book are the only known pre-twentieth century, complete game records of Chu. In the game record, as is standard in shogi, "+" at the end of a move indicates that a piece promotes, while "+" before the name of a piece indicates that it is a promoted piece. For example, "+S" means "promoted silver," and is used rather than VM to distinguish it from an unpromoted vertical mover. Igui capture is indicated by "x!." For further explanation of the notation, see Appendix A.

Black: Mori
White: Fukui

1.P-8h P-5e 2.Ln-6h P-8e 3.P-5h Ph-5d (If White brings out his lion with Ln-7e, White usually plays Ln-6g, maintaining his spatial advantage in the center. The general chess principle of not developing strong pieces too early does not apply to the lion.) **4.Ph-8i P-6e 5.P-7h Ky-6d 6.Ky-7i DK-6b** (In the opening, it's a good idea to move strong pieces back to make room for the advance of weak pieces.) **7.DK-7k P-10e 8.FK-6k P-3h DK8c-7b 9.P-3h DK8c-7b 10.DH-2h FK-8c 11.P-12h C-9b 12.C-9k C-9c 13.C-8j C-8d 14.Ln-6g FK-10a 15.C-4k R-8c 16.C-4j C-4b 17.C-5i Ky-7e 18.P-5g P-6f** (Freeing pawn sacrifices such as this are common, especially for the second player. If instead White tries to defend 5e with his copper, then after 18. ... C-5c 19.P-5f C-6d 20.Ky-6h, P-3h 21.Ky-5g DH-2e 22.C-6h R-5c 23.P-7g, Black threatens P-7f, which will force White to play Px5f. This is better for Black than variations in which White plays Px5e for two reasons: first, as in all forms of chess, the player who initiates an exchange loses a tempo; and second, if White plays Px5f, Black can play Lnx5f, putting the lion in position to make an igui capture of 4e or 6e.) **19.Lnx!6f Ln-6e 20.Ln-4g** (If 20.C-5h, the Black lion would come under attack again as soon as White plays P-8f and Ln-8e. On 4g, the lion can also be attacked quickly, by P-3e and DH-2e; but Black does not mind this possibility as much, since he expects to attack on the 1-5 files and to be able to use the dragon horse at 2e as a target.) **P-3e** (Ln-6f instead does not win a pawn on account of the reply Ky-6h.) **21.C-5h P-8f** (White could play DH-2e to prevent Black from winning a pawn with Ln-2f and Lnx!3e, but he reasonably prefers to build pressure on the 8 file, and on 8h in particular, while the enemy lion is some distance away.) **22.Ky-6h** (If 22.Ln-2f? P-8g gives White too rapid an attack. It is important for Black to be prepared to defend 8h with the copper. That way, if White exchanges, the copper gets to advance.) **C-8e 23.C-7i C-5c 24.SM-12i VM-10c 25.P-12g P-12e 26.GB-9g** (This invites 26. ... DHx9g 27.Ph-10g DH-9f Phx12e 28.SM-11c Phx10c+ 29.SMx10c, SM-12h with strong pressure on the 12 file that more than compensates for the slight material loss of phoenix for vertical mover [the go-between loss is insignificant]. But the move is dubious, as Black now spends four tempi with GB-9g-9h and Ph-10g-8i, without provoking any bad moves by White.) **Ln-7f 27.Ph-10g SM-12d 28.GB-9h DH-2e 29.Ln-5i P-8g 30.Ph-8i C-8f 31.SM-12h FL-11b** (If 31. ... Px8h 32.Cx8h C-8g 33.Ln-7i, or 33.GB-9g followed by 34.Ln-7i, defends. White correctly maintains the tension at 8g and 8h as long as possible, since that keeps pressure on Black to defend 8h from a slightly cramped position.) **32.S-9k S-9b 33.FL-11k S-9c 34.S-8j S-8d 35.DH-9k S-8e 36.P-1h P-1e 37.P-1g FL-2b 38.SM-1i FL-11c 39.GB-4g FL-10d 40.P-4h P-10f 41.FL-2k BT-9b** (This is a key position, with numerous strategic plans possible for each player. White's choice of BT-9b prepares to defend 5e with B-9a. Better, though, may have been BT-9c, advancing the tiger toward the front on the right flank. Other alternatives are S-4b, C-6d, and FL-10e.) **42.S-4k FL-10e 43.S-4j FL-11f** (The more patient GB-9f-9g may have been a better plan, since White must eventually break down the strong point around Black's go-between to achieve real progress on the wing. But it is hard to resist trying to exploit the exposed position of Black's side mover.) **44.SM-11h** (An odd-looking but effective move. White may have expected P-11h, which would have temporarily safeguarded Black's side mover but left it without much of a future.) **B-9a 45.S-4i Ln-9f 46.BT-4k FL-11g 47.SMx11g** (White may not have expected this, since it means a sacrifice of not only the side mover for the leopard but also the 12-file pawn. Black no doubt planned this before playing his 44th move. Black hopes to get compensation by acting in the center while the White lion is on the wing.) **Lnx11g 48.Px8g** (Black prepares to free his position with P-7g, which will also open

the bishop diagonal from 10k to 4e.) **Cx8g 49.Ky-7g S-8f** (If 49. …
Kyx7g? 50.Lnx7g wins the copper.) **50.Kyx7e Px7e 51.P-7g P-10g
52.P-11h Lnx12g-11f 53.P-11g Ln-9f 54.C-7h Cx7h** (This costs
White a valuable outpost and gives Black's lion too good a square.
Correct was P-7f, planning C-6d-7e. Playing C-6d first may look
more solid, but it allows the reply Ln-6g.) **55.Lnx7h P-7f 56.B-4l
Px7g 57.Ln-9j DH-9c 58.Ln-11h** (Here the lion prevents P-10h,
making further progress by White on the wing much more difficult.
Black, meanwhile, is ready to advance on the other wing.) **P-7h
59.B-3k** (A calm, positional move. Bringing up a weak piece to
defend 7i was possible, but would have left Black's forces disorga-
nized. Black accurately judges that he will be better off sacrificing
the phoenix, if necessary, and using the time he saves to press his
own wing attack.) **C-6d 60.DH-5k Ln-8g 61.P-2h S-7g 62.P-3g
R3c-7c 63.P-2g S-8h 64.P-2f** (If 64.Ph-6g? P-7i+ is much better for
White.) **DH-1d** (This becomes a target on the edge. Better is
DH-4c.) **65.S-3h Sx8i+ 66.FKx8i Ln-6f 67.FK-7j Lnx5g-5f
68.SM-4i** (This both defends against Lnx4gx4h and threatens P-1f.
Black must have felt confident after being able to make such an
efficient double-purpose move.) **Lnx4g-4f** (White is trying too hard
to justify his decision to put the dragon horse on 1d. Better was
68. … VM-3c, to start fixing up the "bad shape"—a go and shogi
term for inefficiently organized pieces—on his left wing. The capture of the go-between only helps Black open lines of attack more
quickly.) **69.B-6h Ln-6f** (69. … Lnx3g-3f? would allow 70.Bx7h
and would leave the lion vulnerable to further attack by S-2g or S-
3g. Black could also play 70.P-1f at once.) **70.P-4g Ph-7f** (White
must have played this out of impatience or desperation. He should
have tried 70.... VM-3c 71.P-1f Px1f 72.RCx1f DH-2c 73.P-2e
VM-3d, although 74.P-3f! yields Black a strong initiative.)
71.DH-3i Phx5h (Plunging into this combination is now inevitable
since, after 71. … Ln-8g, White is in trouble after either 72.P-1f or
72.B-5g.) **72.DHx6f Phx7j+ 73.BTx7j DHx6f** (White has had to
give back the earlier exchange of a weak piece for a phoenix, and in
return has managed to get two strong pieces—a free king and a
dragon horse—for his lion. Other things being equal, such a trade at
this stage of the game might have given roughly equal chances to
both sides; but here, Black still has his powerful next move available, which ensures a clear advantage. From here on Black demon-
strates flawless technique. He patiently eliminates White's
advanced pawn, brings up weak pieces to control the center, keeps
them carefully supported, and advances his lion as close as possible
to the enemy king.) **74.P-1f VM-3c 75.Px1e DH-2c 76.P-2e
VM-3d 77.P-3f Px2e 78.Px3e VM-2d 79.S-3g FL-3c 80.S-3f B-4c
81.BT-8i B-10b 82.BTx7h DH-5f 83.DKx5f Px5f 84.S-8i P-5g
85.R10j-7j DH-3b 86.VM-10j VM-2b 87.VM-9j C-6e 88.VM-8j**

C-5f 89.BT-5j P-5h 90.VM-8k FK-11a 91.SM-1i C-5g 92.B-7i R-5c 93.BT-4i C-4h 94.BT-6h Cx4i+ 95.SMx4i Bx2j+ 96.Rx2j R8c-7c 97.S-7h FK-6f 98.DK-3k G-4b 99.B-6j R-5d 100.VM-7k G-8b 101.B-4h FK-6c 102.FL-10j FL-2d 103.G-6k G-3c 104.Lnx10g-9g DH-4b 105.Ln-7i P-2f 106.BT-5g FL-2e 107.Lnx5h G-2d 108.R7j-3j VM-3b 109.S-6g VM-9c 110.P-4f GBx4f 111.Lnx4f DH-6d 112.Ln-4g DH-4b 113.S-5f FLx3f 114.Lnx3fx2f DH-3c 115.Ln-4f G-2c 116.S-5e R-8d 117.BT-4g DK-8c 118.Bx8d+ DKx8d 119.VMx7c+ FKx7c 120.DE-7k FK-7f 121.Ln-5g P-4e 122.B-6g FK-7e 123.S-6f FK-7c 124.BT-5f GB-9f 125.R-7j FK-6c 126.BTx4e P-9e 127.BT-5e P-11e 128.B-4e FK-5c 129.Ln-5f G-7c 130.P-6h VM-8c 131.G-8k BT-6c 132.Ln-4f FK-5b 133.FL-3j BT-5c 134.R-5j S-4b 135.FL-3i DK-8b 136.FL-4h DE-6b 137.G6k-7j DH-2b 138.DK-2k (Black's pieces are perfectly placed to begin the final assault.) VM-3c 139.P-1d+ SMx1d 140.Bx2c+ VMx2c 141.Rx2c+ DHx2c 142.DKx2c+ DK-2d 143.R-2j DKx2c 144.Rx2c+ BT-4d 145.DH-9j BT-3c 146.+Rx1b Lx1b 147.DHx1b+ B-3b 148.RCx1d+ SMx1d 149.Lx1d+ Bx1d 150.HFx1d FK-8e 151.HF-3d BT-4c 152.HF-9j BT-5b 153.G8k-8j P-12f 154.K-8k P-12g 155.S-6e GB-9g 156.S-6d+ P-12h 157.Ln-5d K-7a 158.P-10h P-12i+ 159.FL-10i DK-9c 160.BT-6e GBx9h 161.BT-7d+ Gx7d 162.+Sx7d K-6a (This loses immediately. After 162. ... K-8a, Black would still have had some work to do, but might have proceeded positionally with 163.+S-7i [threatening +S-8i] FK-9d 164.Ln-7e K-9a. Black could then play FL-11h and Lx12i to eliminate the threat of P-12j+, thereby freeing the horned falcon from the defense of the third rank.) 163.HF-3d S-5a (If 163. ... VM-7c 164.Lnx4b K-7a or 7b 165.Lnx5b-6a mate.) 164.HFx5b Resigns (If 164. ... Sx5b 165.Ln-4b mate; if 164. ... DEx5b 165.Ln-7b mate. Such mating possibilities are abundant when a lion is near the enemy king.)

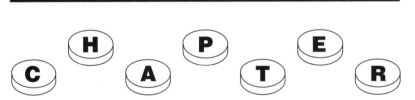

CHAPTER

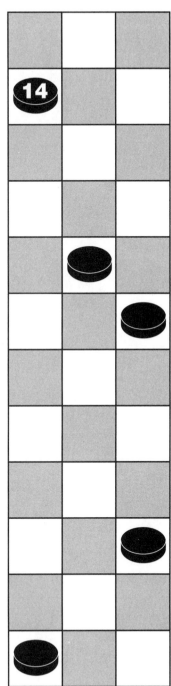

PLAYING BY MAIL

Playing games by mail is a passion for tens of thousands of people around the world. Chess is undoubtedly the game most widely played by mail. There are national and international postal chess tournaments, prizes, and rating systems. For information, contact the U.S. Chess Federation, 186 Route 9W, New Windsor, NY 12553, or Max Zavanelli, U.S. Secretary for the International Correspondence Chess Federation, 729 South Prospect, Park Ridge, IL 60068.

More informally, postal game clubs such as NOST (Knights of the Square Table) play numerous kinds of games by mail, including chess, chess variants, checkers, word games, and a variety of abstract games. For information about NOST, write Les Roselle, 111 Amber Street, Buffalo, NY 14220.

Postal games are ideal for many kinds of people, especially those who:

- Have trouble finding nearby "over-the-board" opponents.

- Are looking for a new way to pass the time on a daily train or bus ride.

- Feel rushed when they play over the board and like to be able to take their time considering their moves

Almost any game can be adapted for postal play. It's a good idea to play more than one game at once with the same opponent, since you'll have twice as much fun for the same amount of postage. It also gives each player a chance to go first in a game.

Postal games are often played on postcards, using as brief and clear a notation as possible to describe each move. Many games have standard notations, but it is not difficult to develop a notation system for games that do not.

There are also many games that are designed specifically for play by mail. Most of these are complex, multiplayer simulation games, coordinated by computers, in which players act as a country and use diplomatic and military assets to improve their positions as much as they can. Information on such games can be found in some of the numerous specialized magazines carried by stores that sell wargames and fantasy role-playing games. Often these magazines will also contain a classified section in which players advertise that they are looking for opponents to play games by mail.

SIMULATING DICE ROLLS

What if you want to play a game by mail that involves throwing dice? It's pretty hard to trust your opponent to report all his dice rolls accurately, and it's also hard to resist the temptation to "reroll" the dice a couple times for yourself at a critical juncture of, say, a backgammon game. Worst of all, perhaps, is the embarrassment that can come if you are perfectly honest and find that you legitimately have just thrown the only dice roll that could win the game for you. How do you think your opponent will like hearing that in your next letter?

One way around this is to have an impartial third party act as a referee and do the dice rolling at each turn for each player—but this method causes delay and extra postal costs. Yet dice rolls *can* be simulated in postal play, without the question of honesty ever arising and without involving a third party. The trick is to make use of random numbers that are being generated all the time in the world. Stock and commodity prices, city-specific weather information, and numerous professional sports statistics are uniformly published both in local newspapers and in widely distributed sources such as *USA Today*.

Players might agree, for example, to let the game's next dice roll be determined by the closing Dow Jones Industrials average on the first business day after the postmark of the letter in which the previous move was sent.

Suppose, for instance, that Player A sends a move postmarked January 7, and the closing Dow Jones average on January 8 is listed as "2,687.24, down 1.49." The closing average is used to determine one die roll, and the amount the average changed (whether it went up or down makes no difference) is used to determine the other die roll. This is accomplished as follows:

1. Drop the decimal from each number. Thus, 2,687.24 becomes 268,724 and 1.49 becomes 149.

2. Divide each number by 6 and determine the remainder. In this case, 268,724/6 = 44,787 with a remainder of 2, and 149/6 = 24 with a remainder of 5.

3. If there is no remainder, the roll is considered to be a 6. Otherwise, the roll is considered to be the remainder.

   In the example, therefore, the roll is 2-5.

Other kinds of numbers you can use are the high temperature in London, the total number of hits in a certain baseball game, or the number of points a certain basketball team scored. All that's important is that the source of the numbers be agreed to in advance by both players, and that the numbers be accessible to both players so that each player can check that the opponent did not make a mistake.

There's also an entirely different way to get around the dice problem: Change the rules to eliminate them!

DICELESS DICE GAMES

One of the nice things about playing a game that involves at least some luck is that a player's ego needn't be bruised when he loses. He can always blame the luck of the cards, dice, or whatever is used to create random moves.

But some players dislike losing on account of bad luck and feel less than fully satisfied when they win because of good luck. These kinds of players may enjoy trying the system set forth below. It can be used with backgammon, Monopoly, or any other game in which dice rolls determine movement. It is also ideal for postal play.

Each player begins with a list of all possible dice rolls. For a game using two dice, the list would look like this:

1-1	2-1	3-1	4-1	5-1	6-1
1-2	2-2	3-2	4-2	5-2	6-2
1-3	2-3	3-3	4-3	5-3	6-3
1-4	2-4	3-4	4-4	5-4	6-4
1-5	2-5	3-5	4-5	5-5	6-5
1-6	2-6	3-6	4-6	5-6	6-6

Each player, in turn, chooses one of the dice rolls on his list and plays it. Then he crosses that choice off his list. Each turn, a player may choose any roll that he has not yet crossed off. Note that on turn number 36, a player will have no choice about his roll—he will only have one roll left. After the 36th turn, each player gets a fresh sheet and once again has the full range of choices.

Strategy is not simple. Probabilities don't mean anything anymore: The odds that your opponent can throw a certain number are either 100 percent or zero, depending on whether the roll is still listed on his sheet—something both players can keep track of. And no one is ever going to win simply because he threw more double 6s than his opponent.

When you have a chance to do something really good with a roll, you usually should. But you should also try to leave yourself with as many choices as possible. In backgammon, for example, a player who first uses up all combinations that contain a particular die roll will have the disadvantage that his opponent can keep blots that distance from the player's pieces—and the situation will not change until after move 36.

The advantages of this system for postal play are clear. There is no need to resort to any randomizing method to determine and verify dice rolls. The disadvantage is that the nature of the game changes dramatically—but for some games, players may find that the new variation is a change for the better.

OPEN SCRABBLE

This variation of Scrabble is ideal for players who habitually complain about their bad luck in drawing tiles, as in "My opponent always gets both blanks and the X, while I always get stuck with the Q and no U..." It can also be used to play Scrabble by mail without a third person acting as a tile-drawing "referee."

One player randomly arranges all 100 tiles, face up, in the shape of string. On a table, this is most conveniently done by making a ring of tiles around the board. Don't close the ring into a complete loop, though—you will want the string to have two ends. For postal play, the string of tiles is simply written out on paper, taking into account the letter distribution that comes with the set, and which is given on the board—that is, there should be a total of nine As, two Bs, and so on.

At the start of the game, each player in turn takes one tile from either end of the string, until each player has a total of seven tiles. Then the players take their turns normally. After each turn, a player replenishes his rack by drawing tiles from either or both ends of the string, as he chooses.

It's in the spirit of the game for both players to keep their racks exposed at all times, since each player can see what tiles the other has chosen anyway. Theoretically, a game such as this has no element of luck; but in practice, it is not possible to see very far ahead. Figuring out which tiles to take to make your own best score is hard enough, but also calculating what tiles will then be available to the opponent, the value of his best counterplay, and then trying to see what your next turn will be like, becomes close to impossible.

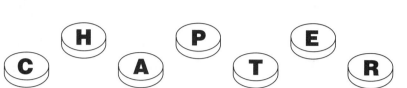

CREATING YOUR
OWN WINNING
VARIATIONS

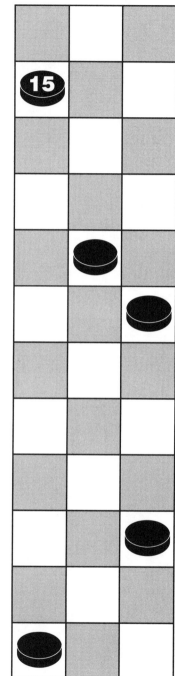

If you're an avid game player who buys new games every year, you probably own a lot of games not discussed in this book. This chapter offers general advice on how to make up your own game variations for nearly any game, either to improve or just to vary the play.

What makes a variation worth trying? If it's because the variation is better than the original game, then what makes one game better than another. But what makes a game good in the first place?

To me, the best measure of a game's quality is what happens when it is played repeatedly: Do the players become *less* interested or *more* interested in playing again? This is a question that cuts across different game genres and player tastes.

Tic-tac-toe is an excellent game for teaching children about basic game principles and spatial relations. But for adults, it fails the "lasting interest" test miserably. After just a few games, two players will learn enough about the game so that every game, unless played carelessly, will result in a draw. By contrast, a game such as go or chess contains many secrets; and the more players learn about these games, the more they appreciate and enjoy them. Some people spend their entire lives playing go or chess professionally, yet never stop learning new things about the games.

When a game is rich enough in strategy and tactics to give rise to many different levels of understanding by players, it is said to have "depth." Depth may seem like a vague concept, but in fact it can be measured empirically, at least for games of pure skill (i.e., ones that have no random moves or hidden information), simply by having many players play the game against one another for a long enough period of time. By analyzing the results, it is possible to assign players different ranks according to their abilities.

Ranks can be assigned in a way that is uniform from game to game; for example, as in amateur go and shogi rankings (described in Chapter 6), two players can be defined as one rank apart if one of them beats the other, on average, two games out of three. Once enough players are ranked, a game's depth can be defined as the number of ranks that separate the average beginner from the world champion. For the game of chess, that number is probably somewhere around 20 or 25; for the more complicated games go and shogi, it is closer to 40. The greater the depth of a game, the longer players are likely to keep learning new things about it, and the longer their interest in the game will last.

But depth is not the only quality needed for a good game. A good game should have drama in the form of at least the possibility of reversals of fortune and close finishes. It should have some element of originality that distinguishes it from all other games. It may have complicated rules, but it should never have rules that are *unnecessarily* complicated. It should not end too frequently in draws, nor should it be noticeably unbalanced in favor of one player or another. There are also aesthetic considerations, the question of playing time, and other, harder-to-verbalize factors that make some games "better" than others.

Generally, game variations should be created to improve games. But if they wind up merely varying a game, without improving or harming it, that's okay too—it just means a new game has been invented that is as interesting to play as the original one.

Here are some specific examples of rule changes to consider in new games. Not all of these suggestions will apply to all games, of course. And watch out for unintended side effects of rule changes you make. Sometimes a rule change that looks good will have some undesirable consequence that is hard to foresee.

1. Rule changes that give players more choices are usually good. The more choices a player has, the more chance he has to control the outcome, try new strategies, and distinguish himself from his opponent in terms of skill. For example, in a game in which a player throws two dice to determine his moves, you might try one of the following variations:

a. Let players throw three dice instead of two and let them choose which two numbers to use.

b. Let each player begin the game with a limited number of "rethrow options." When a player doesn't like the dice throw he just made, he may use one of his rethrow options to throw the dice again, in which case he uses the new roll (unless he doesn't like that one, either, in which case he may use up another rethrow option). Players must keep track of how many rethrow options they have left. Giving one player more rethrows than another is an interesting way to handicap a game or to offset the advantage of going first.

Note: In some games, players may think of new ways to use rethrow options. In Monopoly, for example, players may agree to allow rethrow options to be traded for properties or bought for cash. It is a good idea to keep the number of rethrows per player to a minimum, such as four or five. This will make it harder, but more interesting, for players to decide when to use them.

c. Let each player begin with a certain number of tokens (pennies will do) that may be "spent" throughout the game to adjust the number rolled on a die. By spending one token, a player may change his dice roll, up or down, by one. Whether or not a player should be allowed to spend more than one token in a turn is up to the players.

2. Try out rules that improve players' offensive capabilities and weaken their defenses. I have seen many games in which the best strategy, unfortunately, was to sit back and do nothing, waiting for the opponent to weaken his position by trying to attack. When both players realize that defense is the best strategy, some long, dull games will result, and they may never even end.

In general, it is better to increase the offensive capabilities of pieces, such as by making them more mobile, rather than their defensive capabilities. It is also good to consider ways to reward the player who takes the offensive. In chess, for instance, this is done in part by means of the pawn promotion rule, which gives players incentives to advance their pawns even though doing so creates permanent weaknesses in their own positions. Chessboard geometry also plays a role: Players have an incentive to contest the center of the board because most of their pieces have more mobility there.

It may also be a good idea to weaken the defense. A simple way to eliminate the large number of 0–0 and 1–1 ties in world-class soccer competition, for example, without changing any other rules, would be to increase the size of the goals. A size change of just 10 percent would probably increase scoring by much more than 10 percent.

3. Try increasing the amount of player interaction. The more a player can interfere with what the others are doing, the more interesting a game usually is. Adding a challenge rule to Trivial Pursuit, as suggested in Chapter 1, is an example of this kind of variation.

4. Try changing the object of the game. For example, reduce or increase the number of balls you must capture in Abalone or the number of pieces that must be captured in Pente. One-Capture Go (see Chapter 5) is another example.

5. Try adding alternative victory conditions, as Extinction Chess (see Chapter 1) does for chess. Suppose you could win a game of checkers either the usual way or by getting three kings in a row on a diagonal; or a game of Monopoly by getting hotels on six consecutive colored properties anywhere on the board.

6. Try increasing or decreasing the number of pieces a player starts with—or the amount of money, the number of cards, or any other kind of equipment in whatever way seems most likely to make the game more interesting.

7. Try giving players two moves per turn instead of one. In some games, this may be a way to increase offensive potential, while also shortening the playing time.

8. Try changing the board's geometry. Pretend the left and right edges, and/or the top and bottom edges, are connected, allowing "wraparound" movement of the kind found in many computer games. Or try adapting a game that is normally played on a square grid to a hexagonal grid, or vice versa.

9. Try simultaneous movement instead of sequential movement, as in the Simultaneous Risk variation in Chapter 5.

10. If a game seems unbalanced, try to equalize the chances by adding a pie rule or bidding rule, as discussed in Chapter 2.

11. In many strategy games, rules fail to cover the possibility of a repetition of moves by both players—or, if it is covered but is treated as a draw, it can sometimes result in there being too many draws. A good variation to try in such situations is to apply the "superko" rule from go. This rule states that *no player may make a move that recreates a prior board position.* Thus, a player must vary rather than make even a single repetition of position.

In some games, using this rule may result in interesting tactics analogous to those in go known as "ko fights." Suppose that, in one part of the board, players are attacking one another in such a way that whoever varies first from a sequence of moves will suffer some sort of disadvantage. If the ko rule is in effect, this repetition cannot occur—but the situation is not necessarily lost for the player who must vary. That's because when a player needs to make a reply that is forbidden because of the ko rule, he can instead make a threatening move somewhere else on the board. If the opponent needs to answer that "ko threat," the player can then come back and make his desired reply—which is no longer prohibited by the ko rule because the position has changed somewhere else on the board. Now, in fact, it is the opponent who cannot make the desirable repetitious response and who must himself look for a threat that is important enough to force the opponent to answer. A ko fight can go on for many turns, until one player runs out of threats that the opponent must answer.

12. Even if you're not interested in chess, you may find it worthwhile to look through Chapter 13 for ideas that can be applied to other games. For example, the principles of Refusal Chess and Compromise Chess will work with almost any two-player strategy game. In a Refusal game, each time a player makes a move, the opponent may reject it, forcing the player to make a different move (which must then be accepted). In a Compromise game, a player must propose two alternative moves each turn, and the opponent selects which of the two moves the player is to make.

These ideas can be combined in any fashion to produce still more variations. Just remember that the point is to have more fun when you play. And never be afraid to experiment—that's how many of the best games are discovered.

APPENDIX A

ALGEBRAIC NOTATION

Most games can be recorded with a simple "algebraic" notation in which board space (squares, hexagons, intersections, or whatever) are identified by a combination of a letter and a number. After a system is worked out to give each space a name, a move can be specified by naming the starting and ending spaces of the move.

Some games, such as checkers and xiang qi, have established notation systems all their own. But generally, in games with square or rectangular grids, files (vertical columns of squares) are given letters, starting with "a" as the leftmost file from the point of view of the player who goes first. Ranks (horizontal rows) are given numbers, starting with "1" as the rank closest to the player who

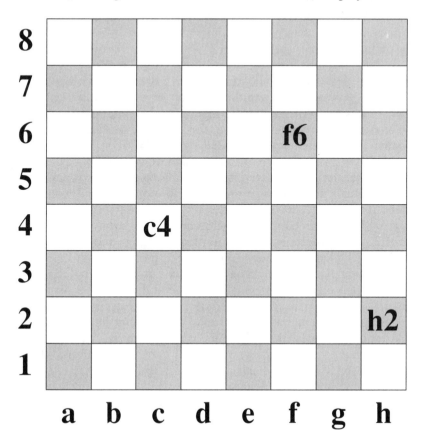

Diagram A.1

In algebraic chess notation, each square is named for the coordinates that intersect there, as the three labeled squares in the diagram illustrate. The same system of notation can be applied to any game that is played on a rectangular grid, and the system can easily be modified for use on hexagonal grids.

Algebraic notation is simpler than the "descriptive" notation that, until recently, was used in most English language chess books. One disadvantage of descriptive notation is that each square has two different names (for example, White's "king four" is Black's "king five"); another disadvantage is that it cannot readily be extended to chess variants or other kinds of games.

goes first. In chess, for example, ranks and files are given the letters and numbers shown in Diagram A.1.

A two-square advance of White's king's pawn is then recorded as "1.Pe2–e4," where the "1" indicates that it is the first move of the game, the "P" indicates the kind of piece moved, "e2" is the starting square of the move, "–" means "moves to," and "e4" is the destination square.

> *Note:* In shogi, shogi variants, and certain other Oriental games, files are customarily numbered from right to left, and the ranks are lettered (or numbered using Oriental characters) from top to bottom, from the point of view of the first player.

Since chess notation is widely used in books, magazines, and tournament records, certain conventions have become popular that shorten this notation. It is normal now, in what is sometimes called "short-form algebraic notation," to omit the starting square unless confusion would otherwise result. Also, although piece symbols are always given (K = king, Q = queen, R = rook, B = bishop, and N = knight, or the pictorial equivalents), the abbreviation P for pawn is dropped. Thus, "1.Pe2–e4" is normally written as " 1.e4."

In many games, a capture is indicated by replacing the "–" (meaning "moves to") with "x." In chess, there is a trend toward economy of space, and the use of "x" is falling out of fashion; and so "Nf3" is now used to mean both "knight moves to f3" and "knight moves to f3, making a capture there." Pawn captures, though, have a special shorthand. A capture such as "Pe4xd5" is written as "ed" in short-form algebraic. In the unusual case in which more than one e-file pawn can capture more than one d-file pawn, the destination rank is added, as in "ed5."

Pawn promotion is indicated by adding the symbol of the new piece after the move, sometimes placed in parentheses or preceded by an equals sign. A pawn promoting to a queen on e8 would be recorded as e8Q, e8(Q), or e8=Q.

Many chess books use "+" at the end of a move to indicate check, but sometimes this is omitted. In shogi and a few other games, "+" indicates instead that a piece promotes, and "=" indicates that a piece that could have promoted did not do so.

When captures are made by a method other than displacement—that is, when the moving piece does not occupy the square of the piece it captures—players may wish to indicate the locations of captured pieces in parentheses, preceded by an "x," as in the Tablut game on page 24. As a special case, the notation "x!" is used in Chu Shogi to indicate a capture by igui (see page 213).

Game annotators generally place "?" after a bad move, "!" after a very good move, "?!" after a dubious move, and "!?" after a move that is interesting but that may or may not be the best.

APPENDIX B

IMPROVISING GAME EQUIPMENT

Many games in this book can be played with equipment that can be improvised quite easily and inexpensively.

Rectangular Grids

Suppose you have only an 8x8 checkerboard, but you want to try International Checkers, or one of the many other games that require a 10x10 checkerboard. If you're a skilled woodworker and have the right tools, you can create a fancy wooden board with inlaid squares. Most people, though, will want an easier option. Here are two methods.

1. Buy 100 mosaic tiles about $1^1/2$ inches square. Half the tiles should be light and half dark. Lay them out on a piece of plywood that has already been cut to the desired size, using spacers (available at tile stores) to keep them a uniform distance apart. Glue down the tiles, adding a wooden trim around the edge of the board if you wish. Add grout between the tiles, and you'll have a beautiful—though somewhat heavy—100-square checkerboard.

2. At a plastics supply store, have a sheet of acrylic plastic cut to size. At an art supply store, buy some artist's ruling tape that is $^1/16$ or $^1/8$ of an inch thick. Measure the distances between squares and place pencil marks on opposite edges of the board, then place the tape across the board to form the edges of the squares. This tape will stick to the acrylic and form straight lines.

The latter method will result in a one-color board rather than a checkered one. But for some games, such as go, Reversi, or Turkish Checkers, a one-color board is traditional. For a checkered board, mark lines on the acrylic sheet and, before placing the tape, paint the squares to create a checkerboard pattern. When the tape is placed, it will hide irregularities in the edges of the painted squares.

It's also possible to substitute wood or heavy cardboard, such

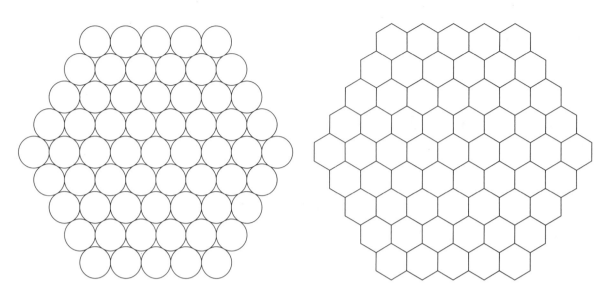

Diagram B.1

Poker chips, stickers, or other circular objects can be pasted into the pattern shown at left in order to simulate the hexagonal grid shown at right.

as oak tag, for the acrylic, using tape in the same way.

Once you have your board, getting extra checkers is as easy as picking up an extra set at a toy store or a garage sale. Or you can use poker chips, coins, bottlecaps, buttons, or any other objects of suitable size and color.

Hexagonal Grids

Wargame supply stores often have sheets of paper or vinyl with hexagonal grids on them. They come in various sizes and can be cut or colored to make them suitable for virtually any game played on a hexagonal grid. Alternatively, hexagonal tiles can be found at stores that sell bathroom and kitchen tile; these can be glued onto plywood in whatever pattern is desired.

Grids of interlocking circles make suitable substitutes for hexagonal grids for many games. Poker chips or other thin, circular objects can be laid on a flat surface to create a grid in which the circles have the same geometric relationships to one another as the hexagons do in a regular hexagonal grid, as shown in Diagram B.1. The poker chips can be glued to a stiff surface, if necessary, and then used as board spaces.

INDEX